HENRY BOUCHA, OJIBWA, NATIVE AMERICAN OLYMPIAN

HENRY CHARLES BOUCHA

ISBN: 0615717446
ISBN-13: 9780615717449
Library of Congress Control Number: 2012922821
Henry Boucha, Ojibwa, Native American Olympian
Anchorage, AK

Dedicated to

My parents, Alice and George Boucha; my children,
Tara Marie Boucha, Henry Boucha Jr., Bridgette Ann Boucha,
and Jean Paul (JP) Boucha; and my grandchildren, Shalese Marie,
Sky Two-Clouds, Deon (Gaabi), Jace (Doot), and Andy,
with love and respect. May you learn from my experiences,
both good and the rough patches, and everything in between
as our experiences make us who we are.

ACKNOWLEDGEMENTS

Thank you to those people who have knowingly and unknowingly contributed to the success of this book. Your contributions, no matter how big or small, have made this book more compelling:

Aunt Irene Boucha Bobcznski; Dixie Boucha Johnston–the Boucha family historian; Dale Thrasher Boucha–family historian; Fred Kelly–Descent of the Eagle; Shirley Boucha Flick; James Allen Boucha; David Louis Boucha Sr.; Elaine Boucha; Tara Boucha; Henry Boucha Jr.; Bridgette Boucha; JP Boucha; John Boucha; Rosie Boucha, Becky Johnson, Roger and Janet Dorion, Ed and Linda Boucha, Jeff Parker, Jeanne Erickson, Bob and Pam Wenzel, Dale Bleau, Kenny and Elvira Kvarnlov, Kaydelle Kvarnlov Leverty, Deb Green, Pat Holland Stotts, Amanda Brinkley, and all the others that I have not have mentioned.

HENRY'S FAVORITE WISDOMS

"I have seen that in any great undertaking,
it is not enough for a man to depend simply on himself."

—UNKNOWN

I often think that people we have loved
and who have loved us,
not only make us more human,
but they become part of us
and we carry them around all the time,
whether we see them or not.
And in some way we are the sum total
of those who have loved us
and those to whom we have given ourselves.

Margie Boucha
1921-1997

TABLE OF CONTENTS

FOREWORD

After many years of consideration about writing my autobiography, I found the time to think, remember and write while living quietly in Anchorage, Alaska. Although Mary Halverson Schofield had written a book about me, published in 1999, I wanted to write my own. Her book is called *Henry Boucha: Star of the North.* This autobiography is more detailed. It is a story of my people- maternal, and paternal, and my life: my ups and downs, my achievements and downfalls, my relationships, and the places I have lived. The story is in chronological order from the "beginning time," as we say, to my induction into the United States Hockey Hall of Fame in 1995.

I wanted to share this story since 1992, when I was being honored during the Gathering of Nations in New Mexico for being one of ten Native American Olympians (now we know of eighteen). Before then, I had not thought about the honor or distinction of being a Native American Olympian. I was surprised at that time to hear that there were only ten Native American Olympians. Amazingly, only four of us were living. Billy Mills and I were the youngest. Billy, a Sioux, is eleven years older than I. He won a gold medal in 1964 in Tokyo, Japan. The other athletes in attendance were: Wilson "Buster" Charles, an Oneida who competed in the decathlon in Los Angles in 1932 (He was elderly and fragile when I met him, but his mind was clear.); Jesse Bernard "Cab" Renick, a Choctaw who competed in London in 1948, winning a gold medal in basketball; also, Grace Thorpe, Jim Thorpe's daughter, who brought and displayed her dad's medals. Grace was a joy to meet. Thorpe, of Fox and Sac Potawatomi heritage won two gold medals at the 1912 games in Stockholm, Sweden.

The other known Native Americans to compete as Olympians, as of 2012 (listed are their tribal affiliations, year and location of the Olympics they competed in):

Frank C. Pierce, Seneca, 1904, Saint Louis, Missouri
Frank Mount Pleasant, Tuscarora, 1908, London, England
Louis Tewanima, Hopi, 1908 silver medalist, London, England
Andrew Sockalexis, Penobscot, 1912, Stockholm, Sweden
John "Taffy" Abel, Ojibwa/Chippewa, 1924 silver medalist, Chamonix, France
Ellison "Tarzan" Brown, Narragansett, 1936, Berlin, Germany
Ben Nighthorse Campbell, Northern Cheyenne, 1964, Tokyo, Japan
Naomi Lang, Karuk, 2002, Salt Lake City, Utah (the first Native American woman to participate)
Callan Chythlook-Sifsof, Yupik/Inupiaq Eskimo, 2010, Vancouver, British Columbia, Canada (still on the US team and expected to participate in the 2014 Olympics in Sochi, Russia).

Please watch for forthcoming books and television documentaries about the Native American Olympians, and the Canadian Native Olympians available to the public starting in 2014 or soon after. The series of Canadian Native Olympians and the US Native American Olympians stories' is a work in progress. Boucha Films, LLC will executive produce the films.

CHAPTER 1: THE BEGINNING

In the beginning, the Great Spirit placed the four colors of human-kind in the four directions: the yellow to the east, the black to the south, the red to the west, and the white to the north. To each was given the special gift of life and freedom. Each was shown its own way to live in peace and harmony with all creation. We (the Ojibwa), were placed to the west on Turtle Island (N. America), from where we have looked at the Universe and lived by the laws of the Creator. We were a thriving and expanding people.

There is only one Creator, the maker of all life. Because the Great Spirit makes everything, all life is filled with the sacred. From the smallest insect to the biggest animal, from the tiniest grain of sand to the largest galaxy—all is alive, and everything is intimately and spiritually connected. There is no such concept as animate or inanimate.

The quest for the good life in the Creator and overall well-being is the story of the Anishinaabe (the first people of N. America) from time immemorial. This forms the basis for our worldview upon which our life ways are founded.

We need to know who and what we are if we are to maintain ourselves as originally intended by the Great Spirit. Our language, Anishinaabe-mowin, is our history, and it is also the essence of our community. Through our language we recall and celebrate sacred events passed on to us by our ancestors over countless generations.

These become traditional teachings that embody our spirituality and define our sacred relationship to the land and all life in creation. To understand our teachings is to understand our culture and who we are as Anishinaabe.

There are two explanations for the word *anishinaabe.* First, there is the spiritual meaning derived from its two components: "niisiina," which means "descended," and "naabe," which means "male"—hence, the being descended from the Creator through Mother Earth. Secondly, in colloquial terms, "anishaa" means "of no value." Combined with "naabe," it translates as "male of no value." In this sense, we do not place ourselves above any other life form; instead we are an intimate part of the universal interconnectedness and interdependence, but life can continue without us. Yet, there is no mention of the women, and that is because she already carries all spiritual powers and is by nature sacred, a most worthy being.

Our spiritual genesis reveals that we came down through the star constellation Paagoneliizhig (hole in the sky). This is the beginning of Pimatiziwin, which can be translated as "Sacred Life of the Great Spirit". Thus being placed upon our Grandmother Earth, we received the seven laws of Pimatiziwin: Respect, Love, Honesty, Courage, Humility, Wisdom, and Truth. In time, we were also given the sacred ceremonies and the ways to pursue Pimatiziwin, including the four lodges, the four drums, and the grandmother and grandfather pipes.

These are the ways in which some of our beliefs are explained. In effect, Pimatiziwin-Life is more than mere existence or a chronological progression of age. It is a quest to fulfill our purpose. Our traditional elders carry the teachings to help us achieve it in the good way.

Pimatiziwin being the Sacred Gift of Life, we are told, is not only the right path but also a duty, for we do not own life. Our ancestors, therefore, believed that life was to be regarded as a sacred trust of the benefit of other life, including our children and generations yet unborn.

We have come to view our interconnectedness as an individual with the family, community, and nation in a holistic way. We have come to seek the social, cultural, economic, and political balance of life's ways as the well-being of the collective. Individually, we seek mental, emotional, physical, and spiritual balance as the quest of wellness.

Pimatiziwin also entails the use and care of the land, air, water, and all life in our environment, which defines our sacred relationship with Grandmother Earth. In the universal order, we learn that we have "everything that we need to survive and exist as a people." This is a perfect definition of "culture" and sets out how we are to govern ourselves on the land. This is what we mean by "Bimiiwinitisowin Omaa Aking."

Thank you to Fred Kelly (Kizhebowse Mukwaa-Kind Walking Bear) for sharing this spiritual, cultural and historical information.

CHAPTER 2: THE OJIBWA MIGRATION

When the seven prophets came to the Ojibwa with instructions about life from the Creator, the Ojibwa were living east, on the shores of the Great Salt Water, the Atlantic Ocean. There were many people, and for many, many generations were they lived in harmony.

The people were so many and so powerful that if one was to climb the highest mountain and look in all directions, the person could not see the end of the Ojibwa Nation. Life was full and there was abundance from the land and the sea. Because things were good and plentiful, some people doubted the predictions of the prophets and there was much discussion about the migration and the prophecies of the seven fires.

The prophecies said that the light-skinned race would land on our shores and bring death and destruction to our people. Many huge gatherings were held to discuss the purpose of the migration. Some didn't want to leave because things were good. There were some that stayed behind to guard the fires and the eastern doorway as the others followed the instructions of the seven prophecies and started to migrate to the west. Like most migrations, and like military columns, the front, the right and left flanks are protected as was the rear. If something happened, the flank columns in any directions would send runners to notify the main column of the danger. The people who stayed behind moved west sometime after the main migration took place.

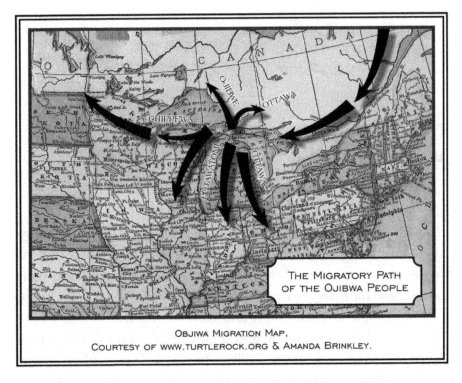

OBJIWA MIGRATION MAP,
COURTESY OF WWW.TURTLEROCK.ORG & AMANDA BRINKLEY.

Figure 1

Please note the word Ojibwa has different spellings but mean the same thing, also "Chippewa" is the same as Ojibwa. People speak in different dialects of Ojibwa from east to west.

The large Ojibwa migration separated by clans, families, and small bands started the migration westward, as the first prophecy instructed. Some found an island that was shaped like a turtle somewhere near present-day Montreal on the Saint Lawrence River. Again, ceremonies were held to find further instruction. Some of the bands stopped and set up camps as others moved farther west along the southern and northern shores of the Saint Lawrence River.

There was conflict along the way with other tribes, including the Iroquois. The dispute was negotiated and the Iroquois gave the

Ojibwa a wampum belt made of a special *megis* shells. A pipe was shared and a peace was settled.

Some bands of Ojibwa made it all the way across the State of Michigan to Lake Michigan. Some bands separated and went south, and others decided to stay, but most moved and traveled north into what is now Canada, met up with the others and found what was Manitoulin Island, where they stayed for a long time. The island became known as the Ojibwa headquarters for generations. However, according to the instructions gathered through ceremonies, their journey was not yet over.

When the instructions came: "Find the food that grows on the water" they were looking for the wild rice of the upper Midwest of North America and what is now called Michigan, Wisconsin, Minnesota, and Northwest Ontario. The main body pushed on into what is now Sault Saint Marie. They split and moved south along the southern shores of Lake Superior and others traveled north along the lake's northern shores.

Some of the bands stayed along those routes to make permanent settlements, on both the south and north shores. However, many of them continued and found the west end of Lake Superior, and some moved even future north and west.

The northern bands varied in a northwest direction, and a few were to arrive at the west end of Lake Superior. When they did not find the others who were traveling along the southern shores, they followed the south shore back east around the lake to meet up with the bands. Some bands stopped at a place called Madeline Island, near Red Cliff, and Bay Field, Wisconsin. This land the Ojibwa call the center of the Universe and their spiritual headquarters. After staying there for a period, many of the Ojibwa bands traveled farther west and to the north to the Lake of the Woods area and beyond. As they moved west and north, some warred with the Sioux who had settlements in the Minnesota area and in southern Manitoba and

Northwestern Ontario. The Cree and Assiniboine were friendly and moved further north and west.

Some of the bands had discovered, or maybe were shown, by the Cree, Sioux or Assiniboine, a portage from Lake Superior. It was a westward route through what is called now, the Boundary Waters to Rainy Lake and into Lake of the Woods and Lake Winnipeg, composed of the Pigeon River and other strategic interior waterways, as well as the Grand Portage Trail and many other land portages. The route provided quick water access from Canada's Northwest Ontario to the Great Lakes.

The Grand Portage Trail is nine miles long, connecting to Fort Charlotte on the Pigeon River. Voyageurs from the interior of Canada would carry furs by canoe to Fort Charlotte and transport the bundles of furs to Grand Portage, Minnesota. There they met the traders from Montreal and exchanged the furs for trade goods and supplies.

At first, the Ojibwa started guiding the French explorers to the west through Grand Portage. Some explorers wanted to find the Northwest Passage to the great salt water to the west, and others wanted the furs from that region. During that time the Ojibwa and French were collaborating and the Ojibwa were used as interpreters and guides. When the French started trading directly with the Sioux, the Sioux took offense toward the Ojibwa, and looked at them as intruders and warred with them, which lasted a long time. The Ojibwa managed to push the Sioux further south and west. There are variations of the story of the migration of the Ojibwa. There were bands that split from the main body of the Ojibwa and became other tribes throughout the United States and Canada.

CHAPTER 3: SIEUR DE LA VÉRENDRYE AND FORT SAINT CHARLES

FORT ST. CHARLES

FORT SAINT CHARLES. COURTESY OF WARROAD MUSEUM.

Figure 2

Not long after the first explorers came into the midwest region, Pierre Gaultier de Varennes, sieur de La Vérendrye, established a fort on Lake of the Woods in 1732. La Vérendrye had the ambitious dream of finding the fabled "Western Sea" and sought to establish French outposts along the way.

VOYAGEURS. COURTESY OF WIKIPEDIA.

Figure 3

On the western shore of the lake he built a fort named after and in honor of Charles de Beauharnois, Governor of New France. Fort Saint Charles became the western capital of the French empire in the northwest. From it, expeditions were launched and supplies dispatched to newer posts around Lake Winnipeg. Indians brought furs to trade for white men's goods, and these pelts were sent by canoe to Fort Charlotte, Grand Portage, Fort Michilimackinac, and Montreal. The scarcity of food and the war between the Ojibwa and Sioux made life precarious.

In 1736, from Fort St. Charles, La Vérendrye's oldest son, Jean-Baptiste, nineteen voyageurs, and Father Jean-Pierre Aulneau, a Jesuit priest, were sent on an expedition to the east for supplies. They were massacred by a Sioux war party on a nearby island, now called Massacre Island on Lake of the Woods.

An Ojibwa/Cree war party assembled quickly, and warriors pursued the Sioux party south across the lake and found the bloody Sioux canoes abandoned at the southwestern part of the lake near

present day Warroad, Minnesota. The Sioux war party escaped to
the west down the ridges called the war trail.

In the LaVerendrye lineage, Pierre Gaultier de Varennes, Sueur
de La Vérendrye, born November 17, 1685-December 5, 1748 in
Trois-Rivieres, Quebec, was the youngest son of Rene Gaultier de
Vannes, who came to Canada as a soldier in 1665, and wife Marie,
the daughter of Pierre Boucher, the first governor of Trois-Rivieres.

It is noted that Jacques de Noyon had reached the Rainy Lake
area in the 1620's, and maybe the Lake of the Woods. In 1717, Zach-
arie Robutel de La Noue tried to reach Rainy Lake but succeeded
only in establishing Fort Kaministiquia.

In 1731 La Vérendrye, three of his sons, and fifty others left
Montreal. That fall his son Jean-Baptiste built Fort Saint Pierre on
Rainy Lake. The next year they built Fort Saint Charles on Lake of
the Woods, and it became their headquarters.

La Vérendrye explored the area from Lake Superior to the mouth
of the Saskatchewan River. He also reached North Dakota, and his
sons reached Wyoming.

CHAPTER 4: WARROAD, (KAH-BAY-KAH-NONG), ROSEAU COUNTY

Kah-Bay-Kah-Nong is the Ojibwa word for Warroad. The Warroad River is located at the southwestern end of Lake of the Woods in Minnesota. It is where the Ojibwa and Sioux pursued each other when making war up and down the war trail and it is how Warroad got its name. During the wars and skirmishes, there were hit-and-run battles from both sides throughout the area.

I remember my mother telling us that when her grandmother Laughing Mary Thunder was little, she had to hide in the reeds along the Warroad River when a Sioux war party came into Warroad on a raid. In Warroad/Buffalo Point, the same bands of families and clans lived together as a community. They would move to Buffalo Point in the summer and then to Warroad in the winter. They traveled to other communities like Red Lake, 100 miles away, as well as other Indian communities in the area. Later on, the US/Canada border cut between the sites, splitting it into two countries. Still the families moved back and forth. Under the J-Treaty we were to be exempt from screened border crossings and able to trade openly.

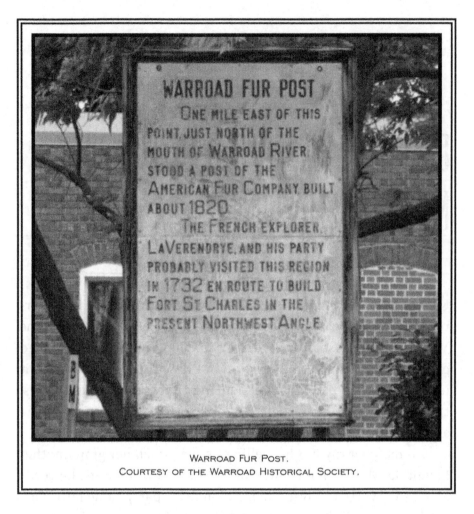

WARROAD FUR POST.
COURTESY OF THE WARROAD HISTORICAL SOCIETY.

Figure 4

The Sioux and Ojibwa warriors used the path from the Warroad River west along the sand ridges to pursue each other. It was considered a dangerous area because you never knew when the other would attack you.

My Ojibwa family settlement known as Kah-Bay-Kah-Nong (War-road) is where my family stories begin, and the lineage on my mother's side.

My Great-Great-Great-Grandfather Ay-Ash-A-Wash, aka O-sow-we-gene-big, born circa 1790, died before 1895 at Warroad. He is buried at Buffalo Point Reserve First Nation in Manitoba. He was the son of Bwan, aka Boin-aince or Bwan-aince, and Nah-wah-je-ge-shig-oquay. Ay-ash-a wash was called the first chief of Warroad and Buffalo Point. He signed Treaty #3 as Chief of Buffalo Point along with twenty-eight other Ojibwa Chiefs around Lake of the Woods, all in Canada.

Ay-Ash-A-Wash's father, Bwan, was related to other well-known Minnesota Ojibwa Chiefs. Ay-Ash-A-Wash was in the battle at Two Rivers west of Warroad when the Ojibwa repeatedly tried driving the Sioux out of the area. Ay-Ash-A-Wash was badly wounded in one of the final skirmishes and he played dead, as a Sioux warrior took half of his scalp. He continued to play dead, and then crawled away and hid. Everyone thought he was lost in battle, but he made his way back to Warroad a few days later.

Some believe that was one of the last battles with the Sioux. Peace came to the region after that, but there was always a threat of war, even after the whites started coming into the area. The pioneers migrated from the Mississippi River near St. Paul, west up the Minnesota River and then north down the Red River to Pembina, North Dakota. Because there is a north/south continental divide, the Red River flows north from southern Minnesota to Hudson Bay. The settlers then traveled by wagon train east from Pembina and Kittson County. Most stopped at what is now called Roseau (a French word for "lake of the reeds"), Minnesota. Some came through Canada via Rat Portage at what is now called Kenora, Ontario or overland through Manitoba. Some traveled down the Rainy River, as did the fur traders and voyageurs in the past.

The French explorers and voyagers built Fort Saint Charles in 1732 on Lake of the Woods. They also explored and built forts in Winnipeg and other places. The settlers and pioneers found the forests teeming with wild game, including moose, caribou, elk, and deer. The animals gathered into large herds and were easy to hunt. The partridge, grouse, ducks, and geese were also plentiful. Settlers found only a few people scattered in the valley, most arriving just two years before. The trail followed the high sand ridge, which offered convenient access across the territory, which was dotted with bogs, swamps, and marsh. These trails where used earlier by the Sioux and Ojibwa.

Incoming settlers were attracted to the timber and the fertile land to farm and grow vegetables in the Roseau River Valley area. The new settlers faced many burdens, including floods and rain, as the Roseau River was fairly flat. The mosquitoes were horrible with all the rain and standing water. Money was a curiosity; no one had any or used it. The frontier period was one of bartering, free giving, and cooperation. By 1889 hundreds of people began moving into Roseau Valley.

When the pioneers arrived they found the Indians peaceful and friendly. But in 1891, rumors flew that there was to be an Indian uprising. Some white settlers who were drinking instigated the rumor, and it scared a lot of people in the communities. Some of the white settlers packed up and headed west out of the supposed danger. When the Roseau settlement sent a representative to Warroad to talk to the Ojibwas about the uprising, the Ojibwas were surprised, concerned and scared. It was not that long ago that the Sioux and the Ojibwas were battling, but the rumors were not true and life moved forward.

In 1892, the first newspaper was printed, and in 1895 the County of Roseau was established. In 1900 the Canadian National Railway built a track that came through Warroad, around the southern shore of Lake of the Woods.

CHAPTER 5: LAUGHING MARY THUNDER AND ALICE CARON

Laughing Mary, born in 1850, was the daughter of Ah-Ne-Me-Keence (Little Thunder), born circa 1830. Ah-Ne-Me-Keence was the son of Ay-Ash-A-Wash, 1790–1895, the great chief of Warroad and Buffalo Point. Chief Ay-Ash-A-Wash's mother, Nah-wah-je-shig-oquay, is listed by Ransom Judd Powell as the head of family #1 in his genealogies. He was called Chief Ay-Ash-A-Wash, Chief O-zow-we-ge-nay-big, and it shows him as having had four other brothers and sisters. Ah-Ne-Me-Keence's (Little Thunder) other siblings where Ka Ka Geesick, 1844, Na-May-Poke, 1840, Mrs. Major 1855, Mrs., Blackbird, Mrs. Elliot, and Mrs. Bombay (Bambi).

Chief Ah-Ne-Me-Keence (Little Thunder), aka Chief Francis H. Animikins, was born in 1830 and married O-ka-kam-i-gi-ji-gok at Red Lake, Minnesota. He died in 1864 while making a treaty at Washington, DC, and was buried in Warroad.

Laughing Mary Thunder married Ok-zee-mi-bee-tung, son of Chief Powassan, at the Northwest Angle of Lake of the Woods, in Canada. Chief Powassan signed Treaty #3 as one of the twenty-eight chiefs representing the twenty-eight First Nation Bands of Ojibwas surrounding Lake of the Woods on October 3, 1873, at the Northwest Angle on Lake of the Woods.

CHIEF LITTLE THUNDER, HIS WIFE AND GRANDCHILDREN AS PHOTOGRAPHED IN 1897.
COURTESY OF THE MINNESOTA HISTORICAL SOCIETY AND BOB AND SANDY THUNDER.

Figure 5

Laughing Mary, through tragedy or sickness, or maybe both, lost her husband, children and family members sometime in the early 1900s at the Northwest Angle. Annie Thunder Powassin, my grandmother, died in 1913, leaving a child Alice Powassin Caron (my mother). John Baptiste Caron, aka Louis Caron, was her father. Laughing Mary and my mother were the only survivors of the family. Laughing Mary and my mother, Alice Caron, moved from the Northwest Angle back to Buffalo Point and Warroad.

Louis (Louie) Caron was living in Warroad. He wanted Laughing Mary to raise my mother. My mother stayed with her dad in Warroad while attending school. Louie later married a white woman named Jessie and left the area. My mother only knew her father in her early years and while attending school. Later, when my mother tried to contact him, Louie's white wife Jessie would tell her to stay away. Mom wanted to hear it from her dad, but she was never allowed to talk to him. Years later, she went to Washington State or Oregon to see her dad. When she went to their home to visit him, Louie's wife Jessie met her at the door and stopped her. She told my mother he didn't want to see her, never come back, and she slammed the door in her face. After that my mother never went back or tried to contact him again. She had tears in her eyes when she told us the story. This bothered me and the rest of the family. It bothered us to think of what my mother had to go through.

Laughing Mary raised my mother, and they stayed close throughout Laughing Mary's lifetime. Laughing Mary died in Warroad in 1936. She was an extraordinary woman. Everyone liked her because of her kindness and laughter. She didn't speak English confidently but she could understand it. She was small in stature. Her Indian name May Mush Ga Waabik, means "standing firmly". She was said to be very spiritual and a healer. Sam Gibbons, now a native elder, told me about how he had pneumonia when he was a young boy. His mother Maggie brought him to the doctor's office. The doctor attempted to treat him, but unsuccessfully, with medications to get the fluid out of his lungs. The doctor sent him home to rest and gave him a fifty-fifty chance of survival. Maggie, found Laughing Mary and ask her to see Sam. Sam said that when she knelt over him, prayed and examined him, her eyes looked glowing red with great intensity like she was looking inside him. She then took a hollow goose leg bone from her medicine bag and used it to suck out the phlegm from his lungs, right through his chest. She spit out the phlegm into a bowl that Maggie had given her. Once finished, she said her prayers and gave him some herbal-medicinal tea, made of bark and roots and she told them to make sure he drank it and that he needed to rest. He recovered.

My mother told me that she and Laughing Mary went to the Badger, Minnesota area to pick roots, a 35 mile trip one way. They travel with Tommy Lightning and his wife Ethel. Ethel was from Eagle Lake, Ontario. Tommy and Ethel went everywhere together. Tommy had a two wheel cart and a horse. They all rode in that cart and walked some too. Tommy had his leg amputated after he cut it at Buffalo Point when falling a tree. He walked on crutches. He also had a canoe. Ethel and Tommy would paddle their way to Kenora some 90 miles by water. They followed the shoreline and camped out each night. If the weather was bad, they waited until the weather changed, then traveled again. The trip to Badger was a two day trip, they stayed overnight on the trail and would stop and have their lunch during midday. Money was scarce during that time. Bartering and trading was the way most people lived.

There was a time when old Tommy went into the store to buy a shell for his rifle. He asked to buy one shell. The owner told him "They didn't sell shells that way. He needed to buy the box". "Why in the world did you only want to buy one shell?", he asked. Tommy's reply was "I only need one deer."

Laughing Mary took good care of my mother and made sure she attended school, and taught her well. She graduated 8th grade, as was the custom in those days. Laughing Mary and my mother lived at Buffalo Point in the summer and Warroad in the winter, as did most local Ojibwa in those days, traveling by canoe, and walking. Laughing Mary died in 1935 in Warroad after living a long and full life.

In the 1990s the younger of the Caron children came to the Warroad Heritage Center looking for information about their dad, Louie Caron. It was at that time they found out that my mother was their stepsister. The Caron children knew nothing about what their mother Jessie had said to Alice Caron. Jessie had withheld all information and kept it a secret. They wanted to meet us. We agreed to meet and visit with them. It was hard for me as I remembered my mother's grief, about not being able to see her dad, and how much it hurt her. We were cordial with the Carons. It was a nice visit and in the end, they knew the truth. My mother passed away earlier in 1988 and never met them. The Caron's were writing a book about their dad, and family, and were looking for information while in Warroad. As of this date, I have not read their story.

CHAPTER 6: BOUCHERS/BOUCHAS

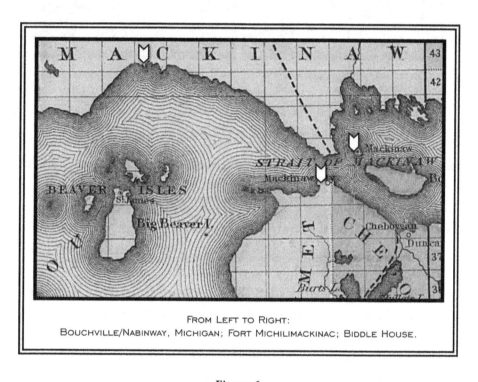

FROM LEFT TO RIGHT:
BOUCHVILLE/NABINWAY, MICHIGAN; FORT MICHILIMACKINAC; BIDDLE HOUSE.

Figure 6

Sometime in the year of 1820, a lovely house was erected on Mackinac Island, not far from the French Fort of Michilimackinac. Edward Biddle, a cousin of the more famous "Biddles of Philadelphia," owned the home. The assumption is that he, like John Jacob Astor and other

WILLIAM F. BOUCHA
BORN: NOVEMBER 1, 1826
LA PRAIRIE, QUEBEC,
DIED: FEBRUARY 8, 1905
BURIED ST. IGNACE, MICHIGAN.

CATHERINE TROTOUCHEAU
BORN: 1834
PLACE OF BIRTH UNKNOWN
DIED: AUGUST 27, 1920
BURIED ST. IGNACE, MICHIGAN
MARRIED TO WILLIAM F. BOUCHA
DECEMBER 10, 1849.

Figure 7

affluent easterners, was in the fur industry, procuring pelts at very nominal prices from the Indians. Edward Biddle married an Indian girl named Angelique. They did not have any children.

However, on December 12, 1840, they indentured two little sisters—Catherine, age six, and Nancy, eleven. Catherine Trudeau/ Trotochaud/Trotochow was born 1834 and Nancy in 1829. The indenture document states that "they shall well and faithfully serve their master and obey all his lawful commands as a faithful servant ought" and that Edward Biddle was to "provide and agree to cause the said Nancy and Catherine to be taught and instructed to read and write, if they are capable to learn, and to provide for the said girls good and sufficient food, clothing, lodging, and other necessaries fit for a servant."

When Catherine was fifteen, a large sailing vessel dropped anchor in the harbor at Mackinac Island, Michigan. Among the crew was a boy of seventeen by the name of William F. Boucher/Boucha, born 1829, my great-great grandfather. He was originally from La Prairie, Province Quebec. He had at the age of fifteen traveled to Detroit, where he stayed with an uncle and worked in the Detroit area and on the Great Lakes. After meeting Catherine, visiting and getting to know her for a few days, he decided to stay and the ship sailed without him. For a couple of years, he worked at the Biddle house in winters and sailed between Buffalo and Chicago during the summers. William and Catherine were married on December 23, 1849, when Catherine was 15 and William 17. According to records, they had their first child when Catherine was 16 and William 18.

That first child was named William Henry Boucha, my great-grandfather. His parents searching for a place of their own looked over the area and found a place to build a cabin on the northern shores of Lake Michigan in the Upper Peninsula of Michigan. An Ojibwa Indian camp was on one side of the bay, and they decided to build their log cabin on the other. Eventually, the William F. Bouchers/Bouchas had sixteen children, eight boys and eight girls. Fourteen of the children were born in the two-story log home that William built in Bouchaville, Michigan.

The Indian camp proved priceless because they helped each other through the hard times. During all of those births, the Ojibwa women served as midwifes and provided medicines and cures that were handed down through generations of Ojibwa. William was in the fur trade with the local Ojibwas and would go on long journeys to Chicago to sell his goods. He began to accumulate money. Most of the trips to Chicago were good, although some were not. On one trip his second-oldest son, Edward, was washed overboard during a storm on Lake Michigan and drowned. He was eighteen years old. William F. Boucha was also in the timber business as well as boatbuilding and fishing. The community became known as Bouchaville, Michigan. Eventually the village name was changed to Naubinway, Michigan.

My Great-Grandfather William Henry Boucha was in born 1851, on Mackinac Island. He was the oldest of the sixteen children. His is first wife was Mary Ann Pemble and they had seven children in ten years. The youngest child was an infant when Mary Ann died in March of 1884. Five months later their son Charlie also died, at the age of two. William Henry's second wife was Mary Paquin and he had three more children with her but they lost the youngest, a daughter, at the age of two weeks.

According to newspaper articles and family obituaries William Henry Boucha was invited to come to Lake of the Woods in 1893 or 94 to show fisherman how to use pond nets. He was good at building boats, and knew how to make sturgeon caviar. Commercial fishing had started on the Ontario side of the lake just a few years before and these were valuable skills and much needed. Around 1895 his son William Allen Boucha joined him on Lake of the Woods. Not long after the rest of the boys also came to Lake of the Woods.

In 1896, William Henry took ill and spent some time back in Bouchaville/Naubinway, Michigan. When he returned to the Lake of the Woods area he married his third wife Maria Beecham in Norway House, Manitoba. They married in 1904, while William Henry was working with the Booth Fisheries. Along with Maria's children, they lived in Manitoba for some time and then returned to French Portage where his son's William Allen, John, Joseph, and Elmer were living. All became naturalized British subjects (Canadian Citizens).

The Bouchas were commercial fisherman, boat builders, carpenters, lighthouses builders and keepers. They had fish camps at Northwest Angle, Painted Rock Narrows, and French Portage among other places.

WILLIAM HENRY BOUCHA, SONS, AND OTHER RELATIVES IN KENORA, ONTARIO.

Figure 8

The Bouchas built some of the first steamboats on Lake of the Woods. The *Hunter* and the *Savage* vessels were used to fish and tow booms of timber. On Lake of the Woods, the Bouchas opened a fishery at the Northwest Angle, on Boucher Island on the Canadian side near Northwest Angle Band #33. They stayed there for a time and then decided to move to a place called French Portage, a nice spot in the middle of the lake that had deep water and was well protected from the elements and weather. All the Bouchas lived there at one time; twenty-three families worked and fished, built boats, lighthouses, channel markers and built their own homes and had large families. French Portage had a church, school, and tourist camp, and most residents fished commercially. There was a big market for timber, so logging and towing booms from the lake to Rat Portage (Kenora) also provided work.

ALYMERS BOUCHA, LIZZIE BOUCHA, WILLIAM HENRY BOUCHA, AND JOSEPH BOUCHA.

Figure 9

My grandfather Joseph married into the native population, as did many other family members. He married Rebecca Ellen Morrisseau (Morrison) in 1906. Joseph's brother John married Rebecca Ellen's sister, Catherine. They all lived and worked on the lake at French Portage. The Morrisseau sisters were the daughters of a famous guide/voyageur who worked for the Hudson Bay Company, Jonathan Morrisseau. He was said to be able to carry five hundred pounds on his back. During those times, all guides and voyageurs knew the water system and could travel from fort to fort with ease by canoe.

CHAPTER 7: PAINTED ROCK NARROWS/BERGLAND, ONTARIO

Rebecca Ellen Morrisseau (Morrison, my grandmother) was born in 1888 in Kenora, Ontario. Her dad was Jonathan Morrisseau. He worked for the Hudson Bay Company, as a boatman, and later a lighthouse keeper at Bishop Point on Lake of the Woods, not far from French Portage. Jonathan had a twin brother by the name of Jacob. (Jacob's great grandson, Phil Fontaine from Fort Alexander, is a former Grand Chief of Canada, and now owns a consulting company in Canada). My dad, when showing me around while on a family houseboat trip in the 1990's showed me the grave site of Jonathan (my paternal great grandfather) and his wife Mary Daniels (my paternal great grandmother) at Bigsby Island on Lake of the Woods. Also buried there is my dad's sister Elizabeth Boucha. Elizabeth died in 1920 at the age of 13. She was bleeding from the nose, and they could not stop the bleeding. It was springtime at French Portage and they could not get her to town or to a doctor.

JOSEPH AND REBECCA ELLEN MORRISSEAU BOUCHA, TAKEN AT RAILWAY STATION IN KENORA, ONTARIO.

Figure 11

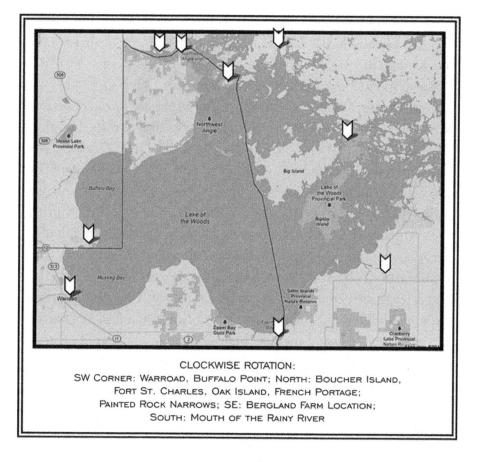

CLOCKWISE ROTATION:
SW CORNER: WARROAD, BUFFALO POINT; NORTH: BOUCHER ISLAND,
FORT ST. CHARLES, OAK ISLAND, FRENCH PORTAGE;
PAINTED ROCK NARROWS; SE: BERGLAND FARM LOCATION;
SOUTH: MOUTH OF THE RAINY RIVER

Figure 10

Joseph and Rebecca Boucha (my paternal grandparents) had a beautiful cedar log home at French Portage and a good life there. Joseph wanted to go off on his own and start a fishery. Rebecca Ellen's parents Jonathan and Mary Daniels Morrisseau lived at Dawson Narrows on Bigsby Island, thirty miles southeast of French Portage. Joseph found a nice site nearby at Painted Rock Narrows. It was suitable for a fish camp. Painted Rock Narrows was about three miles from the Morrisseaus' place on Bigsby. The family lived there and fished. They also kept their French Portage log cabin.

31

Joseph and Rebecca had eight children while at the Lake of the Woods. Elizabeth, the oldest, was born in 1907, Janet in 1909, my dad George in 1911, Edward in 1915, Fred in 1919, Clarence in 1922, Howard in 1923, Alvina in 1925, and Irene in 1929.

Sometime after building and operating the fish camp at Painted Rock Narrows, in 1926, Joseph, Rebecca, and family bought a 320-acre farm in Bergland, Ontario on the Little Grassy River. The purchase included a house, barn, and a sawmill all for $850. He made lumber for Bergland and the surrounding area. It was a very successful operation and he employed several men in the area. During the Great Depression years, everyone struggled for survival. Joseph, operated his fishery, managed the sawmill and a small farm of chickens, cows, sheep, and horses in Bergland. They had a large garden and picked wild berries and canned quarts of fruit, vegetables, and meats, and they always had fresh eggs from the farm. Rebecca and the kids helped with all of the chores on the farm. During harvest everyone worked together, putting up hay, canning and stocking the cellar for winter.

In 1932, my dad (George, a young man at that time), was working at Painted Rock Fish Camp. He visited the family in French Portage where he met my mother, Alice Powassin Caron who with her grandmother Laughing Mary Thunder, was also visiting and they attended the spring dance. I was told that every weekend one of the fish camps had a party and people would travel from all over the lake to attend. People would sleep in their boats, which was common in those days and go back to work when finished.

In July 1932, my dad jumped in his small kicker boat at Painted Rocks Narrows and traveled across Lake of the Woods to Buffalo Point, twenty five miles one way by water. When he arrived, he parked his boat on shore, walked up the bank, and went to Laughing Mary's cabin and walked in. He said to Alice: "Come on, let's go get married." She stood there for minute looking at him, and finally said "ok". Laughing Mary and mom packed up their belongings and left in dad's boat. They traveled back to Painted Rock Narrows for the marriage ceremony.

Dad told grandpa Joseph about his plans to marry Alice and grandpa sent the word out. The news of the wedding traveled around the fish camps. When they arrived back at Painted Rock Narrows Fish Camp, the bay was filled with fishing boats. Family and friends were gathered there for the wedding. They married and everyone celebrated. They lived and worked there for a time, while they talked and made plans for moving and fishing at Buffalo Bay. Dad made arrangements for acquiring boats from grandpa. Dad packed supplies, including nets and poles on a thirty-eight-foot wood boat. He also took a small kicker boat and motor.

George and Alice (my parents), decided to move to the north side of Buffalo Point and fish Buffalo Bay in Manitoba. They stayed at Laughing Mary's cabin while they built their own cabin on a small strip of crown land on the north side of Buffalo Point near Buffalo Bay.

Dad would fish and haul his catch to the fishery in Warroad. Buffalo Bay was part of Lake of the Woods. Fishing was abundant. The bay is ten miles long and four miles wide. It is filled with sandbars, weed beds and more than a few creeks running into it from the west and north side. The cabin was small and modest. It was a summer cabin only with one room, a bed and a cook stove. It had small single pane windows, tarpaper roof and tarpaper walls. It had an outdoor toilet and no running water or electricity. They used a kerosene lamp for lighting. They bathed, cooked with and drank lake water. They bought ice at the fishery in Warroad, which they used for icing (preserving/cooling) the fish in wooden boxes. The fishery in Warroad had other goods that the fisherman could trade for or buy when dropping off the fish during the summers. The fishermen had running credit for supplies such as gas, ice and other fishing supplies. They would also receive cash when they needed it. They shopped at the local grocery store for goods and supplies. It was nice for the people of Buffalo Point to have dad running to town on a regular basis. Many of them caught rides with him.

Dad would take a deer or moose once in a while, and would share the meat with others living at Buffalo. They shared their fish and sometimes traded for meat. The berries were plentiful and they had a small garden and canned and stocked for winter. The wild rice was plentiful. They harvested and processed it in late summer. Weather permitting, dad hauled his catch to Warroad on a daily basis. He had enough ice so he could hold the fish for a couple days. They stayed at Buffalo in the summers and moved either to Middleboro, Manitoba, or Warroad, Minnesota for the winters.

Dad was like a taxi service on some occasions. When someone needed to go to town, they rode with him. One time he gave Bemis Handorgan a ride back to Buffalo Bay. Bemis was drunk but dad was nice and gave him a ride anyway. During the ride back Bemis wanted to fight and took a swing at dad. Dad put the boat in neutral, and wrestled Bemis down and tied him up. When dad got to Buffalo, he pulled close to shore, untied him and threw him in the lake and watched him swim to shore.

Dad trapped in the fall and cut pulp in the winter. They rented a house for the winter in Warroad. Dad fished Buffalo Bay until it was closed to commercial fishing in 1957 by Manitoba Fisheries. They lived and traveled back and forth for years before buying a house in Warroad.

We made several family trips to Bergland in the summer. Dad would pull his nets and load the family in the thirty-eight foot boat. We usually stopped several places and stayed the night sleeping in the boat. We stopped especially at Big Island and picked blueberries. After a couple of days dad would maneuver his boat up the Little Grassy River to grandpa and grandma's farm. There were very few bridges. Everything was ferried across the rivers. We stayed and helped with the harvest and canning. Grandma had a summer kitchen and cooked outside to feed everyone. We used only wood heat in those days. Cooking in the main house was too hot in summer and early fall.

BACK: HOWARD, CLARENCE, GEORGE, FRED.
FRONT: IREANE AND JANET.

JANET BOUCHA MATTSON, GEORGE BOUCHA WITH
VI, PHYLLIS AND DARLENE.

FRONT, LEFT TO RIGHT:
REBECCA ELLEN MORRISON BOUCHA,
DARLENE BOUCHA AND JOSEPH BOUCHA. IN FRONT
COUSIN ELMA JOY BOUCHA.

ON THE BOAT WITH FAMILY. AT THE HELM
BELOW IS CAPTAIN GEORGE BOUCHA AND HENRY.

Figure 12

CHAPTER 8: TREATY #3

Buffalo Point is a Canadian Indian Reserve located six miles by water and walking distance from Warroad. It is part of Treaty # 3, along with 28 other Canadian Reserves surrounding Lake of the Woods.

Treaty # 3 was the third in a series of eleven numbered treaties between the Crown and Canadian First Nations. Despite being the third of these treaties it is in fact more historically significant in that it's text and terms served as the model of the remainder of the numbered treaties in Canada. Treaty # 3 is also significant because there exists a written document of the native people's understanding of the agreement. This is known as the Paypom Document. It is a series of notes that were written for Chief Powassin, my great great grandfather. It was taken during the treaty negotiations. It documents the promises that were made to the First Nations people. The promise in the Paypom Document differs in a number of ways from the version available from the Canadian Government today.

The year 1870 was significant to the Lake of the Woods area and western Canada. With lawlessness in the area, the Dominion of Government sent Lt. Cornel John Garnet Wolseley with his 1200 men to maintain peace in the area. It took them 3 months to reach Rat Portage from Toronto. It also left little doubt to the Indians about who was in charge of the area. Soon after the roads were built, portages were improved and travel was easier. Although the Chippewa/ Ojibwa were friendly toward the whites, they were still at odds with the Sioux. They would fight and were hostile toward the Sioux when they met. The Chippewa/Ojibwa through their migration from the east pushed the Sioux into the Dakotas, and the Cree and Assiniboine north. The result was many battles and skirmishes over the years with the Sioux, until peace finally came to the area. The Chippewa/Ojibwa got along with and trusted the French but it was inevitable that the white man's large force meant that the whites were here to stay and bring order to the area. The government wanted title to the land and in return made treaty with the Indians and offered the Indians sums of money, guarantees of peace, protection and education.

It took many years to finally negotiate the treaty. It would have been easier to negotiate the treaties if France was still in control but the British had taken over. With many tribes from Lake Superior to the Lake of the Woods and Manitoba it was difficult to bring them all to the table. The border had not yet been established. Treaty # 3 was concentrated to about 55,000 square miles and with about 14,000 Indians living in the that area.

The Indians (each settlement or band of several families to bands as large as a few hundred) considered themselves sovereign over their area. The headman or Chief of each band had to be in agreement to sign the Treaty. It took years to finally get the Indians all together and to agree to meet. In September 1873 a conference was finally held at the Northwest Angle. In attendance for the Government were: Alexander Morris, the Lt. Governor of Manitoba and the Northwest Territories; Lt. Colonel Provencher, representing the Military; and S. J. Dawson, Explorer, and member of the Canadian Parliament of Algoma. The official Government delegation arrived at the Hudson Bay Post at Harrison Creek Northwest Angle on September 25, 1873.

The Indians were in conference already and for several days talking about the treaty and what it meant. The whites thought the Indians were savages and didn't understand what was happening and they tried their best to convey to the Indians the purpose of the treaty. With the language and culture barrier, the Indians had translators to help them. The Indians were quiet, shy and with few words but they were eloquent, poetic and wise in their own ways and culture. The love of Lake of the Woods by the Indians and all who came to see and take part in its beauty explains why the Indians wanted this territory. Now they were about to be guests in their own land.

The Treaty was signed on October 3, 1873 at the Hudson Bay Post, at Harrison Creek Northwest Angle. Although, it was never followed to the letter, it has been re-interpreted by government officials and lawyers over the years to get out from under many of the provisions' as stated in the treaty. The Indians have been forced into Federal Court to fight for treaty rights and appeal the Government's interpretations on many occasions. The Canadian Provinces, Indian and Northern Affairs Canada and the Canadian Government continue to challenge the treaties on most issues to this day.

Thank you to Duane R. Lund's "Lake of the Woods Yesterday and Today" for some of the information in this chapter.

CHAPTER 9: BUFFALO POINT (NEY-AA-SHIING)

Buffalo Point is an Indian First Nation Reserve located in south-eastern Manitoba. It is a peninsula, 4 miles long by 2 miles wide. The First Nation has reserved themselves six reserves under the treaty land entitlement and they encompass: Buffalo Point Indian Reserve of 5,760 acres; Reed River Indian Reserve of 2,870 acres; Buffalo Point Indian Reserve 1 of 92 acres; Buffalo Point Indian Reserve 2 of 860 acres; Buffalo Point Indian Reserve 3 of 230 acres; and Agency Indian Reserve 30 on the Aulneau Peninsula on the Lake of the Woods in Ontario, which is shared with 12 other First Nations. Total population is 110 registered members and less than 40 live on the reserve currently. There is a Chief and two council members.

Adults L to R: Tom Lawson, Jim Thunder,
Mrs. Hondorgan, Mrs. Jim Thunder, Laughing Mary,
Unidentified, unidentified, Mrs. Accobee
Identified by Alice Boucha

BUFFALO POINT/WARROAD INDIANS. COURTESY OF THE WARROAD HISTORICAL SOCIETY.

Figure 13

Warroad, Minnesota is less than 6 miles by water to Buffalo Point Reserve. Buffalo Point was inhabited by Ay-A-Ash-Wash and family along with other families. His father Bwan was related to other well known Minnesota Chiefs. He and his family along with others lived on Buffalo Point as well as Warroad (Kah-Bay-Kah-Nong). Both places were inhabited and called home by them. When the U.S/Canadian border was established, it cut them in two. The Ay-A-Ash-Wash's family consisted of: Ah-Ne-Mah-Kneese (Little Thunder—the Boucha's come from his lineage), Ka Ka Geesicks, Nah-May-Poke, and the daughters who married; Mrs. Major, Mrs. Blackbird, Mrs. Bombay, Mrs. Elliot and my great grandmother Laughing Mary Thunder. Also other members on the reserve were the Lightning's, Cobiness's, Handorgan's, Ka Ka Geesick's, Nah-May-Poke's family, the Jones', Goodin's, and there were others coming and going as the Indians traveled and married into various bands around Lake of The Woods and elsewhere. Some of the other names that come to mind are the Blackbirds, Major's, Powassin's (Laughing Mary Thunder married a Powassin), Accobee's, Elliot's, Bombay's and others.

Before the dam was built in Kenora, the Indians called the Big Traverse Bay "The Lake of the Sand Hills." It was dotted with sand islands from east to west, and south from Warroad to the islands at the Northwest Angle. The islands had large pine trees on them and the Indians could paddle their canoes anywhere on Lake of the Woods. There was a large long island that ran from Buffalo Point past Springsteele Island to the north shore near Warroad. The Buffalo Point Indians would travel at ease to and from Warroad by canoe.

Most of the Buffalo Point Indians made their homes in Warroad while keeping a place at Buffalo Point. Buffalo Point was a sacred place and they held many sacred ceremonies on the Point on the east end of the peninsula. As a child growing up on the north side of Buffalo Point, I felt that it was a magical place. I would often look out across the lake and I could see Buffalo Point from Warroad. Mom and dad would always talk about Buffalo Point after moving to Warroad.

Dad once told me that Bemis Handorgan was sitting at his table in his cabin smoking a rolled up cigarette, when he looked up and there was a Sasquatch looking into the window at him. Startled, Bemis jumped up and the creature ran off. After Bemis calmed down, he could not find his cigarette anywhere and he realized that he must have swallowed it.

At Buffalo Point there were many cabins and most of the Indians stayed there throughout the summer and into the fall and they lived in Warroad in the winter. There was good fishing, berry picking, and vegetable gardens. Wild rice was plentiful and harvested in late summer. Hunting was always good at Buffalo Point which had abundant game. After the dam was built, the lake was raised by 9 feet and it washed all the sand islands away in the Big Traverse Bay. It was hard to travel back and forth with high seas at times. You had to pick your times to cross and follow the shoreline.

Later on, Tom Thunder married Sara Conover who had two children: James and Catherine, both caucasian (white by birth). Tom and Sara had two other children Dorothy and Frank. In the late 1960's James Conover took control of the band. It has been tragic for the real members of Buffalo Point ever since. There are very few band members who live on the reserve and they are under constant threat to be removed from their homeland. Other members would like to move back but are hesitant to do so. They no longer have the right to vote, obtain their inherent rights or entitlements, and do not have transparency with the current Chief and Council. The members are seeking a democratic election to restore the reserve to its members.

CHAPTER 10: WARROAD

In the early 1900's, the Canadian government built a dam in Kenora to make the lake more navigable. It raised the lake level by nine feet. Before that, a person could go by canoe along a long sandy island that ran from north to south from near Buffalo to Warroad. There were sandy islands with pine trees on the south end of the lake. The dam raising the lake level and high water washed all the trees and sand islands away. The Indians could paddle to most places within the islands making for good, safe travel.

There were early stories about the south end of Lake of the Woods even as far away as Fond du Lac, Wisconsin. The stories told of people walking on water. It may have appeared that way because if you were on the lake and saw someone walking on the sand beaches at a distance, it could look as if they were walking on the water. It is amazing to think how much the native people traveled in those days. They would go from band settlement to band settlement within the Chippewa/Ojibwa tribe region to trade, visit and intermarry.

GEORGE G. MARVIN CAME TO WARROAD IN 1904 TO MANAGE THE GRAIN ELEVATOR. HE SAW POTENTIAL IN LUMBER AND OPENED UP MARVIN LUMBER AND CEDAR COMPANY IN 1912. IT GREW INTO MARVIN WINDOWS AND DOORS EMPLOYING THOUSANDS. MARVIN ALWAYS GAVE TO THE COMMUNITY OF WARROAD QUIETLY AND NEVER SOUGHT TO TAKE ANY CREDIT. GEORGE MARVIN SET AN EXAMPLE OF HARD WORK, INGENUITY AND INTEGRITY.

HAROLD HENEMAN, BANKER, JOINED SECURITY STATE BANK IN 1918 AND ASSUMED PRESIDENCY IN 1943. THE BANK IS A INDEPENDENT COMMUNITY BANK COMMITTED TO THE PEOPLE OF WARROAD PAST, PRESENT AND FUTURE. THAT SAYS IT ALL, THEY HAVE BEEN THERE THROUGH THICK AND THIN FOR THE PEOPLE OF WARROAD. SON, JOHN HENEMAN NOW RETIRED TURNED OVER THE REINS TO HIS SON RHODY.

COURTESY OF THE WARROAD HISTORICAL SOCIETY.

Figure 14

Some of the people at Buffalo Point, while living in Warroad, received land allotments from the US government on the US side. Some of those land allotments were at the Northwest Angle and others in the Warroad area. In Warroad, Ka Ka Geesick's received a land allotment of 120 acres on the south east side of Warroad. It ran north to south and almost to the blinker on the lake. Most of the land is now underwater because of the dam. Na-May-Poke had another allotment in Warroad that was everything north of the Warroad River (Christian property) to Marvin Windows Plant. Na May Poke was able to sell land to the school, and then his family was able to sell the rest over the years through the Bureau of Indian Affairs.

In 1864, under the Nelson Act, the US government was brokering Indian land and opened it up to homestead. It gave a few allotments to the Indians. The US government was to pay the Indians a few cents an acre for brokering the land. It never happened, until the tribes took it to court in the 1950s. The case was finally settled in the 2000s, after millions in legal fees were paid. Finally, after over a hundred years, the Indians received payment for the land.

The Buffalo Point Indians moved to Warroad or Middleboro in the winter. Most had homes in Warroad on Na May Poke's allotted land which is now the Christian property. There is a gravesite on the property where there are a few marked graves. For work most Indians cut pulp, trapped, worked at the mink ranches or worked odd jobs to get by. Most people hunted, picked blueberries, and harvested wild rice in late summer and fall. Most hunted birds, ducks, geese, moose and deer. Everyone stocked up for winter. There were not many luxuries. People survived, raise their families and helped each other.

ALICE BOUCHA HOLDING HENRY
WITH MOOSE BELLANGER HARDY
ON GEORGE BOUCHA'S FISHING BOAT ON
BUFFALO BAY.

GEORGE BOUCHA PELTING MINK.

WARROAD FISHERIES.

FISH CLEANING.

LODGING AND SAWMILL SOUTH OF WARROAD.

MARVIN LUMBER AND CEDAR CO.

Figure 15

There was no electricity on the lake. The fisheries cut and hauled ice in winter and stored it for the summer. They built huge buildings to store ice on various strategic places on the lake. The buildings were insulated with sawdust. They cut, hauled and stacked blocks of ice with sawdust between the blocks for easier separation. The ice would last all summer. Without refrigeration, putting up ice for the commercial fisheries was monumental.

Getting around in the winter on the ice was hard. With the ice full of cracks it was difficult to maneuver, they would lay boards across the cracks to get across. Some developed and used the wind sleighs or puddle jumpers. Most people walked, often wearing snowshoes when going across the lake or cross country. Trying to travel on the ice and snow was a challenge. Some ice roads were plowed locally. Some would try going across the lake and would wander off the roads. They used cars or trucks with chains, skis and anything else they could think of to cross on the ice. They tried to find a better way of getting around in winter. It is evident even today when in the islands on Lake of the Woods; you can see old cars and trucks from the 30's and 40's left to rust where they were abandoned.

The Booth Fisheries were large and successful. The fisherman contracted and sold the fish to them. There were also other smaller fisheries at the south end of the lake. The fisheries shipped fish to markets to the east and would send their fish to Kenora. Later the railroad came through Warroad and the fisheries shipped from there. With no refrigerated cars everything was iced down. I remember the old steam engines coming through town when I was a kid. They had whistle-stops with coal and water every six miles. The train ran from Winnipeg to Fort William and Port Arthur, now Thunder Bay. The rail system came around the south side of Lake of the Woods in the early 1900s.

There were no lights on the road crossings. You had to pay attention and look for trains. Over the years there were a lot of train/car accidents at the crossings. In Warroad, at the Lake Street crossing, they had a little shack which was not any bigger than an outhouse. The railroad hired Herb Hardy to sit in there and wait for trains to come. He would walk out to the center of the road and hold up a sign to stop traffic when the trains came through. As a kid going to school we would stop, poke our heads in and say hi to Herb sitting in there. In winter he had a coal stove, to stay warm.

The logging business was good with many sawmills around the area. Trapping and cutting pulp was a good seasonal job for the commercial fishermen in the winter. In the spring they worked on their boats, and prepared nets for the fishing season. All boats then were made of wood and needed yearly repairs.

Buffalo Point had navigable waters on three sides, and on the west side it had a big shallow swamp. Elm Creek ran out of the south side, and Tamarack Creek out of the east side of the swamp. Some of it drained into Reed River on the north. Dad told me that he would walk or wade through the swamp to go to the store in Middleboro. He did that many times while they lived at Buffalo Point. He had to lift the groceries on his shoulders because the water was up to his armpits. He said his arms got tired, and he had to rest once in a while. It took a long time to go round trip and he never got anything wet.

Most of the other Band members lived on the south and east shore of Buffalo Point on reserve land. Buffalo Bay was on the north side. From our cabin, it was about ten miles to Warroad by boat. Dad set his nets in Buffalo Bay, a great fishery. It still is today, but only open to sport fishing. East winds would wreak havoc with dad's fishing, and it was rough. The east end of Buffalo Bay was wide open to Big Traverse Bay that ran 55 miles east to the Ontario shore. Large fishing boats around Buffalo Point had to anchor out in deep water, and people came ashore in small kicker boats. There was no harbor at Buffalo Point.

Warroad had a nice harbor up the Warroad River. It was dredged and made navigable. The fisheries were along the river, and the railroad brought the tracks right to the fisheries. It currently has two channel marker towers, one 50' and one a 100' and a blinker a mile out to find the channel.

Most days while at Buffalo we would ride into Warroad to drop off the catch and pick up a few things at the store. We would sometimes spend the night and sleep in the boat. We would go out early in the mornings.

We also had a cabin at Reed River. A river that ran into the bay from the west side. It is part of the Buffalo Point Reserve. At Reed River, the cabin was used to fish and hunt. They would catch big northern pike in the spring. The mouth of the Reed River was shallow and difficult to access except with a small boat. Dad trapped and hunted there in the fall, and used it in the winter when logging in that area. Most cabins in those days had one room, a bed and a woodstove for cooking and heating. There was no electricity or running water, and we used an outdoor toilet or the woods. There were other cabins up there too. One summer the Ministry of Natural Resources destroyed our cabin by mistake. Mom said she lost everything she had in the cabin including old pictures and family keepsakes that were passed down to her and dad. I asked her if the government compensated them or paid them for it, and she said "no". The government workers just said "sorry" and left.

Dad trapped in the fall and cut pulp in the winter. He walked from Warroad or Middleboro to Buffalo Point, Reed River, Stony Creek and north to Sandy Beach. He stayed at the cabins and would walk back to Warroad when finished. He also trapped on the south shore out of Warroad, and out at Marvin Lake north of Warroad. He got a ride to Hay Creek some 13 miles from Warroad, then walked Hay Creek north to Marvin Lake and then east to the road north of Warroad. It would take him all day. He would do that a couple times a week. Sometimes Don Hanson, a local pilot, would drop him off in the mornings at the head of his trap line at Buffalo Bay, and Stony

Creek and pick him up late in the day. He paid Don by sharing some of the profits from his pelts.

All of my older brothers and sisters went to school in Middleboro. You could ride the train in those days to Warroad and up and down the line for 25 cents. Middleboro was a small community with a few stores, a hotel and a post office. After spending the summer at Buffalo Bay fishing, the family would usually rent a place for the winter in Middleboro, and later go to Warroad. There were other Buffalo Point families living in Middleboro, and in Warroad. The towns were only 9 miles apart.

In Middleboro, dad had two draft horses and a sleigh. He contracted with the Canadian National Railway to cut railroad ties. He spent a few winters cutting near Reed River and hauling the ties to Middleboro on a big sled with his horses. They cut pulp in those days with a bow saw and an axe. Dad told me that he hired old man Kostynic, who had a store in Middleboro. Dad found it amusing that all the man would bring for lunch was a few sausages. It would last him all day.

My dad was still fishing in Buffalo Bay when we first moved into Warroad for the winter. Dad would pull his fishing boat up on the Warroad beach for the winter. Many other big boats were pulled up there also. They used a tractor to pull them totally out of the water. Then in the spring they used a tractor to push them back out.

All of the boats were made of wood in those days. There were many skilled boat builders in the area. They used local oak for the beams and cypress for the planking. The cypress was shipped in from Florida. Large boats were used for trips from Warroad to Kenora for freight and passenger service. Warroad was thirty miles across open water from Garden Island and the start of the Islands at Northwest Angle. Big Traverse Bay was thirty miles north to south and fifty-five miles east to west. It was dangerous at times with high winds, large waves. Kenora was 90 miles one way with a stop at the Northwest Angle, some 45 miles from Warroad.

Warroad's population in the early 1950s was around a thousand people. It had several businesses including: Security State Bank, Warroad Hotel, Bar and Café, Cal's Cabins, Marvin Lumber & Cedar Co., Pages, Lu-J Cafes, Roberts Hardware, Coast to Coast Hardware, Rouses Variety, Carlson's Appliances, a bakery, Magnan's Pharmacy, Warroad Hospital, Warroad Clinic, Warroad Public Schools, Wing's Department Store, Meek's, Red Owl, Hartz Grocieres, Warroad Memorial Arena, Poole's and Silver Dollar Taverns, Warroad Liquor Store, American Legion, Warroad Railroad Depot, US Customs, Pete's Mobile and Café, Phillip 66, Johnson's Chevy, Percy's, Anderson's Jewelry, a dentist office, a dry cleaners, a butcher shop, and other businesses.

There were several mink ranches in the area early on and they sold furs to the New York market. Heinen Mink Ranch was the biggest with over forty thousand mink. Most mink ranches had their own fishing fleet using gill and pond nets to catch marketable fish for the fisheries and rough fish to feed the mink. The mink ranches mixed ground rough fish with dry cereal and for mink feed. There were a lot of Indian people working at the mink ranches and working on the lake. My dad worked for Heinen Mink Ranch for many years. Dad managed the ranches fishing fleet. They had a trawler, and several other boats used for gill and pond nets. In winter they dropped nets through the ice for burbot, tullibee, and other rough fish that were used for mink feed. The market fell out in the 1970s, and all the mink ranches are now closed. Dad later worked at Christian Brothers' hockey stick factory making wood hockey sticks.

The economy was steady with commercial fishing, timber, lumber, mink ranches and small farms. Warroad shipped fish, timber, crops, and lumber to the markets on the rail. The commercial fishing was eventually terminated by the Department of Natural

WARROAD IN THE EARLY 1900s.
COURTESY OF THE WARROAD HISTORICAL SOCIETY.

Figure 16

Resources. Sport fishing and tourism took over and Warroad is now mainly known for manufacturing windows, sport fishing, tourism and hockey.

For many years commercial boats provided passenger service to the islands of the Northwest Angle and to Kenora. Flying services provided travel for sport fisherman and tourists to lodges, and fish camps until economics and regulations drove them out of business.

Warroad, because of the cold climate had a gym at the school, and the children did very little outside. Very few communities had indoor arenas. In 1947, as a young man, Cal Marvin had a dream of fundraising and building an arena. He fulfilled his dream and it created an opportunity for youngsters to skate indoors and out of the elements.

EARLY 1900S WARROAD. COURTESY OF THE WARRAOD HISTORICAL SOCIETY.

EARLY 1900S WARROAD. COURTESY OF THE WARROAD HISTORICAL SOCIETY.

Figure 17

Morris Taylor, the mayor of Warroad during the 1960s, deemed Warroad as Hockeytown USA. Hockey was our life, with the Warroad Lakers, Warroad High School and the Warroad Youth Hockey programs. Over the years the United States Hockey teams had strong representation from the Warroad players on their teams. Billy and Roger Christian won the gold medal while playing on the US Olympic Hockey Team in Squaw Valley in 1960. Their brother, Ginny Christian won a silver medal in 1956, and Cal Marvin managed the US Hockey Team in 1958 and 1965. The Warroad Lakers were one of North America's finest senior amateur teams ever to assemble. Founded in 1947, the team continued for fifty years, winning many National Championships in the US and Canada. Many other notable players from Warroad would follow.

The only theater in Warroad was the Fox Theatre. It was owned and operated by Loren Fox and family. From our home on the south side of the Warroad River we had a trail directly to the theater. It was all snow packed and well used. We followed the trail down to the river, stepped on the docks, jumped down on the ice, walk across the little channel, across Government Island, across the main channel, and then climbed up the docks and walked a block to the theater. Admission, pop, and popcorn were only a quarter. Sometimes we had trouble scrapping that together. If it was a scary movie, we ran home over the rail road bridge and stayed away from Government Island. Walking the trail meant we had to walk through the willows and small trees. You just never knew what would jump out and get you. Now, when I see the old movies, I remember many of them from the Fox Theatre. Good or bad movies, we saw them all. We did not have a TV so the movies were entertaining and educational for us.

Here is a tidbit for all; Sheila Terry aka Kay Clark was born in Warroad, Minnesota March 5, 1910. She was an American actress appearing in 42 films. She played on Broadway in New York and was signed by Warner Bros. Then she appeared in films in the 30's with John Wayne, Cary Grant, Loretta Young, Joan Blondell, William Powell, George Brent and many others. She died in New York on January 19, 1957 at the age of 46.

Growing up in Warroad like many small towns, it was safe, quiet, with neighborhoods where people trusted each other. We knew most people in town and in other towns close by. Most people got along and helped each other.

CHAPTER 11: THE EARLY YEARS IN WARROAD

I was born June 1, 1951, at the Warroad Hospital at around 4 p.m. My sister Darlene, the oldest of the family graduated from high school that very same day. Darlene was seventeen years old when she graduated. She would not turn 18 until December of that year. My sister Phyllis was sixteen, Georgie twelve, Dave ten, Shirley seven, and Jim was five. We were all living in a small two-bedroom house. Our first tragedy was the death of my sister Susan Jeanne, born November 16, 1949. She lived only three days before passing away. She is buried at the Riverside Cemetery in Warroad. I often wonder how life would have been if she had survived. In the small house in Warroad, the young ones slept in homemade hammocks, and the rest doubled and tripled in the beds. Everyone seemed to have a place to sleep, cozy, but no privacy. Most houses were small in those days.

DAVID BOUCHA

DARLENE BOUCHA

GEORGE BOUCHA JR.

PHYLLIS BOUCHA SARGENT

COURTESY OF ED & LINDA BOUCHA AND ROGER & JANET DORION.

Figure 18

Darlene met Jim Dorion, a boy from Roseau who was on leave from the Navy. They would write each other while he was away and see each other when he would come home on leave. Jim was getting out of the Navy in early 1951, the year Darlene graduated. Jim asked Darlene to marry him. She said. "yes." Jim had an older brother, Henry Dorion, who lived out west in a little town called Lewiston, Idaho. Henry Dorian set up a small TV repair business in Lewiston and it was going quite well. He invited Jim to come and find work after he was discharged from the Navy. Jim moved to Lewiston, stayed with his brother Henry, and started working as a bus boy at a local hotel. He sent for Darlene as soon as she graduated. They were married and lived in a small apartment in Lewiston. Jim eventually was employed at the mill and bought a house and raised four boys. The Dorion's live there today. Darlene passed in 2012.

Our house in Warroad, was on the south side of the river. The south side homes did not have city water or sewer, and if you did not have a septic system, you had an outdoor toilet. You had a potty inside the house that you would dump a couple of times a day in the outhouse. If you sat outside, toilet paper was a luxury. Most of the time we used pages from a Sear's catalog or something similar for toilet paper. It smelled bad in the summer heat, and it was biting cold in the winter.

Every house had its own well. We bathed out of the tubs in the kitchen. When we did bathe, we hauled in water from the outside well. Mom heated the water on the stove and then dumped it into the tubs for our baths. It seemed at that time, that everyone had a barrel outside their house to catch the rainwater off the roofs. It was soft water, and they used it to wash their hair, especially the women.

Dad was on the lake commercial fishing when mom bought the house on the south side of the river in Warroad. Before going on the lake, dad talked to a family about buying a house on Lake Street in Warroad. The house had three bedrooms, a basement, and a small garage. It also had city water and sewer. Dad planned to surprise mom and was going to show her the house when he came from the lake. Mom did not know about his plan and she selected and bought another house. She had already moved us in. When Dad pulled up to the dock mom told him that she bought a house, and dad was surprised. He was disappointed but easygoing and went along with the deal. Mom grew up without a well or septic at Buffalo Point. She thought that house was fine. It had its own well and electricity, so she was satisfied.

At home, we did not have many toys or things to do. We made up games and kept busy. Early on, we did not have a TV. We had a radio, and we listened to the stations in Winnipeg or Crookston, Minnesota, some 100 miles away. Crookston had a "Warroad Report" where Margaret Marvin gave the local news. She gave the report live via telephone. When that was on, we all had to sit still. Also, Les Lightning broadcasted from the same station. Mom would drop everything and tell us kids to settle down as Les was coming on the air. We listened to the news, and the radio show. We also listened to hockey games and sometimes music.

Phyllis was sixteen at the time, and helped manage the kids. In the winter, I sometimes watched the kids playing road hockey through our picture window. My brothers and sisters were playing outside with the neighborhood kids. They used old broken hockey sticks that had been nailed together and taped, or they used home-made sticks. If you had a new hockey stick it was a luxury. We made sticks out of just about anything we could find. I watched the older boys play in the living room with a rolled-up socks.

SHIRLEY, DAVID, GEORGIE, JIM, HENRY, PURP.

Figure 19

I vaguely remember Georgie or David being around the house. I was two when my brother Edward John was born on November 23, 1953. Phyllis got married in 1954 to William "Rink" Sargent. She was nineteen. When I was five I started kindergarten, Darlene had been gone for five years. Phyllis was married, and Georgie was seventeen, quit shool and enrolled in the Navy. Mom signed for him to join. Dave, Shirley and Jim were still in school.

I remember my first day of school. I was excited, as we all walked to school. While walking out of the yard that morning with the others, I was worried and I turned around to mom and asked, "But how do I learn?" She laughed, and so did the others. I felt embarrassed. I kept my mouth shut the rest of the way to school. I am sure my sister Shirley took me to the right class. Kindergarten was alright. Going to school was different. I liked being with other kids my age. They taught us how to tie our shoes, among other basics. We had class all day. My teacher was Vickie Berg, who became Vickie Meek after she married Harlan Meek. Harlan's parents owned Meeks Grocery. The grocery store was close to the school. Everyone stopped in and bought candy when they had money. Vickie was originally from Baudette and was attending the University of Minnesota-Duluth. That year was the first year the government required school districts to hold all-day kindergarten. Warroad did not have a teacher to fill that position. The district was in a bind and contacted the University of Minnesota. Vickie being from the Baudette area was given permission and credit to come to Warroad to teach kindergarten.

I remember bringing home a list of things we needed to for school. We had to bring a rug to class to take a nap on in the afternoons, among other things. We had a milk break in the morning, lunch and in the afternoon another milk break. I loved milk, so I had a couple glasses (paper-cone cups) each time. We marched single file out of the room to the milk coolers and stood there in line against the wall while drinking the milk.

When recently visiting with Mrs. Meek, she reminded me of the separation of the Indian people and the non Indians in Warroad in the early 1950s. There was definitely a difference in the way we were treated and depicted as people. It brings back some memories of how I felt when I was a child dealing with those thoughts and emotions. We did not have a lot of self-confidence when outside our home. I was always quiet, and didn't say much around people in those days. I knew my place and kept my mouth shut. I remember how some of the elders felt. Tom Thunder would talk about how he felt when at the theater, watching westerns and how the Indians were depicted and always defeated. He would jump up and walk out of the building and go home. The roles of Indians in the old John Wayne and western movies were not positive depictions or descriptions of the Indian people, to say the least. It impacted us all. I know I had low self-esteem and never wanted to be an Indian. Those emotions ran deep and were hurtful. There were some people in the community then and still today that identify our living areas and homes as reservations. You overhear them at times when you happened to walk up unexpectedly and they are making statements to that effect. I have overheard them several times over the years. Racism and discrimination are still a social problem. During Ms. Meek's tenure at the Warroad School, she observed a time when one of our native children came to school without a jacket, hat or mittens and it was over 20 below zero. She tried to get help for the child but no one seemed to care. They seemed to believe the situation would take care of itself and they simply said, "Oh, he will survive".

HENRY, GEORGE, SHIRLEY, ALICE AND EDDY AT CHRISTMAS.

Figure 20

The Poole family (Bill & Helen) had thirteen kids and one was in just about every age bracket. They owned Poole's Tavern. I played with both Billy and Tommy who were close to my age. They both played goalie during the early years, and Billy played goalie in high school. Tommy was our goalie at the Bantam State Tournament in1964. He later moved to California, but kept in touch with everyone. I saw the Poole's in California in the 1970's, when I played with the Red Wings. I always had a great time while visiting them. Earl was quite the hockey player. The Blackhawks owned his rights, but he never signed with them.

The Joe Oshie family lived in Warroad too. Joe's wife, Sally Jones, my cousin, was part of the Na-May-Poke family. Joe Oshie worked at one of the mink ranches and commercial fished. He was from across the lake. Their youngest, Mike and I played a lot of hockey. Mike, Tommy Poole, and I were the same age and good friends. Mike was really good at sports. Aside from playing hockey, we played all sports. One time while playing baseball near our house, I was batting and Mike was the catcher. I swung that bat around and it hit Mike squarely on the forehead. I put a dent in his forehead and he did not bleed or cry, and I know it hurt. He still has that dent today. I told him that he would never know whether I did that on purpose or not.

Jim and Phyllis Gibbons family lived nearby with their kids Clinton and Carol. Carol was near my age and both went to school in Warroad. Jim Gibbons was a guitar player and singer. Clint learned the guitar as well. Clint taught my brother Jim to play. Clint and Jim were close in age and would sit and play at our house. Jim picked it up fairly quick. They taught me a few things, and I remained interested.

My mother spoke Ojibwa, and she knew the old ways. But as kids growing up in a predominately white community, watching those old westerns, and going to public schools, we did not want to hear or learn the Ojibwa language or about the culture. I thought there was nothing to be proud of for being an Indian. For me, the impact and impressions came from the movie depictions and the comments of others when they did not know you were listening. It was the way people talked about us and how they looked at us that lessened our self esteem. A person can tell and feel when people are talking and looking down at you. You know how they feel about you, even though they may say something to the contrary. Just study the old movies depicting us as savages, drunks, dirty and observe the way people thought of us. You will see. That is what prevented us from wanting to learn our ways. Being Indian was embarrassing, and it seemed we were all trying to get out of the characterization that white people put us in. As a result, we did not want to learn our language, heritage and culture. We had low self esteem. We felt like second class citizens. We self-doubted about who we were and wanted to be. The comments were hurtful and degrading. When we played cowboys and Indians, all the Indians wanted to be cowboys and the white kids wanted to be Indians. Without the prejudices, it would have been easy for us to learn the Ojibwa language and ways. Amazingly, during our childhood and youth, not one of us wanted to learn.

We had a lot of company from dad's relatives from Kenora and Morson, Ontario. It was always nice to see them and get to know them. On my mom's side, we had visits from the Powassins from Windigo Island and the Thunders and others from Buffalo Point. Many had homes in Warroad and stayed there most of the time. Tom Thunder used to cut our hair. He would sidewall us and leave a little bit on top. He loved to sit on the floor on his knees and visit with my mom and talk Ojibwa. Also, Verna (McPherson) Ka Kay Geesick , Mrs. Rose Cobiness and Mrs. Mary (KaKaGeesick) Angus would stop by frequently to visit and have coffee. They would always talk in Ojibwa. They would laugh and laugh. My mother had a great sense of humor and a great belly bouncing laugh. I often wondered what they were laughing about.

In Warroad, the liquor establishments would not let Indians drink or enter the bars. As youngsters, we would walk down the streets in Warroad and several Indian men and women would be sitting on the steps outside businesses. Some were from out of town and they would just hang out downtown. They would sit there passing the time and watching what was happening around town and sometimes they would be drunk. It was embarrassing for us to see that. As kids and while walking to the beach, we had to go through the downtown area. Some of the Indians would ask us to go into the drugstore and buy them a bottle of shaving lotion or cologne. They drank it because they could not get alcohol at the liquor store. Most times we would run away from them. But the first time they asked me, I took their money and went into the store for them. Marge Keeney, the clerk at the drug store immediately asked me, "What's this for?" I told her the truth: "It is for those Indian men out there in the street." She said, "They cannot buy this stuff", and scolded me. She took me out there and gave those guys heck. She told them not to ask the kids to come in and try to buy anything like that again. She gave them their money back. They just sat there and looked at her. I was embarrassed and took off running.

The Accobee brothers were from Roseau River Reserve in Manitoba, and lived at Buffalo Point and Warroad. They were great baseball players and played for the Warroad Muskies, a senior amateur baseball team. After the games, the team would go to the bar—all except the Indians, who were not allowed into the bars. Sam Gibbons, who had a great sense of humor, told me that he thought he was the only Indian living in Warroad during the 1940s and 1950s. I said, "What?" He said with a laugh, "All of the Indians were claiming to be French Canadian so they could get in the bars."

Come to think of it, dad always claimed to be French Canadian too. So we all grew up claiming to be French Canadian. He had no trouble getting into the bars. During our lineage search, it was discovered that we have very little French Canadian other than the name Boucha, which in Canada is spelled Boucher (Boo-shay). We were brought up being called Bushie. It was common and still is in some parts to be called Henry Bushie. The name Boucha or Boucher was pronounced Bushie for some reason. With 16 kids, 8 boys, and 8 girls coming from Naubinway, Michigan, the name has many spellings. I heard the name Bushie many times, and from many parts of the country. My relatives in Michigan were called Bushie. Everyone seems to prefer Boo-shay.

HENRY, DRESSED FOR THE BASEBALL GAME.

HENRY, EDDIE, BILLY.

JIM, EDDY AND HENRY.

Figure 21

Sometime in early 1960s my sister Shirley was in a house fire. She stayed with friends across town, and was sleeping upstairs. The house had a chimney fire during the night when everyone was asleep and the house caught fire. Shirley was trapped upstairs and tried to make it down the stairs but the flames were too high. She was burned by the high flames as she tried to come through the fire and down the stairs. She ran back upstairs and had to jump out the upstairs window into the snow. Her hands and arms were burned, and she spent time in the hospital. She still carries the scars today.

In 1961, my parents got a tragic call about a house fire that killed Margaret Oshie, our cousin. Her older brother Buster was burned badly, too. Buster had gone back to try to save Margaret. Everyone else got out okay. The house burned to the ground. Margaret was a year older than Shirley, and they were friends. Margaret was often at our house. Buster was a great hockey player and athlete. He played for Warroad in the State Hockey Tournament in the late 40's. Buster is the grandfather of TJ Oshie (who currently plays with the Saint Louis Blues of the NHL). Delores, Joanne, and Max Oshie were living in Everett, Washington at the time. Max Oshie was a great athlete, and was one of the best hockey players out of Warroad. After the house burned, the whole family moved out west. In those days, houses were not built very well. All the homes were wood built with boards inside and wood board siding, with sawdust or paper insulation. Most were heated with fuel oil or wood, and the chimneys were prone to overheating and catching fire easily. The rest of the house would burn quickly. There were many house fires during that time.

When I was eight, Dave was seventeen and had quit school and joined the Navy as did our brother Georgie. Shirley was fifteen, Jim was thirteen, and Eddy was six. After losing Susan in 1949, tragedy struck our home again on September 28, 1959. Georgie was killed in Lewiston, Idaho. He was visiting Jim and Darlene Dorion. A jealous ex-husband killed Georgie while he was visiting the man's ex-wife. He was shot at close range while walking up a sidewalk to the house. The shooter was cleared of charges by telling the courts he thought that my brother had a gun. He did not have a gun. He was only 20 years old. I remember the phone call that my mother received from my sister Darlene. Both dad and mom were devastated, as was the rest of the family. I remember sitting there in disbelief. I was too young to remember much about Georgie. Mom talked about him constantly. He left for the Navy when I was very young. After the funeral he was laid to rest at the Riverside Cemetery in Warroad. I remember mom running into the bedroom and crying, sobbing and wailing while lying on the bed. Dad and the rest of us sat there not knowing what to do. Mom would do that from time to time over the next few months. Whether she would be in the kitchen or out in the yard, she would come into the house and go to the bedroom and cry. I felt so helpless during those times. I remember the hollow feeling and the loneliness. I wanted to help her but did not know how. It was a horrible time.

CHAPTER 12: ROAD HOCKEY

Anybody who lived in Warroad in the 1940s, 1950s and 1960s played road hockey. I never knew who actually started it or when it began. It was during the late 1950s that I started to participate in hockey. When growing up at that time, playing road hockey was fun and it was a good past time in winter. They are the first memories I have of playing any type of hockey. We played in the house too. We used cutoff sticks, or just blades and played with rolled-up socks. Most of the neighbors enjoyed and had fun playing road hockey and skating on the river.

While the older kids were playing road hockey one day, they were short on a goalie. They came into the house and asked mom if I could get dressed and come out and play goal for them. I was about five. I was excited and was jumping up and down. She said "okay". I bundled up and went out with the big kids. We used a taped up chewing tobacco can of my dad's for a puck. We did not have equipment, so we needed something lighter than a puck. We were often injured. It still hurt sometimes when we were hit with the home made pucks. I had a few black-and-blue marks here and there. The experience was the great. I was a regular after that. Mom would get after them when they made me cry, usually because they hit me in the face or a shot was too hard. I always came back to play. During the school year kids played intramural hockey on Wednesday evenings and Saturdays. On all other days they played road hockey or skated on the river.

We did not have snowmobiles, four-wheelers, color TV, computers, or cell phones. To use the phone, you had to pick it up, and tell the operator the number and she would connect you. If it was a long distance call, you would need to ask for the long distance operator. Some lines were party lines with a number of other people on the same line. If someone was using it, you had to wait your turn, also they could listen to your conversations.

There was not much for kids to do except make our own games. We had fun times playing road hockey and creating other things to do. I had a lot of "hand me downs" of either Dave's or Jim's. Usually, the skates were too big. I pushed newspaper into the toes and wore several layers of socks to make them fit. When I stood up, my ankles bent over to the inside. I wore them anyway. I walked out through the snow, tried to skate on the road to a big ditch that was covered with ice. I struggled to skate around and somehow I managed. It was hard to keep skating without falling down a lot. I was hooked. I loved it. I could get going but did not know how to stop or turn very well. My skates were always too big and the skates in those early days did not have much support. When the skates got wet the leather stretched and had to be re-tightened. I skated whenever I could, in the ditches, on the road, on the river, and at the arena. I kept getting better each time.

When I played in goal, I took some pretty good shots in the head and body. I had my share of black-and-blue marks. It was part of the game. Almost every kid in town played road hockey at one time or another. There was not much else to do outside, beside skate on the river or build forts and play in the snow. There were no hills to slide down as it was flat country. Road hockey was just something we could do outside. "Pickup" (spontaneous) road hockey games were a natural thing to do. Sometimes we played all day long, and sometimes under the streetlights at night. I remember the sound of the sticks and pucks on the road. I still can see the snowflakes falling under the streetlights as we played, stopping every once in a while

WARROAD, MINNESOTA. COURTESY OF THE WARROAD HISTORICAL SOCIETY.

Figure 22

clearing the road with our sticks so we could see the Snoose can. We would sometime shoot it over the snow banks, and have to dig to find it. They used to get pretty beat up and end up like a ball. We were constantly looking for new cans. Most of the games were right outside our house. I guess it was because we were playing all the time and had things set up. If we were playing, the next thing you knew the neighbor kids were out there too. We all watched out our windows for something to happen, and then outside we would go.

The Isacksons (Tony & Bernice), an older couple lived next door to the east. Frank and Lil Rose and kids lived to the east of them. The Roses were all basketball players, but they liked to play road hockey with us too. Mike and Dave, who were my age, would play. Their older brother Chuck still holds the state high jump record for the scissors jump. He was a great high school athlete but a real character. He loved to get Mike and Dave fighting, sometimes, we could hear his dad, Frank, yelling at Chuck from inside our house. One day we saw Frank chase Chuck down the street with a board in his hand. Mom used to chuckle about it. Chuck was like Charlie Brown, always in trouble, and would do some hilarious things. The neighborhood was entertained many times by the Roses. Lil was a character who you could hear calling the kids for dinner nearly down to the beach in Warroad, a couple of miles away. You knew who's voice it was when she yelled. She was always a treat to be around. Her wit, antics, and loud voice were entertaining. She would come over and play cards with my mother and the other ladies of the neighborhood. You always knew when Lil was in the house. Those women used to laugh and laugh. One time Lil had been shopping in Roseau with some friends. The girls decided to go into a local bar to have a quick drink. Lil went along but hardly ever set foot in a bar. When she walked out, she ran smack into her pastor from church that was walking down the street. Lil just about died of embarrassment and went running down the street screaming all the way to her car.

Our other neighbors were Jim Fish, Willard Krahn, Brewsters, and Gordy Palmquist families, as well as others on the south side of the river. Gordy played in the state tournament with the Warriors in the late 40's. Also the Sargents rented across the road for a while before they moved to Bemidji. Tom and Sarah Thunder were there for a while before moving. Toward the river there was Laurance Saurdiff, the famous boat captain of the Bert Steele, the Gerries, and John Pick. We had Joe Umhauer to the west that raised their grandkids Ron and Cookie. There was a house in between the Umhauers and our house, where Lil Rose's father Harry and uncle John lived. John played fiddle, and he would sit out on his porch and play. I enjoyed that, and never heard anyone play where I could stand there that close and listen. Before they moved, they lived in an old railroad car near the river. It was a nice place but probably not very well insulated, so the Roses moved them to the house next door. We called our neighbor Ron Umhauer, Eli for some reason. Deb Green, a former classmate, thought maybe it was from that song, "Eli Coming" from our days in junior high school. He did not play sports, but he played road hockey with us. He was our version of Johnny Cash. He bought a guitar when he was about twelve and started playing Johnny Cash songs and never stopped. He still plays today. When he was teenager he made himself a cabin out of one of the old sheds on their property. He bought a red electric guitar with an amp and microphone. He waited for that guitar for weeks, and showed us a picture of it every time we were there. He would invite us to listen to him play and sing. He had a record player and had all of Johnny Cash's albums and 45's. He taught himself three chords, and that is what he played most of the time. He sometimes let us play a chord or two on his other guitars. He taught me how to play, and I still play today. We spent a lot of good times at the little cabin. Eli was a little older than us. He was our neighborhood bully. We were scared of him. He was tough as nails—so we thought. He acted tough in school, and was about to get into a fight, when our football coach stopped him. The football coach said, "If you are that tough come play football with us." Eli tried it and got knocked around a lot and then quit. He was not very big. He was a nice guy, "pure country and before it was cool." Mike Rose was left handed and would play the guitar upside down, and play pretty well. He figured out a rock 'n' roll song, "Dream Lover," on his guitar. He taught it to me. Eli got mad at us and took the guitar away and said, "You're not playing that shit on my guitar." He hated anything rock "n" roll, and refused to play it.

During the road hockey games, we would sometimes get under Eli's skin. He would knock us in the snow bank. It was fun for a while and our games did not last long after that started, as someone always went home crying. When finished for the day, we would clean off the road and leave our sticks in the snow banks for the next game. We would have two dozen sticks sticking in the snow banks and a few Snoose cans sitting on top of the bank ready for the next game. We saved blocks of snow that we used for goals by shoving them off to the sides of the road so the cars would not run over them.

My brother Jim came home one day with his front teeth knocked out. He was playing road hockey down the street at Jim Fish's house when Jim Fish Jr. took a shot and brought his stick up too high and knocked Jim's teeth out. He had to have them pulled and replaced with false teeth.

Our dentist, Dr. Larson was a character. As he was sticking the needle with Novocain into your gum, he would chuckle and ask "Does that hurt a little?" He worked on my teeth and did the same thing. Kids dreaded going to see the dentist.

During our road hockey games, some people would come by and run over our goals (blocks of snow) just to be spiteful, and some people would be upset with us for playing on the road. We had our interruptions when cars came by and we let them through. Most people were nice and they would go between the goal posts, smile, and wave.

When we were bored with road hockey, we would sit on the snow banks and talk. Sometimes we would hitch a ride down the road on a bumper of a car. We knew which cars had good bumpers. If you were wearing just wool socks in those buckled-up rubber boots the ride would tickle your feet. The best ride was when we were wearing leather-soled shoes. We would hang on the bumper with our hands while in a squatting position. Some of the people would know we were there, and would try speeding up and would start to zigzag down the road trying to shake us off. We fell off sometimes, but it sure was fun. Then there were those who would be looking in their mirrors watching us, and as soon as we got on they would stop and get out of the car and cuss us out. Everyone loved Dave Hallett, the milkman. He had the best bumper. It stuck out and was easy to grab. We could get four of us on that bumper. I think if it were up to him, he would have let us ride. I think some of the parents may have said something to him. Sometimes he would let us ride, and other days he would stop and chew us out.

When the Sargents moved to Warroad in the 1960s, Gary, Earl Jr. (June bug), Buck, and Rosie lived across the road. They lived there for a few years before moving to Bemidji. We played road hockey all the time when not in school. I think we played every day after school, and all day long on Saturdays and Sundays. We played at night under those old streetlights that were fairly dim. If there were only two of us playing, we would set the goals close and we would shoot back and forth with both of us playing goal. We had a series going up to best of seven and we would usually go up to five goals in each game. We would not blast the puck but we made it fun, enjoyable and competitive.

CHAPTER 13: GRADE SCHOOL AND RIVER HOCKEY

My brother Dave was the first in our family to play the game of hockey on an organized team. It was Jim who excelled and was getting noticed for how good he was in the intramurals. As a kid in Warroad, you played intramural hockey up to the sixth or seventh grade. You would get picked to represent the Warroad Pee Wee or Bantam team from those intramural teams. It was in the late 1950s the local youth hockey program was taking off with more kids playing than ever. This was thought to be the direct result of the new indoor arena.

In the mid-1940s, Cal Marvin talked the University of North Dakota into venturing into hockey and allowing Cal and his teammates to develop a team. He started UND Hockey. After he left the university, Cal came home and started to promote the idea of a new indoor arena in Warroad. With his fundraising and enthusiasm, he was able to obtain enough support to build an arena. The arena went up in 1949. Prior to that the teams played on an outside rink next to the school and practiced on the Warroad River. People told me that they stood on the snow banks and watch the games.

HARTZ TEAM. COURTESY OF JEFF PARKER.

ROBERTS HARDWARE TEAM. COURTESY OF JEFF PARKER.

Figure 23

WARROAD HOCKEY TEAM ON THE WARROAD OUTDOOR RINK.
COURTESY OF THE WARROAD HISTORICAL SOCIETY.

1940S HOCKEY TEAM OUTDOOR RINK AT
WARROAD SCHOOL.

Figure 24

In Warroad, the youth hockey program developed an intramural league and asked community businesses to sponsor teams. They provided the coaches for the team and the players with jerseys. The hockey board divided kids into age groups and abilities to make the teams competitive. Most kids had no equipment, other than skates and sticks. We wore jerseys that were provided by the sponsors and played in our blue jeans. Some of the kids had gloves and shin pads, and some of us played in our mittens with no equipment. We did not care or know any better. We had fun.

There were enough players from grades four through seven to make an intramural league. The teams played on Wednesday evenings and again on Saturday mornings. The teams were competitive and would play hard to have bragging rights in school. We taunted each other and made fun of each other relentlessly. It was a real battle at times both on and off the ice. We skated in the ditches and then on the river in late fall until the arena opened. We did not get into the arena until the first of December.

I remember playing in a big game on the river one Thanksgiving Day. We had plenty of snow and good ice. We scraped a rink off and played hockey all day. The weather was beautiful. My mother called us to come have Thanksgiving dinner in early afternoon. We took a break to eat and then went right back down there to play until dark.

In early fall, it was nice if the river froze over with no ripples or defects in it. Sometimes it was like glass and it was easy skating and we could glide forever. I practiced my stride as I skated along. You could see on the ice how you were striding and self-correct yourself. There was an island separating the main channel to our small channel. The island was five to seven acres and long and narrow. It was made with dredgings when the government dredged out the channel. They sucked up the mud, dumped, piled it, and eventually turned it into an island. Everyone called it Government Island. Later on everyone seemed to claim it—the city of Warroad, the county, the state, and the federal government. We skated around and around

WARRROAD RIVER LOOKING TOWARD TOWN.
COURTESY OF THE WARROAD HISTORICAL SOCIETY.

Figure 25

the island, built forts on it and made it our playground. In the early 1900's they used the island as a dry dock for the dredges and other large boats. I remember seeing the rails that were used to pull the boats up to the big cribs used to house the boats while under repair. There was a wooden bridge over to the island from the south side of the river. It was old when I was a kid and was not safe. Billy Quinn fell off the bridge and drowned, so they tore it down. The city of Warroad and the Chamber of Commerce wanted to clean it up, and use it as a park or tourist attraction. Funding was always a problem. Nobody knew who owned it. They started projects to clean it up, cut trees and brush, but it fizzled out and it never happened. It is in the same condition now as it was many years ago.

During those times skating on the river, there were no snowmobiles. Without snowmobile tracks on the river, the river was pristine. There would be a few ski planes that would come and go on the river. It was easy to scrape a rink off almost anywhere. We had pickup hockey games everywhere. It seemed there were a dozen rinks up and down the river. We played across the river with other neighborhoods kids and really had fun. Skating was a good way to burn off energy and to get around. When I was in high school, a newspaper article stated that I would skate to school every day. Of course I never did, but I played along anyway. I may have skated to school, but only a time or two.

Dad would sit and tell us how he used to skate in the old days, at French Portage, and how they used to skate to town (Kenora, Ontario). We thought, yeah, right. We didn't think he could skate at all. Until one day he said, "Okay, let's go." We walked down to the river, and he strapped on the skates and came skating with us. I was amazed. He actually could skate and very well. I could not keep up with him. Later Mom laughed and said, "I told you so."

It was amazing that no one drown when we skated on that thin ice in the fall. Thank God that our parents did not know what we did. At night we would dare each other to go out into the middle of the main channel to see if the person could make it all the way across without going in. Usually, we would get 10 or 20 yards away from shore and the ice would start cracking and we would take off toward shore. The river was deep, and if we had fallen in, there was no way someone could have rescued us.

The place where we first skated in the fall was a branch off the main channel of the river, and it was not very deep or very wide. Our branch froze over sooner than the main channel. We skated in the ditches until the river was ready. As the days got colder and the ice started getting thicker, we would challenge each other to go farther out in the main channel. We usually stayed pretty close to the shores of Government Island. We played tag at night and hide-and-seek in the weeds along shore. Sometimes we would drop a foot through or even a leg, but we would jump right back out and take off. If you want to learn how to skate fast, take off on thin ice.

When you hear the cracking all around you, you seemed to get a little more spring in your legs. The more scared I was, the faster I could skate.

Some nights on the river were absolutely beautiful, with crisp air and clear skies. I can still see the streetlights shining on the ice from downtown and the stars glistening off the ice. There were no other sounds than those of your blades on the ice as you skated around. I can close my eyes and see it as if it was yesterday—a bright, crisp, clear night, with a million stars shining down on the Warroad River, and the streetlights glistening on the ice as you glided around, and the sounds of your steel blades on the ice as you skated.

One day, I was feeling cooped up. It was cold and windy outside, and nobody wanted to play road hockey or go skating on the river. After begging my brother Jim, he finally said, "Okay, let's go." I was half-dressed and nearly ready anyway, so I took off right away and made my way down to the river. Jim said he would follow me down in a few minutes. I started skating and playing around with a puck. It was cold as heck, a north wind and about twenty below. As I moved around and skated, I started warming up. For some reason I had forgotten my hat, but I didn't care, like most kids going out to play. I knew my ears were cold, but I didn't pay much attention. After awhile I could not feel them anymore. When Jim finally got down there, my ears were frozen solid and were pure white. He said, "Jeez, you better go up to the house and get a hat." I stopped and felt my ears; they were hard as a rock. I had no feeling in them. I took off and went up to the house. When I walked in the door, my mother took one look at me and said, "What the heck are you doing without your hat? You better take a look in the mirror at those ears. They are frozen solid white." She made me stay in, get undressed, and warm up. As I sat there, my ears started to thaw, and swell, they started dripping, and then they began to sting. The more they thawed, the more they hurt. I was crying, as they thawed and they turned red. It felt as if I had elephant ears. I really suffered over the next couple of days. They ached a lot. I even stayed home from school. As the skin started to scab and peel off, they itched like crazy. I was miserable and I learned my lesson.

Another time we were all down on the river playing hockey and just messing around in the snow banks. I had snow pants on. I developed cramps in my lower abdomen. I had to go! I started home to get to the toilet but did not make it. I was struggling in the knee high snow and I would stop now and then to minimize the discomfort. It was slow going. I made it half-way home before I lost it. So I walked home the rest of the way feeling relieved but pretty uncomfortable. Mom was having a card party with some neighborhood ladies. Of course they were right at the kitchen table as I walked in the door. Sure enough a woman sitting at the table looked down at my boots and said, "What in the world is that?" It was oozing out of my pant leg. Then everyone started laughing, and I could have died. So, I went into the bathroom and got undressed and washed up and changed. I stayed in the house the rest of the day and stayed far away from those women.

Some of the best games we played on the river were at the Roberts' rink on the north side. We played with the Roberts kids several times. There was also a rink in Hospital Bay where we played some pickup games with kids from that side of town. It was great on sunny days when the wind was down, everyone wanted to get out of the house and enjoy the beautiful winter day. Another place we played a lot was over on the west side of the railroad bridge. It was well protected from the wind, with a high wall holding back the bank, and tucked away in between the two bridges. The high school team practice there sometimes.

One fall, I cannot remember how old I was, maybe eight or nine, I decided to quit hockey. This may have been the turning point in my life. It was late fall, and I was sitting in the house. My skates had broken when the rivets came out of the rotten part of the boot. So I decided not to play. I did not have any skates. I knew there were hockey games at the arena that morning and I was supposed to be there. I did not go. I just thought to myself that was it, accept it, stay home, and do not play. For some reason I felt okay with it at that moment. Maybe in a day or two, I would have changed my mind. As I sat there, there was a knock on the door. It was John Parker, president of Warroad Youth Hockey and a big booster of youth hockey. John was a game warden and was a good family man. He raised his family in Warroad and was an all-around good person. He wanted to know if I was sick or something because I was not at the arena. I was always up there skating, horsing around, or just hanging out. He saw me and asked me why I was not at the rink to play hockey that day. I told him, "I did not have any skates. They were broken." I told him that "When I get some skates, I will join them." He said "okay" and asked me "What size skate I needed in case he could find an old pair that I could wear?" I did not think much about it after he left.

WARROAD HOCKEY GODFATHER CAL MARVIN. ED HOLLAND. COURTESY OF JEANNE
COURTESY OF BETH MARVIN. HOLLAND ERICKSON.

LEFT: JOHN PARKER AND SON JEFF. RIGHT: CAL MARVIN AND SON MIKE.
COURTESY OF JEFF PARKER.

Figure 26

Not long after, there was another knock at the door. It was John Parker again. He came in and had a brand-new pair of skates, still in the box, for me. "Here. these are for you. Now, get dressed and let's go. We just have time to make the game," he said. It was amazing. I jumped up and sprang into action.

I really do not know if I would have gone back to skating or not if John had not shown up that day. It was a big moment for me. They were my first new skates. All I ever had was secondhand skates that never fit well. I was extremely proud to have those new skates. They fit well. I was so proud to have them that I probably wore them to bed.

During the spring thaw in Warroad, there was not much to do, but we managed to find a few things; most of them were not too smart or safe. The ice was out of the arena, and the river was too dangerous to play on, as the ice was honeycombed. There was open water in the main channel. As the snow melted we would play along the deep railroad track ditches full of water. The water was rushing down and we would throw cans in the ditch and run down along the tracks trying to sink them with rocks. We threw cans in upstream and took off running down to the river, as the cans came down, I was standing on a construction crib that was holding up a telephone pole. It was partially in the main river. The river was running fast at that time. I was wearing tall rubber boots and had a big rock over my head. I was going to trash this can that was coming down the ditch when my friend bumped me and I ended up falling into the river. I managed keep my head above water, but the boots were full of water and they were pulling me down with the currant. I was panicking and I was swallowing water and was about to drown. My brother Jim was standing on the bridge with his friend Marvin "Feen" Shaugabay. Jim jumped in and tried to save me, but in a panicked state, I just about drown him too. Feen jumped in and together they got control of me and pulled me out. It was a very close call, but I was okay.

We played along the tracks, and would stand back when the trains came by, I am sure it bothered our parents as they told us many times to stay off the tracks. Being kids we were always on the verge of getting into trouble. Mike and Dave Rose, Eli and I noticed the insulators on the poles and the wires on the telephone poles along the tracks. Well, of course we had rocks at our feet. We managed to break a few dozen of those insulators and shut down the communications lines of the railroad. When they discovered the broken insulators, it was not hard to find us. We were charged, and ended up in court with our parents, and we were scared to death.

The first time I saw anyone drown, I was in my early teens. I was at the beach in Warroad when I heard someone drowned at the railroad bridge. I heard they were searching for them, so I ran to the bridge as fast as I could. When I got there, people were standing on the bridge watching. Mike Rose was there along with Chirb Hardy and we watched the Warroad lifeguard, Cookie, diving the river channel to find a boy and father who had drowned. They said it was Les Lightning and his son, my cousins. The boy had fallen in the river while playing down there with some other kids. One of the kids ran to the boy's house and told his father, and the father ran down to the river to help him. The father jumped in and had a hold of his son but could not pull him to safety. They both drowned. His father had only one lung and he ran down to the river from his house, about a half mile away. He may have not had the strength to pull him to safety. Later Cookie, the summer life guard, found them, and they were pulled up into a boat. It was the first time I had seen a dead body. When they pulled them up, they were all blue colored and bloated. I felt sick inside and just wanted to go home. I think everyone felt the same way. No one talked they just left and went home. When I got home, there was no one there. Then the phone rang, it was my mother who had been calling and calling. She was at work at the hospital. She had heard that someone drowned and was checking on us. She heard it may have been the Lightnings. Dad was out on the lake commercial fishing. Eddy had just walked into the house as she called. So everyone was safe.

CHAPTER 14: WARROAD YOUTH HOCKEY

Out of the intramural teams, the Warroad Youth Hockey Association would pick a team of the better players to play against other towns in the area. I was versatile, playing goalie and I played forward or defense. I didn't care as long as I could play. I just wanted to wear one of those uniforms. Depending on your age and birthday, they picked one Pee Wee team of players, ages ten to twelve and a Bantam team, ages twelve to fourteen.

After we turned 15, we played for Warroad High School, most likely starting at the B Team (junior varsity) level. We could not play both youth hockey and high school in Minnesota at the same time.

The Warroad Pee Wee and Bantam teams had uniforms, with pants (breezers), socks, and jerseys. We were proud to wear them and represent the community. They were red, white, and blue, like the New York Rangers or USA Hockey. Wearing the uniform was my first goal in life, something to set my sights on. The first time I saw the uniform, I made up my mind to earn and wear one.

During the summers, we lived for baseball, and of course swimming. We swam at the beach almost every day and just hung out there all summer. Warroad had several youth teams in various age brackets, and they traveled to other towns in the area to play. We were involved in Cub Scouts and Boy Scouts. Eddy and I went to church on Sundays, and eventually attended confirmation. My parents did not attend church. Others encouraged my mother and dad

WARROAD ARENA WITH NATURAL ICE. COURTESY OF THE WARROAD MUSEUM.

WARROAD MEMORIAL ARENA. COURTESY OF THE WARROAD HISTORICAL SOCIETY.

Figure 27

to send us to church on Sundays, so we went and sometimes rode with our neighbors the Rose's.

I attended Boy Scout camp one summer at Lake Agassi near a town called Holt, Minnesota. It was a week-long camp and there were a lot of other boys there from other communities. We stayed in tents, and they taught us about shooting .22-caliber rifles, tying knots, crafts, and all the basics of survival. We earned our badges during the week. It was the first time I was away from home, and I was homesick after a few days. I remember my mother sending me a dollar and a short note in the mail. I do not know how in the world she got the address. I just about cried. I was surprised to get the money and used it to buy a treat. It sure made me feel better. I was the youngest of our group. Jack Ploof kept me under his wing. The older guys while sitting around the campfire at night would tell those awful scary stories. Yes, I believed most of them and had a miserable time going to sleep. I hated it and after a while I would not listen to them. I received my mile swim badge and a few other badges while there.

A week before we left on the trip, I rode my friend Eli's twenty-four-inch bike. He said it was the fastest bike around. I was going to see how fast I could go on it. I jumped on and took off over the railroad tracks and down the road. When I got to top speed, the chain slipped and I could not control it and I took a fall. It was on a tar road, and I was wearing shorts with no socks, just tennis shoes. I landed on my side, skidding down the road, and scraped all the skin off my left leg from my hip to my ankle, and my elbow and forearm. I just left the bike there in the middle of the road and ran home. I was in pain and home bound for a few days. I managed to get better by the time we left for Boy Scout camp.

It was during this time that I bought a bike. It was unique. I bought it from one of the Palmquist's relatives from International Falls. It was a contraption and cost me twenty dollars. It was a 24" bike that was rebuilt. The frame was turned upside down and long pieces welded to make a long high seat, and long handle bars to steer. I rode that thing around just like any other bike for two summers and got a lot of attention. I rode it down the sidewalks in Warroad and had to duck under the store signs when I road it. People would pull over to take pictures of me riding it down the road. I rode it everywhere.

The Warroad Muskies were Warroad's amateur baseball team. We went to all the home games. Warroad had a nice old park. It was made of wood fences, and covered grand stand bleachers behind home plate, rows of bleachers down 1st and 3rd baseline, and dugouts for the players. It was painted dark green with high 10' fences surrounding the park. It had a food concession below the Grand Stand bleachers. We went to shag foul balls and earn some much-needed money. I think we got a nickel for a foul ball and dime for a home run ball. We had to get there early to get a spot on the fence. We stood along a high fence and watch the game. There were long planks that leaned up on the fence so we could run up there and hang on the fence. We stood and watched for foul balls. It was a good way to make pop and popcorn money during the games. The Muskies played at night under the big lights and Sunday afternoons. Outside the fenced walls, the grass was tall and made it hard to find balls. We needed to pay attention and watch the balls go over the fence and estimate how far out they were. It was competitive. Even with the others like Tuny and Willie Shaugabay, Ed Huerd, Mike and Dave Rose and many others, we got our share and made enough to buy treats. The Muskies made several trips to the state amateur baseball tournament. I was a batboy for some of the teams. During the summer, I played for the Muskies while I was in high school. At one point when I was fourteen years old, I played on the high school team, the 14 under team, the Legion team, and the Muskies team. I played every day of the week that summer.

CHAPTER 15: WARROAD ARENA/NATURAL ICE

The Warroad Arena had natural ice until the 1970s, when they installed artificial ice. We skated on the river until it got cold enough to put ice in the arena. Whenever it was cold enough in late November, the local volunteer fire department and a few other volunteers from the community built ice. It took hours and hours, and it usually had to be flooded late at night or early morning when it was the coldest. They used big hoses from the fire truck to put the water down, layer by layer. Painstakingly, they would build ice that way until they had a good base. Then, they used a 50 gallon barrel with a burlap drag to smooth it out. They hand painted the lines on the ice, then sprinkled water on the paint to freeze it. Then tugged a 50 gallon barrel on wood skis, and a burlap drag to smooth out the hot water. They pulled that around and around to get another few layers of ice before it was ready. We usually did not get into the arena to skate before December. The high school team practiced on the river if the arena was not ready.

WARROAD, MINNESOTA
"HOCKEY-TOWN, USA"

COURTESY OF THE WARROAD HISTORICAL SOCIETY.

Figure 28

During pre-Zamboni days, it was clever the way they resurfaced the ice. They used a fifty-gallon barrel on wood skis with a exit pipe coming out the back end with a T pipe on the bottom attached to a piece of burlap near the holes on the bottom of the cross pipe. They used hot water that would melt the ice and make it smooth, and the burlap would spread the hot water evenly. It would refreeze almost instantly. The caretaker for the arena had a rope attached to the wood skis, and would pull the tank around the rink to flood the ice. The rink needed to be scraped of snow first, if a game was played. They would resurface only once a day unless there was time enough between games to flood. They flooded late at night when no one was using the arena, or early in the morning before it was to be used. During the day, the rink was scraped between periods and games. The ice could get pretty chewed up during the day if not flooded.

Ralph Kling was the arena caretaker–manager. They used to call him "bear trap." He had big feet, and wore those buckle up rubber boots. He always had a big fur hooded parka and when you saw him coming down the street in the dimly lit street, he looked like a big bear. Ralph was a commercial fisherman in the summers. Jim Jaros had a dry cleaning business next door to the arena and was the caretaker for some time. My favorite was Gene Knutson. He could tell stories like no one else. Gene had a prosthetic leg and walked with a limp. That never stopped Gene from trapping, hunting or anything else for that matter. He would pull that 50 gallon barrel around the rink with no problem. Gene made some pretty good ice. When hanging out at the arena and that was most of the time, Gene would love to sit and tell stories. We were all ears and he had some good ones. He was an excellent storyteller. Gene and Donna's kids all played for the Warroad youth program and high school. My friend Eli loved to spend time up there listening to the stories. Although Eli never skated he would go there anyway. Gene hated it when dogs would come into the arena. He would chase them out with a broom, cussing at them as they hurried out the door. If a dog came back too many times, Gene had a solution for that. He would get a hold of the dog by the tail, and slap some turpentine on his rear end with a paint brush and the dog would go skidding across the floor and could not wait to get outside to the snow to cool his burning behind. The dogs never came back.

MAN FLOODING ARENA. COURTESY OF THE WARROAD HISTORICAL SOCIETY.

Figure 29

Usually the Pee Wee or Bantam age players scraped the rink. The caretaker had five or six kids to scrape the rink. He gave the volunteers pop and popcorn and let us into the games for free. We never had any money, so it was great to have a job. We scraped for the high school and the Warroad Lakers games. We had four scrapers and two guys at the end of the arena shoveling snow over the boards, and the caretaker sweeping along the boards. The Shaugabay's, De De Dumais, the Huerds, the Kvarnlov's, the Krahn's and many others scrapped the rink. I still hear the military marching songs they used to play over the PA before the Laker games, and during the periods. I think they had an old record player and an album in the gondola, and they would set the mic next to it and let it play over the speakers. Everyone went to the warming room during periods to have coffee or hot chocolate. When I close my eyes, I can still hear dull roar of the sounds of people talking, smell the cigar and cigarette smoke in the warming room. We would run in there to get our pop and popcorn after we scrapped. There would be smaller kids playing hockey in the corner, just like we did when we were younger.

My friend Bob Wenzel was part of that group, and he was my defense partner when we were bantams, and in high school. We had new Bantam jerseys, and he suggested that we wear them when we cleaned the ice. We asked our coach, and he said "okay." We wore those jerseys with pride representing our team and community.

Compared with the artificial ice, the natural ice was fast but snowed up quick. The arena was not insulated. When it was twenty below outside, it was twenty below inside. The arena sat about 1,200, but we had as many as 2,500 people in there during some of the high school games, and maybe more. The Warroad Lakers entertained the US National teams, the US Olympic teams, various European teams, and some great amateur teams from throughout North America. The high school team played the regional area teams. Teams would come from as far away as Minneapolis/Saint Paul (350 miles away).

The arena was a hangout for kids and especially teens. Public skating was free. When I was in my teens we used to hang out at the arena and at Lu J's Café. The Fox Theater changed movies twice a week. My friend Jack Ploof's mother, Luella, owned the Lu J Café, and had a back room where we used to spend time playing pool and listening to the juke box.

The Kruger boys, Melvin and Richard, were always fun to be with. They lived close to the arena, and they loved to play sports. They played road hockey with us. We would play pickup hockey at the arena, and we would scrape ice together. Richard played more organized hockey and other sports than Melvin. They loved to sing, and they could harmonize together, and they were entertaining. Whether it would be on baseball, hockey, or football trips, we could count on Richard and Melvin to sing a few songs. They sang songs like "Last Kiss," "Party Girl," and "Oh, Donna." They were quite good. Melvin used to sing on the spectator's buses and entertain the kids.

The Warroad Lakers, our men's senior team, would practice late in the evenings, and sometimes we would skate with them if they didn't mind. Some evenings public skating was not always full or didn't last very long. On those nights the caretaker would let us take our sticks out and scrimmage or shoot around. We would skate until 10 or 11 p.m. or until our legs ached.

I remember walking home late on school nights. I lived over a mile from the rink. I walked home carrying my stick and skates. I would pass all of the closed businesses and walk across the railroad bridge beside the tracks, and then down the road and up the trail to our house. If I had wet pants from skating they would freeze on the way home. The trail was snow packed and crunched as you walked in the cold winter night. Warroad only had a few streetlights, so it was dimly lit. A million stars would be shinning, and they were amazing to see as I was walking home. I would often be tired and how I would hate to get up for school. Mom used to lay awake until she heard me come in. Everyone else was asleep.

High school and Laker games were the highlights while I was growing up. The teams played a few times a week. When I was eight or nine and too young to scrape ice, I started going to the games, following my older brother Jim and sister Shirley. We played boot hockey under the bleachers, ran around and played with the other kids our age. We always needed sticks for road hockey and would hang out by the penalty box to wait for a broken stick. We would fix them and use them during our games. The sticks were all wood and did not have fiberglass wrap, so they broke easily.

We never took a slap shot. To fix them we used nails and wrapped them with tape.

We had one game stick that we did not use for road hockey. We kept it only for games. We wanted a good stick that had good balance and a nice feel to it; a must for a hockey player. Very seldom did we have new stick. I remember one time though, I bought a new stick. I had been saving for it for a while. I bought it and I was so happy to have it. I could not wait to use it. I had it taped nice, and when I took my first shot with it, it broke. It was not repairable. Wow, was I devastated.

CHAPTER 16: WARROAD LAKERS

The Warroad Lakers were in existence since the mid-1940s. There was hockey back then. There were Canadians that worked in town that played hockey. It was just after World War II. Cal Marvin came back from the war in the South Pacific. He played hockey before the war and was anxious to get back to playing. It was Warroad pharmacist Ed J. Holland, who was originally from Winnipeg, Manitoba, who called a meeting in late November of 1946 to organize a team to play in the States-Dominion League. Warroad won the league in its first season. After Ed's passing his wife Etta continued to support youth hockey through Holland Pharmacy and sponsored a youth hockey team each year. I remember wearing the gold sweatshirt jerseys that said Holland's across the front. Going through the Warroad Museum with Beth Marvin, I found pictures of hockey in Warroad as early as 1909. One picture shows the high fence built with planks they used as boards on an outdoor rink, and fans stood on the snow banks between the blue lines on each side of the rink to watch the game. The end boards were at least twelve feet high and wrapped around to the quarter side to the blue lines. I guess so they would not lose the puck in the snow, and maybe they used it as a wind break. Cal took over the team from Mr. Holland and never looked back. The Lakers played for another fifty years.

WARROAD OLYMPIANS AND FORMER WARROAD LAKERS.
STANDING: ROGER CHRISTIAN (GOLD MEDAL 1960), CAL MARVIN
(TEAM USA 1958 AND 1965), BLAINE COMESTOCK (1976), GINNY CHRISTIAN
(SILVER MEDAL 1956), BILLY CHRISTIAN (GOLD MEDAL 1960), RUBE BJORKMAN
(SILVER MEDAL 1956), DAN MCKINNON (SILVER MEDAL 1956).
SEATED: CHUCK REDDING, JACK, KOONSE AND DEB BIGGS. TAKEN AT
CHRISTIAN BROS. HOCKEY STICKS, WARROAD, MN.

HENRY
AND
CAL MARVIN.

HENRY AT THE
50TH WARROAD
LAKERS
REUNION.

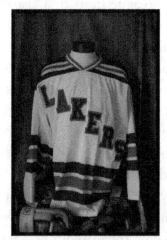

1995 WARROAD LAKERS UNIFORM.
COURTESY OF VINTAGE HOCKEY.

Figure 30

All of those early home games were played on an outdoor rink near the school in Warroad. The away games were the same with hardly any community's having indoor rinks. It was during that time when Cal brought his idea to the University of North Dakota and talked to the athletic director about having a school varsity hockey team. The school approved the team and provided limited funding to start the program.

As a young man, having the Warroad Lakers in town was truly a blessing. It gave us an opportunity to watch with enthusiasm some skilled players over the years. It provided us with some great entertainment and a vast learning experience. We were able to see foreign national teams from Europe and teams from all across the United States and Canada compete in Warroad.

The Lakers played on Saturday nights and Sunday afternoons. Most of the players had day jobs. The Kenora and Dryden teams would fly into Warroad with their big Beaver airplanes with skis and land on the Warroad River. It was quite a sight. Over the years the Lakers competed in a variety of leagues and won just about every championship there was for an amateur team. They did it on both sides of the border in the United States and Canada. The whole town supported the Lakers and all of their games. It was always a social event when they played. The arena sat about 1,200 and would be full most nights and afternoons. There was a portion of the rink that did not have safety wire or glass. Spectators used to stand there and be able to watch the game close by peering over the boards. Sometimes they would get hit with a stick or a puck. It truly gave them a thrill. Between periods they usually ran down to the local pub but were back in time to see the start of the period. That group used to razz and heckle the players on the opposing team and would sometimes get into fights with the players and sometimes cause fights between the players. They were so bad at times; there were some players on opposing teams that would fire the puck at them if they had a chance. Some guys from that group used to stand behind the net, and give it to the goalie through the wire fence. They would hassle and try to distract the goalie from his job. It worked on many occasion, sometimes causing a brawl. Many times the referee would make them leave, after the goalie or coach and players complained.

CHAPTER 17: INTRAMURALS, PEE WEES, AND BANTAMS

When in fifth grade, I made a personal goal to earning a spot on the Pee Wee team and be able to wear the uniform. It was during that time and in late summer when the Warroad Youth Hockey Board announced plans for a candy sale. It offered players an opportunity to raise money for the program and win a trip. The top three players were given a chance to attend an NHL exhibition game being held in Winnipeg. The game was between the Toronto Maples Leafs and the Detroit Red Wings. Wow, what a treat. After we got a TV, we often watched *Hockey Night in Canada* on Wednesday and Saturday nights in winter. So getting a chance to see these guys live was terrific.

If only I could be one of the top three in sales, I thought. Well, I did not waste any time. I went door-to-door selling the candy. I sold a lot of candy and ended up being one of the top three and I was selected to attend the game. The game was great. It was wonderful to see the uniforms in color. When we watched them on TV, it was in black-and-white.

WARROAD BEACH

COURTESY OF THE WARROAD HISTORICAL SOCIETY.

Figure 31

The Winnipeg arena was a huge. I remember seeing 12,000 people at the game, which was more people than I had ever seen in one place and at one time. The Detroit Red Wings won the game over Toronto. They were now my favorite team. Maybe they were before that, but this is my first recollection of having a favorite team. Watching the teams and watching how they played the game was truly a pleasure—I took it all in, watching the passing, line changes, power plays, and penalty killing. My new goal was to play for the Red Wings some day. From that time on, when we played hockey, either on the road or on the river or at the rink, I would try to emulate those players.

Being able to make the Pee Wee team and wear a uniform may have been my first goal as a young player. Playing intramural hockey in grade school was a prelude and a stepping-stone to making a formal team. The first time wearing a uniform was special. I was so proud. We had the word *Warroad* across our chests, representing the community. I played defense and sometimes goalie. The experience was great and it was fun but I was nervous and had butterflies. Our team went to Winnipeg once a year and we traveled to International Falls, a hundred miles away. It was a long way in those days with the cars and roads we had. Certainly not like today, where travel is easy. Some parents took cars, only certain parents would drive, because not everyone had a car. Our family did not have a car, so I rode with someone else.

We never had more than ten to twelve games in a year, so they were all big games. The Bantam team played after the Pee Wee game. I played as a defenseman on the Pee Wee team and then played goalie for the Bantam team in the next game.

We walked to the arena with our gear in just a paper bag from the grocery store, pillowcase, or an old army duffle bag of some kind. We did not have much equipment to haul, mostly hand me down stuff. We had our uniforms (socks, jersey and pants), which were given to us on game day. We carried a helmet and shin pads, with just our skates, and carried a stick. Some of us did not have gloves and we wore mittens, with no shoulder, elbow pads or cup.

As stated, our equipment was poor, with minimum padding and very little protection. The youth program had used equipment that they let us use during the season. After the Pee Wee game, I would come in the dressing room and gather up my clothes and walk over to the Bantam room. Instead of taking off my shin pads or pants and socks, I put the thin goalie pads on over the top. The pads were about an inch thick, stiff and ran straight down to your ankles, leaving the toes exposed. We had soft toed skates so sometimes when you got a shot on the toes it hurt like crazy. They had three straps on the back to hold them to your legs. I took off my jersey and put on a chest protector with arm protection. I did not wear a mask, just a helmet. I had a blocker and a catcher glove that was flat with no pocket. So all I could do was bat down a puck and knock it into the corner.

When I played in Winnipeg the first time as a Bantam goalie, it seemed these players were high school age. I remember all the guys in the locker room saying they shaved already, and some had mustaches. It was all talk. If you ever played on a team, you knew how they exaggerate and how excited some of the players got. I was young and it scared me, and I believed them. When I went out there, I looked at the kids faces to see if they were shaving and had beards and face hair. I was young and impressionable. When the game started, it seemed as if they were shooting pucks at me at100 miles per hour. I was scared, and I did not want to be there. Some of the shots hurt, but I hung on. I batted those pucks down and knocked them into the corner. I ducked a few times as the pucks flew over the net. The big guys came down the ice and were firing the pucks from both sides. We lost that game, but we managed to keep it close, and I was glad it was over. I was a little shocked. Those Canadian kids were good.

The 1961/62 hockey season started with us playing on the river early and then into the arena. We played road hockey about as much as we ever did. We were still playing intramural hockey, and some players were migrating to the Pee Wees and Bantams on scheduled nights to play against other communities. They were scheduling more Bantam and Pee Wee practices for us. The schedules were getting better, as there was more emphasis on competition. We would play more games, practice more as a team, and make a push toward the regional and state tournaments. As in the previous year, I was playing with the Pee Wees as a defenseman and with the Bantams as a goalie. It was good. I loved it when I could play on three teams. I was playing with my intramural team on Wednesday and Saturday mornings, and the Pee Wee's and Bantams on weekends. I would have played more if I could.

1963 WARROAD BANTAM TEAM. COURTESY OF JEFF PARKER.
BACK ROW: ALAN BALDWIN, DE DE DUMAIS, JON HANSON, GEORGE GANYO,
RICK KRAHN, VAN HOLMGREN, DALE BLEAU, BOB WENZEL, COACH DICK ROBERTS.
FRONT ROW: RICHARD SHAUGABAY, MIKE MARVIN, JEFF PARKER, TOM POOLE,
HENRY BOUCHA, GEORGE ROBERTS, BILL POOLE, RON MCKEEVER.

Figure 32

When I was more established as a Bantam goalie in 1962-63 season, I still played games with the Pee Wee's as a defenseman too. The Bantams took a trip to Denver, Colorado. I could not fathom how far away that was. The Warroad Lakers played out there the year before against Denver University. They set up another trip, and the Denver people asked if we could bring out a Bantam team. We were to play against the Denver All-Stars in games prior to the Laker/Pioneer games. What a thrill to make the trip to Colorado. The plan was to have parents drive their cars, with two or three players in each car. We would leave on Thursday night after school and drive to Watertown,

South Dakota. We would stay overnight, get up early and drive the rest of the way to Denver. I rode with Bob Wenzel Sr. and his son Bob and another player. It was a long and tedious time to sit in the car. We talked, told stories, read some, look out the window and slept.

Before we left Warroad, we received beautiful blue jackets with a Warroad Youth Hockey crest on it. The jackets were great, and we wore them with pride. The Warroad hockey community wanted us to look good so they got us the jackets. The Warroad community pulled together for things like that. The American Legion, Security State Bank and the Heneman Family, along with the Marvin Family headed up most of the fundraising. Other businesses and community members would give what they could. Money was always tight in those days

We arrived late Friday night and played two games, one on Saturday night and one on Sunday afternoon. We played a good team of all-stars, and the games were close. We won them both. It was the first time we stayed in a major hotel, like the Hilton. We had fun, and it was an education for most of us who had not stayed in such a nice hotel before. We were amazed how plush it was and surprised to see a rink in the hotel just outside the lobby. It was an ice sheet with artificial ice, and people could rent skates, and skate for a fee. We thought it was crazy, it was warm outside. We never saw anything like it. We did not skate on it. We could not believe they charged people to rent skates and to skate. From our rooms we would look out over the city at the tall buildings and houses, and the mountains. We were amazed at the traffic. It was real education.

The carpet in the hotel was plush. We would shuffle our feet around and give others a shock by touching their ear. It would snap. It really did not hurt, but you got a little sting from it. The food was great compared to what we were used to. In most communities around the country, they were just starting to play organized hockey. Hockey was just taking off in the United States in most places. After the final game on Sunday, we packed up and headed home. We arrive back in Warroad Monday evening after spending a night on the road again. We were full of great memories of the trip, winning the games and the wonderful people we met.

Back in Warroad, it was back to school and back to normal. We had those great memories of the trip. We played our regular Bantam schedule the rest of the season and our intramural games continued. We were into the playoff season, and we were excited. International Falls was the powerhouse for our region. They had a great hockey program, and they were a larger community, so they had more players to pick from. They were the team to beat. We had worked our way into the finals. We could not wait for the game; it was going to be a battle. Winning that game was our ticket to the state tournament that was being held in Hibbing, Minnesota. Before the game, it was intense in the locker room. We were nervous. Coach Roberts was a "rah rah" type guy and would try motivate us for the game. We always had our quiet time with a prayer before we went on the ice. Just before going on the ice Coach Roberts had us yelling out loud, "We're going to win, we're going to win," taking a positive approach to the game. It was a big game and a big opportunity for us. I was young and I was nervous as we stepped on the ice. The game was well played by both teams and close. We won, and we were going to play in the state tournament. In the tournament, we brought home the third place trophy. Our parents and the community were proud of our efforts.

It was my last year playing goalie. It was a milestone for me. The next year was already mapped out for us, and it promised to be a good year. We had most of our team returning. We had playoff experience, and knew the competition. Everyone thought Warroad had a good possibility of a state championship.

During that spring I remembered my earlier personal goal of earning a spot on the Pee Wee team and getting to wear the uniform. The dream came true, and now I felt like a veteran playing with the Bantams. I enjoyed what I was doing; I put in a lot of time on the ice. I worked hard in practice, went to school, and did not miss practice. Looking back it was well worth it. I had fun.

CHAPTER 18: TRAGEDY STRIKES AGAIN

It was January 26, 1963, a night I remember well. I was awakened by the phone ringing and ringing. It was around 1 a.m. Everyone was asleep. I do not know why, but I knew instinctively that something was wrong. I felt the fear right away. I was scared and sick inside. My mother felt the same way. She walked toward the phone and stopped, she did not want to answer it. She said in a trembling voice, "George please answer the phone." She just stood there watching and listening, with her hand over her mouth. I was standing there too, waiting for something I did not want to hear. Then it came. Dad hung up the phone. He said there was a house fire. My sister Phyllis was burned badly and she was taken to the hospital. The two youngest kids died in the fire. The two oldest got out, and they were bringing them over to our house. We all stood there in disbelief, scared and hurt. I watched my mother go into a panic, holding back her emotions and tears. Dad stood there beside her. We waited for the sheriff to bring the boys. Everyone was up and sitting there in disbelief and thinking about the tragedy. We were traumatized and trying to cope with the reality. Mom was on the phone to the hospital. She called Darlene in Idaho. My sister Phyllis was in the ER at the Warroad Hospital with burns on 80 percent of her body. When the boys arrived, they were physically alright, but quiet as they were traumatized also. Mom comforted the kids, and talked to the hospital again. The hospital staff could only do so much. They bandaged

SISTER PHYLLIS'S WEDDING DAY WHEN SHE MARRIED WILLIAM RINK SARGENT.
COURTESY OF JEFFREY DALE SARGENT.

Figure 33

GEORGE AND ALICE BOUCHA. COURTESY OF ROGER & JANET DORION.

Figure 34

Phyllis and helped her with the pain. They tried to comfort her and they were waiting for the plane to arrive to airlift Phyllis to the burn unit at the University of Minnesota, Medical Center in Minneapolis.

We comforted the two boys and they were made to feel safe and cared for. Billy was eight and Tades (Jeff) was seven. Come to find out, both boys had gotten up in the middle of the night and were playing with matches in the basement. They started something on fire, and the fire spread. They panicked and ran outside, not waking up their mother. She was in her bedroom in a different part of the house. She made it outside and then she went back in to try save the little ones, David, four, and Joseph, two. Phyllis collapsed in the heat and smoke-filled house. Firemen pulled her out the bathroom window. She was barely alive.

My sister Darlene came from Lewiston, Idaho, by train, and we picked her up at the Grand Forks train station. Phyllis and Darlene were only two years apart and were very close. Darlene was devastated, as were we all. It was good to have Darlene there. We were all together and coping with the pain. Tragically, on Valentine's Day, February 14, 1963 less than three weeks after the fire, Phyllis died in the burn unit at the University Hospital. My parents raised William and Jeffery Sargent with us in Warroad. Phyllis and the two boys are buried next to Georgie at the Riverside Cemetery in Warroad.

CHAPTER 19: SEVENTH GRADE, STATE BANTAM CHAMPIONSHIP

During the summer of 1963, as we had done most summers, we swam, spent time at the beach, and played baseball. It was a little more complicated now that I noticed the girls. It was that transition time for me. It boiled down to wanting to play outside with the rest of the kids or go where the girls were most likely to be. I guess I did a little of both. We did our share of water skiing and swimming down at the beach, but mostly we played baseball in the summer program. On the 4th of July in Warroad there is a big celebration. George Marvin always gave away nickels to the kids, and there were foot and bicycles races, a big parade, rides, games and food concessions at the beach. Some years they planned canoe and boat races and as always a huge fireworks display. It was a day when most everyone from Warroad came home to visit and attend the school alumni banquet. Warroad continues the annual celebrations to this day.

I mowed lawns to make a few dollars and worked for old Mr. Cherne down at the end of our road. He had a 160-acre hobby farm. He was elderly and needed a hand. He was retired and spent the summers in Warroad. His family was the first white settlers in the Warroad area, and the farm was their original homestead. He and his wife were very nice people. They lived on the Iron Range but came to Warroad in the summers. His kids were living in the Minneapolis area and were successful in business.

We spent time playing on the railroad bridge. We would jump off the bridge into the Warroad River below. It was a little scary, but when there were girls around, we got a shot of courage, and we did it anyway, showing off. Maybe I should call it stupidity. It was about a twenty-foot jump off the bridge. We would dive or jump in the river and then swim over to the shore. The railroad bridge was a main walkway for the people on the south side to downtown. It had a three-foot walkway on either side of the tracks on the bridge. There were a lot of trains coming and going, at least one every hour or so. We would just stand there when the train went by. It was loud and windy, and we got our thrill. We got so use to it we even rode our bikes across when the trains would go by. Something I tremble about now when I think about it. It was dumb, one stumble and it would have been all over. Before I got the bike and when walking across the bridge, I use to run as fast as I could from one end to the other like a track star. There was no one around and I would just do it. It was about 100 yards or so. I would run both ways from town. It may have started when mom used to send me to the store to get something and say run as fast as those little legs could carry you. Other times when on the bridge, sometimes late in the evening, we would try to scare people coming from town by jumping out and growling like a bear. Sometimes other kids would try scaring us at night too. I feel bad about this now but there was a guy who was mentally impared and he would go to every movie. He would walk home across the bridge talking to himself as he walked. He was a little guy that walked fairly fast all the time. We would see him coming and hide under the bridge and we could hear him talking to himself and we would get the giggles.

When he got down by the end of the bridge we would jump out and scare the heck out of him. He would take off running and then stop and look back at us and start yelling at us, telling us he was going to call the cops.

I was voted class president while in seventh grade. I was just twelve. I had a late birthday in June. It was more a popularity contest than one of wit or brains. Maybe it was because I was hanging out with older upper classmen and the kids my age thought that was cool.

Seventh grade was my first year of playing football. It was the first time wearing the equipment and learning the game. We were not allowed to play football prior to that, because there were no other football programs available until you reached the seventh grade. We started in mid-August and played into late October. We practiced more than we played. I didn't like it at first, but then it was something I looked forward to every fall. I actually liked football more than hockey. I thought about going to college and playing football instead of hockey, but I didn't. Eventually, I was offered football scholarships to Notre Dame, University of Minnesota, and a few other universities. I turned them all down to pursue a professional hockey career.

We hunted then too, mostly grouse after school and on weekends when we did not have football. It was a short walk to the woods from where we lived. There were several patches of woods close to our house. I would take the .22 and walk out there; sometimes I took a friend from school. The fall leaves would be coming down so you could see in the woods, and hear the birds walking in the leaves. It seemed the grouse were plentiful. When it was dry, the leaves would crunch and make a lot of noise, but if it was moist you could walk real quietly. I loved the smell of the woods in the fall. I would enjoy it and take my time and try to take it all in. Quiet time in the woods is one of my favorite pastimes, still today.

Henry age 15.

Summer in Warroad.

Hunting anyone?

Mom: Alice Boucha, Henry and Eddie at Nestor Falls.

Figure 35

In 7th grade, we had our classes in individual rooms. It was different from having all of our classes with one teacher in one room. We had our own lockers and had enough time to get to them and exchange books before heading to another class. There seemed to be more freedom as we moved from class to class. Our lunches were served in the old gym; it had a kitchen off the basketball court. We ate at tables that were set up just before lunch, and taken down after. There were kids who worked in the lunchroom and would be credited with their meals. I worked there on occasion. The food was good home-cooked meals, (nothing like they have today). They actually cooked large roasts of beef and pork, and we had real potatoes with vegetables and milk. We also had spaghetti with meatballs, and sausage and sauerkraut; all healthy meals.

The school had a new larger gym where we had our physical education classes. The class involved fitness in the gym and health education in the classroom. As rambunctious as we were, we needed the recreation during the day. In coed gym, sometimes we would have to square dance for an hour. Being scared to death of girls, it was something I could do without. The teachers gave us an option to pick our dance partners; nobody did, so a teacher picked one for us. I usually noticed how everyone dressed. I would notice guys who dressed well with a style that I liked and that was popular at the time. I would try to emulate them, if I had the clothes. Most of the time I did not have new clothes, so I did the best I could. I liked to be dressed nice and neat, even when I was younger.

It was a time when boys and girls were starting to notice each other. I did not have a lot of self- esteem and was self-conscious of how I looked, dressed, and felt. When we went to dances, all the boys would sit on one side of the room, with the girls on the other side. It would take me all night, if ever, to get up the nerve to ask someone to dance. Then, I would be mad at myself for not asking anyone to dance, or just dancing maybe one dance at the end of the night. Sometimes, they had ladies choice, and I would dance if a girl asked me. Girls seemed to have more nerve than boys. With low self-esteem, and being shy, I was scared to death of girls. I thought if I talk to them and if I stuttered, they would laugh at me, so I did not say anything.

I envied boys who could walk up and start a conversation with a girl. I liked to be friends with those guys, because they could get close to the girls. When a girl said "hi" to me, I was stuck for an answer. I was bashful, shy and would hang my head or look away. I would not encourage a conversation. A girl would need to ask me questions before I would answer them. I could not carry on a conversation easily. I was terrified. It was not our Indian way to look someone directly in the eye or talk with someone you did not know.

My friend Jack Ploof who was a few years older than me took me under his wing. He was one of those guys who could talk to anyone. Jack and his mother lived above his mother's Café near the arena. We became friends through baseball, although he was mainly a basketball player. We all spent time together and supported each other's school sports. He loved my mother's homemade bread and cinnamon rolls, and constantly asked when she would be making homemade bread. When I was with him, we spent time with older kids. It gave me a broader, and different view of things. I was moving ahead socially before some of my classmates.

The 1963–64 Warroad Bantam Team was made up of twelve to fourteen year old players. We played a ten to fifteen game schedule. I was twelve and would not be thirteen until June. I played defense that year, my first year of not playing in goal. It felt good not to have that tension of being the last line of defense. I always felt that when they scored a goal on me that I let the team down, although that's not what happened, unless I was completely out of position or made a bad play.

During the season, we took a road trip to Two Harbors and Duluth. It was an overnight trip, and we billeted with the other teams parents. Most teams did that at some point during the season. Rodney Estling and I stayed with a nice family after the game in Two Harbors. We beat them soundly that night. The family was welcoming. I was extremely shy then and would not talk unless I absolutely had to.

While sitting at dinner with the family, I reached across to get the butter at the same time the mother was handing it to me, and I stuck my hand in the dish of soft butter, my hand mashed into it. It was a moment suspended in time until Rodney started laughing and broke the ice. He teased me about that for years.

We played against Duluth the next afternoon; they were the defending state champion. It was a big challenge for us, and we wanted to see if we measured up and compared. We had a good team and played well. We came out of there with a big win, 4–1. The coaches and parents were thrilled and were looking down the road to the play-offs. It was a big confidence builder.

We had 6 good players molded into one good unit. We had a good solid goalie in Tom Poole, and a good defensive unit with Bob Wenzel and me. We had a good older top line with George Roberts at center and Jon Hanson on wing, and Allan Baldwin on the other wing.

Coach Roberts skated this first unit practically the whole game. He would throw in the second line and rotate the others into the games as the game progressed. In tough games he would use the first unit only rotating one player in and out. Before the playoffs, Coach Roberts skated the first unit only at 6:30 a.m. before school. We didn't touch the puck; we just skated for an hour doing just staking and conditioning drills. He wanted to get us to the next level of conditioning. After school we practiced with the rest of the team. We did that for two weeks prior to the playoffs.

Not all the parents were happy or agreed with the strategy. If I were a player on the bench or a parent, I would disagree also. Coach Roberts knew what he had to do to be successful. In the region play-offs, we played our first unit most of the time but rotated in

WARROAD BANTAMS: 1964 MINNESOTA STATE BANTAM CHAMPIONS.
TOP: MIKE MARVIN, RICK MCKEEVER, RENE FOSTER, GARY MOYER,
STEVE STOSKOPF, LEE MOYER, BRIAN HENDERSON, RON MCKEEVER,
ROD ESTLING. FRONT: ALLAN BALDWIN, HENRY BOUCHA, GEORGE ROBERTS,
TOM POOLE, JON HANSON, BOB WENZEL, PETE ROBERTS.
NOT PICTURED: COACH DICK ROBERTS. COURTESY BOB AND PAM WENZEL.

Figure 36

the second line during the quarterfinals and the semifinals. In the finals against International Falls we primarily skated the first unit the whole game, rotating in one other player. Most of the parents were not happy with the coach, but we won the region tournament and we were going to the state tournament in South St. Paul.

The state tournament was being held at Wakota Arena in South Saint Paul. There were eight teams. In our quarterfinal, the coach skated the first unit the whole game, five players, rotating only the left wing from time to time. We won the game. We moved into the semifinals the next day. In our next game, Coach Roberts did the same thing, and we won again. It sent us into the finals the following day. People were wondering if we could stand up to the task of playing the whole game, and playing three games in three days. In the finals, the coach used the same players, and we won again. Amazingly, we were the Minnesota State Bantam Champions of 1964. It marked the first time a Warroad team had ever won a state championship of any kind. We were honored back home the following week at a banquet and were given plaques for our accomplishments. We were also given beautiful red wool jackets with patches of our state tournament championship. We were proud to wear them and to be the first team to win a state championship for Warroad.

CHAPTER 20: EIGHTH GRADE

That Spring after our state bantam championship season in 1964, when all the glory was finally gone and the snow was melting. We were heading into spring, we concentrated on baseball. We started throwing baseballs and playing catch in the gym, along with swinging the bats. There was not much else a person could do until it warmed up enough to get outside. Everyone had spring fever though. It was a great time of year. I was ending my seventh-grade year. I felt good. I had a few dances under my belt and what seemed like freedom by not having to sit in one classroom as we did in grade school. We were growing up. I was enthusiastic about playing sports for the high school in the future.

We were looking forward to school ending and the summer. Everyone seemed to have a lot more energy. Summers would bring swimming, playing baseball and time with friends at the beach. I played baseball that spring for the high school team. I played regularly at third base and held my own for a young player.

At that age, I was into girls and was smitten several times. We had dances that were being sponsored by our new local radio station, KRWB in Roseau. For us kids it was a big event. We wore our best clothes and were all spruced up. They held dances at the American Legion on Saturday nights. The DJs would come in with their sound systems and spin records for us as we danced. The DJs wore green jackets with black ties and matching black pants. Their hair was combed up like Elvis's. They would chat between songs and get the crowd going. We thought they were cool and had great sense of humor.

It was the summer of 1964. The Beatles were popular, but the DJs played oldies, and some Beatles songs and anything to keep people dancing. It was a fun time. I still didn't talk much, but I danced some and had a good time. It was hard to communicate because of my shyness. I kept trying to get the words out, but it was difficult for me. I knew what I wanted to say, but the words were never easy for me. Girls just plain scared me.

Warroad was a tourist town and a fishing destination. So we met all kinds of people coming to fish Lake of the Woods. The tourists stayed at the local city park or at Cal's Cabins. The kids hung out at the beach. So it was easy to meet people. We met a lot of girls who came to town with their parents. We were more than happy to show them around.

I attended my first concert that summer. It was Paul Revere & the Raiders. They were booked at the Winnipeg Arena. My friend Jack Proof met some kids from Winnipeg. They talked to him about the concert. They said they attended a lot of concerts and told Jack to call and get tickets and call if he was in Winnipeg. Jack communicated with them and arranged for tickets to the concert. Some of the older kids from Warroad had been to a few concerts in Winnipeg. The city was not that far away and they would sometimes get a hotel room and stay overnight after the concert. Some of the boys were able to get into a few nightspots by using fake IDs and would tell us of their adventures. We were all ears.

At that point in my life, I never thought about drinking. Jack didn't drink, so going with him I did not have to worry. I had not been away from home that much, so it would be an adventure for me. There was a lot of anticipation and excitement. He drove his mother's car to Winnipeg, and we stopped to call his friend, got directions, and stopped in to see him. He lived near the Winnipeg Arena and was going to the concert too. We all went together. They already knew the routine, so it was nice to have someone lead us around. We had great tickets on the floor about halfway up from the stage. The place was packed, and it was loud and it was exciting.

DARLENE, HENRY, JIM, EDDY, SHIRLEY, DAVID. 1960S.

JOHN AND CAROL PARKER.
COURTESY OF JEFF PARKER.

MAGGIE AAS, SARAH THUNDER, ALICE
BOUCHA AND VERNA KA KA GEESICK.

MAIN ST. WARROAD. COURTESY OF THE WARROAD HISTORICAL SOCIETY.

Figure 37

When they turned out the lights, everyone moved their chairs forward, so we were close to the stage by then. The first band was Chad Allan and the Expressions (later known as the Guess Who), a great local band from Winnipeg. Then came Paul Revere & the Raiders. The crowd was going crazy. The band members were all dressed in their pirate-style light blue uniforms and hats. They played for an hour and a half. It was exhilarating for me. After the concert, I felt so light on my feet; it must have been the adrenaline. We went back to Jack's friends place and hung out, and I think we stayed overnight and went back to Warroad the next day.

Back home we had a fabulous time telling our friends about the trip and concert. I was never the same after that. It broadened my horizons. Still, life returned to normal and we played baseball, swam at the beach, and chased girls—even though I was not sure what I would do if I caught one.

That summer, as I mentioned earlier, the Beatles were big. We were letting our hair grow, and everyone seemed to comb their hair down and have bangs. We had always combed it up like Elvis. To think about it now, holy cow, were we silly. I talked my mom into ordering a pair of Beatle boots with the high heels, ankle-high tops, and pointed toes. Man, I thought I was pretty cool. I wore them to all of the dances that summer and dressed in clothes that mimicked the Beatles. I had my hair longer with the dry look, but it was still short.

Football was just around the corner and I trimmed my hair right before football started. Coach Stukel was upset with all of us. He tried to send some of us back to the barbershop to get it trimmed. Our barber, Don Toulouse, laughed at us. He encouraged us to stand up to the coach and try to keep the look and be stylish. Our hair was not even close to being over our ears. Stand up to the coach? Yea, right!

I had ankle problems when we started football that year. My ankles were used to being elevated and walking on those high-heeled Beatle boots. I was not accustomed walking on flat football shoes. The first thing that happened in football practice was ankle sprains—not one but both. I was miserable. I played like that and kept reinjuring them. I finally figured out the problem one day. It had to be the boots, and I never wore them again—a lesson learned. My eighth-grade football season turned out to be a good season. We won most of our games and had a lot of fun. Pat O'Donnell was a good friend and classmate and we pushed each other to be better.

As hockey season came around and although I still had two years of eligibility in Bantams, I chose to play high school hockey. Our coach, Myron Grafstrom, was happy I made the choice. I played full games on the B team (junior varsity) and dressed for the varsity games. I played sparingly that year, but I received a lot of experience. The game was faster, with better players and more hitting and strategy. I was learning the ropes. I was thirteen years old playing with high school seniors. In the locker room, I kept my mouth shut and went along with everything, listening to the older players' stories, good and bad, continually learning.

There are always characters on a team, and this team was no different. Some people just like to see what they can get away with. They liked to have fun and pushed the rules to the limit. A couple of the seniors asked me what I was doing one day after our home game. I said, "Nothing, why?" One said, "We are going over to Greenbush tonight after the game, do you want to come?" I was surprised to be asked and said "yes." Greenbush had dances every Saturday night, and most older kids in the surrounding area went to them. I had heard about them, but I was never invited to go with anyone. I was only thirteen, but I looked older. I was thrilled to be invited; I felt that I was part of the team. Gordy said, "My friends are picking me up after the game, and we'll leave then." We played the game against Baudette and won. So everyone was in a good mood. I still was not sure they were going to take me. Finally, he said "Come on let's go". His buddies were there and waiting in the car outside the rink. They had the car warmed up and had a case of beer in the backseat. We took off for Greenbush, about forty-five minutes away. As I sat there, we pulled out of town, the other player handed me a beer. I took it, and we drank beer all the way over to Greenbush. I never thought about getting caught or the consequences. We stopped in Roseau to use the bathroom at a gas station. It did not take much beer on an empty stomach to feel buzzed and a little sick to my stomach. By the time we got to the dance and parked, I got sick and threw up. I did not get out of the car. I just hung my head out the back door and let it fly. I'm sure they were laughing at me. I just lay there in the back-seat for a while, thinking this is not good. I did not want to go in and have people see me this way. Sometime during the next couple of hours I went into the dance anyway. I just looked around and used the bathroom, but that was about it. All I remember is someone from Roseau saying "hi", and asking me "What I was doing there?" I went back out to the car, slept it off, and was never so happy to get home in one piece. Those guys teased me about it all season. It was another experience but one I would like to forget.

It was different playing hockey at the high school level, and I had a lot to learn. I knew if I hung in there, the experience would come. I watched the high school team play for years. I could not believe I was playing with them now. I loved the uniforms and the black and gold. I loved the school spirit with the band and the cheerleaders. The atmosphere of the games was addicting. It was all "rah-rah" at its finest. I loved the big crowds of students and the community sup-port that the programs received. I was proud to be a Warrior.

The Warriors never made it out of the playoffs that year, and the season ended anticlimactically. Roseau again represented Region Eight at the state tournament. The Minnesota State High School Hockey Tournament is the largest in the country. The state is divided into eight regions, and each region has a representative at the state tournament. It was a goal of each team to represent its region in the prestigious tournament. Warroad had represented

Region Eight several times over the years, starting in the late 1940s and again in the 1950s and early 1960s. The last time was in 1963. Roseau and Thief River Falls predominantly represented our region over the years, especially Roseau, our big rival. They were the bigger schools with more students, more players to pick from and they had a great hockey program.

CHAPTER 21: NINTH GRADE

As a freshman, I started the school year with great anticipation. We had a new high school hockey coach, John Hopkins, a Bemidji State College graduate. Coach Myron Grafstrom resigned and transferred to a bigger school in the Minneapolis area, leaving the coaching job vacant. Mr. Hopkins was our physical education teacher, and we knew he would be a good coach. Everyone seemed to like him.

In mid-August, we started our football season after another great summer. Coach Tony Stukel was originally from the Iron Range of Minnesota. Tony and his wife, Ruth, were both teachers. Coach Stukel had a way about him that was unique, and he could inspire you when you needed it. Whenever we got out of line or started fighting with one of our teammates, he had a way of making you look like a total idiot. Once you felt that way, you never wanted to experience it again, especially in front of your teammates. He was our baseball coach as well. We were looking forward to school that year and to all of the fun activities that were associated with it. It was that way in a small town with not much else to do, except sports. As a freshman, I started off on the varsity team. I was a running back but did not play on a regular basis. We were too deep in the back-field. I also played on the defensive side, as a safety, so I got my time in. I was in and out of the offense with other backs throughout the first couple of games. I was also learning to play quarterback along with my friend De De Dumais. We had a great team with a lot of talent. I was young but had the spunk and determination to play. The coaches liked having competition for the positions. It made us all work hard to maintain the spots. We had a big offensive line. Our regular quarterback, De De Dumas, was an upperclassman. He was having spotty success and the team did not respond very well to him. He was on and off through our first couple of games, although we were winning. We played Baudette in a big conference game. They had been a real good team the past couple of years. They were good that year too and were picked to run as conference champions.

De De started the game as quarterback. He was calling plays and things were not going well. De De was like Rodney Dangerfield, "He had no respect." Some of the other players and De De would go round and round and would argue. The coach recognized that things we not moving and asked me if I thought I could handle it. I said "yes", but really I was not sure. I was young and a nervous wreck. It was a big game, and I was just learning the position. I knew the basic plays, and he quickly wrote the plays on a piece of white tape that he stuck to my hand so I could remember what to call. I looked at the plays during the huddle and called one out. I mixed up the plays and the team seemed to respond. We had the Baudette defense confused and guessing what direction we would come. Not one of my teammates questioned my calls. We started moving the ball down the field. Our defense held and we had the momentum. We ended up winning the game 19–14 in an upset, and after that, the position was mine. Although, I had the position, De De played full back and rotated in and out of the lineup and was able to contribute to our success. We went on to win the conference championship, the first time in years.

After the break between the football and hockey season, we were ready to start. We were excited, we had a new coach in John Hopkins, everyone seemed to like him, and we were anxious to see what he could do. Our new coach was an avid conditioning person, and we started out with a heavy dry land training program. The first time ever, and after looking at the player roster, he was convinced that I should play goal. I had not played goal for two years, and he thought that a good team should have a good defense, starting with a goalie.

He felt that I could do the job. I agreed. I would have played anywhere, so I did not care. During the dry land training, I kept coming in first in most of our drills. When we did our distance running, I ran in goalie pads and would finish last because of the weight. But with all of the other drills and conditioning exercises, I would run first. He changed his mind about me after he saw what I could do. I had much more endurance than the others, and he thought that my being in goal was a waste of my talents. So he revised his lineup so that I was to play either defense or forward that year.

It may have been the downtown quarterbacks who said something to him after they found out what he was thinking. The downtown quarterbacks were a convincing group of businessmen who could put the pressure on a coach when they felt he was making the wrong decisions. With his coaching style and determination, we were bound for a good year. Most of us were glad to have him and a new system. He brought in new life, techniques, and challenges, and we all bought into it. He was fresh out of college with knowledge and enthusiasm. He was a good motivator. We were trained well, and he made sure we skated to our potential each shift.

Early that year he ordered new uniforms. No one knew exactly what he ordered. He just said they were going to be different. The school had the money budgeted that year for new uniforms and they let him pick them out. Traditionally, the old Warroad uniforms were the Boston Bruins style and colors. When the gear arrived and I looked at it, I was shocked. The uniforms were different. We wore the old uniforms at a few home games before the new arrived. When we wore the new uniforms for our home game, our fans thought that we were the other team coming onto the ice. We had gold breezers (pants) and the same color of socks and gold jerseys with black and white trim, but very little black in them. Our away uniforms had black socks and jerseys with the same breezers. The away uniforms were nice, but I thought the home uniforms were ugly. They were bland. There was not much we could do. We had to wear them.

That year, I played the whole season with the junior varsity and played the varsity game too. So I had a lot of ice time. We were a respectable, good team that overcame and won some of the games with pure conditioning. We had a good record and had beaten some good teams. We were a little short on talent but we worked hard to overcome that. There was hope and excitement about the upcoming playoffs. The thing about the playoffs is, if you lose one game you're out. So anyone could upset you if you did not come to play or if you had a bad bounce of the puck at the wrong time. That year I realized how things worked in the regional playoffs. I realized what it took to win and what it took to become a contender. Now I wanted to win, and all the time. I loved the feeling of winning, the feeling of accomplishment and a job well done.

We went into the playoffs and won our quarterfinal game. Then we won our semifinal game, which took us to the regional finals against our big rival, the Roseau Rams. We lost 5–0 to a fine Roseau team in the finals.

Ordinarily our season would have been over, but there was a glitch in Region Three. They had no representative because no one played hockey in that region. The Minnesota High School League let the Region Seven and Region Eight runner-ups play for the Region Three title. This would round out the 8 team State Tournament format. The winner would represent Region Three in the state tournament. We had another shot at the tournament. We knew that before our game with Roseau. If we lost we were to play again in Roseau at the Memorial Arena against the runner-up of Region Seven.

Just after our loss to Roseau, we found out that we were to play the Greenway of Coleraine High School. The Coleraine team was out of the Iron Range area of Minnesota and was well-known for

144

its hockey talent and skills. We had not played Coleraine but knew it had a great hockey tradition. We were playing well and knew we had a chance to win. It was game day at the Roseau Memorial Arena which was our home rink for Region Eight. The arena was packed to the hilt. Spectator buses from both Coleraine and Warroad were there. It was standing room only. Both teams brought their cheerleaders and their pep bands, and the place was 'rockin'.

After the drop of the puck, both teams came out as if they were shot out of a cannon. We scored first, and then they scored, and then we scored again, and then they scored. It was a back-and-forth game, exciting and fast. In a game like that a player does not have much time to think what he is going to do with the puck once he gets it. Things happen so fast. You might have a second or two before someone is on you, hitting you or trying to get the puck away from you. We led most of the game, but at the end of regulation the score was tied at 3 all. While in the locker room we talked about who is going to get the winner. One shot could end it. As we went into overtime, both teams were determined to win. It was end-to-end action and then it happened: They scored! It was all over in a heartbeat—all of our hard work, the stress of a season, and another loss to our old rival Roseau and now Coleraine. After the game the Coleraine team came into our locker room and congratulated us on a terrific game. We wished them well too. After the loss and some time away from the rink, the sting tended to go away, but the bitter memory remained as to how close we came to play in the fabled state tournament. We could hold our heads high, but the pain would always remain. We were that close.

Baseball could not come soon enough. It seemed as if the break between sports was getting longer each time. We were ready to move into baseball but had to wait for the weather. Springtime was here and we were ready. We had success in football and a pretty good season in hockey, and we were ready for the spring sports to begin. We started off in the gym again, throwing, playing catch and practiced our hitting into a net. When we finally got outside, it was nice but cold. I remember how the bat would sting as we hit the balls. Those wooden bats were all we had during that time. Nobody wore any batting gloves. I was also in track and competed in track meets when we didn't have baseball games. I started competing in both and was doing that since seventh grade but baseball would come first. I really did not train much then and ran only occasionally. I would show up at the track meets and compete. We did not have a track in Warroad at that time. When we would host a track meet, the coaches and teachers would have to go out on the playground and measure the distances and mark off the track with chalk or lime. The pole vault and high jump had either sand or shavings in them to land on. It was primitive.

CHAPTER 22: TENTH GRADE

Once again the summer was exciting and we spent time chasing girls, swimming, and playing baseball. This summer was different. I was working as well. I got a job through the CITA program at the school. We did odd jobs, such as painting, cleaning, moving desks and chairs around, and sweeping. Sometimes we got to use the big buffer. If you never used one, well, it was hard getting use to. If you tilted it forward it would take off to the right, and if you bent it back it would take off to the left. The first time I had one in my hands I knocked over tables, chairs, and anything else that was in my way, including some dented-up lockers. The janitors would stand there and laugh. After cleaning up my mess, I pulled it out into an area with a little more room and got used to it, before attempting to get into places where there was furniture, but I finally figured it out.

The janitors were always playing jokes on the kids who worked there. They would hide our lunch boxes and fool around with you all the time. One time Bill Lewis pulled the ladder down on me when I was cutting limbs on a tree in the playground. He left me up there for over an hour. He said he got busy and forgot about me. I guess I could have climbed down, but I was being paid by the hour, so I stayed up there until he came and got me. We were not making much money—most likely less than $1.25 an hour—but it was a respectable job. I wanted to get Bill back for teasing me all the time; I knew he was working a split shift, so he and some others would be back at the school later. That night at about dark, I got a bucket of water and climbed up on the flat part of the roof leading out from the gym's back door of the school. With the bucket of water up there, I then went back down and peeked through the windows until I saw Bill go toward the gym. Then I pounded on the back door because I knew he would open it and look around. Then quickly I climbed back up on the roof and waited for him to come out. Just as I thought, he came out and looked around; I poured the bucket of water on his head. I took off running across the flat roof laughing all the way and jumped off in front and ran away. I could hear someone swearing as I ran away laughing, but I wasn't waiting around to find out what he said.

After a night's sleep, I could not wait to get to work the next day to find out what he said about it. He came in late that day after working late the night before. I saw him in the afternoon and he did not say a word. I waited. I would go out of my way to ask him certain questions about his night shift, but I did not want to come right out and ask him about the water. I was afraid to. Bill never mentioned it. It makes me wonder if I got the right guy that night.

The summer was winding down, the fun we had during the summer went so fast once again. It seemed when the 4th of July was over, we would start thinking about baseball play-offs in late July, and the start of football in mid August. Maybe it was the climax of the 4th being over. The fish flies were abundant and the city would turn off the lights at night so the bugs would not gather around the poles. Once they started rotting they smelled bad. As July past, you would start getting the sense of fall coming with the nights getting cooler and the sun going down earlier. The Warroad River would be turning green with algae, and we did not swim much. Poisoning in the water was an issue during that time of year and if you went in, it would make you itch for a few days, and make you miserable. Most of the guys who played football started to throw the football around and play some pickup games in the vacant yards and lots. In the evenings we still had our social lives and carried on with our youthful romances.

Once mid August was here; we got our physicals and started football practices. It was hot in August even in northern Minnesota. We survived the heat, and we were looking forward to all of the school activities that would follow. After winning the conference the previous year in football, we were all ready for another season. We lost kids to graduation from the year before, and the makeup of the team was a little different. We had goals set on another conference title. We had a plan, and we went to work. We played well all season and gained another conference title.

Homecoming was a weeklong celebration of activities at school, including the pep fest and the crowning of the homecoming king, queen and all of the attendants. On game day, we had a big pep rally during school. The tradition was that the students would meet around 5 p.m. at the school to begin a snake dance around town and end up at the football field at the old ballpark. There would be a big stack of wood, and we would have a big rally and bonfire before the game. After the game, the homecoming dance topped the evening. We had live bands that played at the dance. The grand march of the homecoming queen, the king, and all of the attendants would follow, making it quite spectacular.

It was great anticipation once again before the hockey season started. It was the year that the state Bantam championship team was all back together. Our former coach, John Hopkins, was moving onward and upward. He decided to move to the Minneapolis area and teach at a bigger school. Our former Bantam coach, Dick Roberts, knowing he had the former Bantam team together again, took over as head coach at Warroad High School. He also was our physical education and health teacher.

The Roberts were longtime Warroad residents. Dick's father had a hardware store in Warroad. Dick graduated from Warroad and went on to the University of Minnesota. He was captain of the university team while playing there. His claim to fame was a kick shot that he developed as a player. The kick shot was outlawed because it was so dangerous. He would come down the ice, have the puck on the stick blade, and would kick the shaft of the stick. It would whip the puck like a slap shot but much harder. It was a dangerously hard shot that a person could not control. You didn't know where it would end up. Dick moved back to Warroad and reopened a hardware store and wanted to raise his family in Warroad. He coached our state Bantam championship team in 1964.

His assistant was Dale Telle from North Dakota. Dale and his wife had just moved to Warroad, and he was helping with our football teams as well as our hockey teams.

It would prove to be a challenging year in Warroad High School hockey, with great expectations fallen by the wayside. We played well as a team from time to time but were not consistent. We did not have the same chemistry as we did when we were younger. As a result we lost games that we should have won. There were a lot of variables during the season with player tensions and sometimes poor attitudes. We had groups of players arguing with other players. We didn't have the camaraderie that we had when playing as Bantams. I guess we were all growing up, and our values and motivation may have changed. At one point there was a petition from some of the "do-gooders" against some of the other players who liked to venture out of the team's rules once in a while. They were never caught doing anything wrong, but the other players knew what they were up to and resented it.

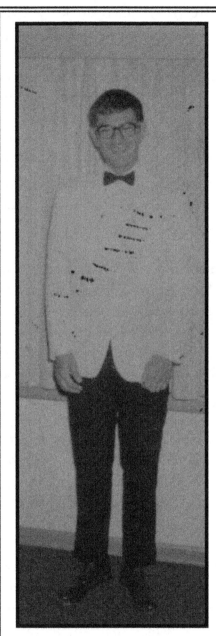

HENRY, ANOTHER PROM.

WARROAD FOOTBALL AND BASEBALL
COACH TONY STUKEL.
COURTESY OF RUTH STUKEL.

WARROAD WARRIOR.

ASSISTANT COAH DALE TELLE AND
COACH DICK ROBERTS.
COURTESY OF KENNY KVARNLOV.

Figure 38

151

While the coaches and the parents did not really know what was going on, the players did. The petition called to have these guys removed from the team. Some of the players presented the petition to the coaches and explained that they knew that team rules were being broken and something had to be done. My friends, Dale Bleau and Bob Wenzel were among some of the players who were targeted. We laugh about it today. That happened early in the year, and it gave way to tensions when playing. As a result we were at odds with each other throughout the year. I got along with both sides, but as a team we were doomed. There was too much resentment and bickering.

It was a long season, but we had our good times too. We played in the Coleraine Christmas Tournament that year. We played well but did not win the tournament. Still, Warroad was the favorite of the fans. It was because of this tournament and the recognition that I was chosen to the All-State Team that year as a sophomore. It was the first time ever a sophomore had been chosen to an All-State Team. That tournament may have been a highlight of the year for me.

We went into the playoffs again at Roseau, but we never did well and were knocked out of the tournament again. There would be no state tournament again that year. I attended the All-State Hockey Banquet sponsored by WCCO Radio in Minneapolis that spring and received honors for being selected. My coach was kind enough to drive me down and back for the special event.

It was again a long spring while waiting for the next sport to begin. We had only a quarter left of our sophomore year. I was thinking ahead now, trying to figure out what I might do with the rest of my life. I had never thought about it much before. But with two years left in high school, a lot of people were talking to me, telling me about the colleges that were interested in giving me a scholarship. My name was starting to show up in various newspaper articles. I was starting to get recognition as a hockey player.

Baseball was just around the corner, and we started throwing and batting in the gym and getting ready for another fine season. It was early April, and a couple of juniors, Rene Foster and Glen Thompson were looking for liquor and asked me if I knew someone who would buy it for them. Even though I was a sophomore and these guys were upperclassmen, they looked up to me, I think because I always spent time with older kids and was a little more streetwise. I felt older and more experienced because I started playing hockey in eighth grade. These guys thought I could help them, and I could. It was a bad decision. I should have said no or told them I did not know. It would have ended it, but no, I was a nice guy trying to please everyone and play big shot. Rene and Glen gave me the money, and I went ahead and bought a couple of bottles through my contact. After I picked up the liquor, I met with Rene and Glen and I gave them the bottles. I made a dumb decision.

They needed a place to stash it, so I helped with that too. Instead of keeping out of it, I said I knew a place. It was near my house and down by the river in a building owned by my neighbor, John Pick. John was a mink rancher and commercial fisherman. We drove Glen's car down near his house to get to the hiding place. John saw us leave while looking through his window. He thought we were stealing his nets. He came out of his house, and ran down the road toward us and we heard him yell. If we would have stopped and explained, he would have laughed, but no, we took off. He called the police and gave them a description of Glen's car. We didn't know that at the time. We went to the school, where the juniors were decorating for prom. We visited for while and the guys drove me home and dropped me off. They went back to the school to help decorate. The police found the car at the school and found the guys in the gym.

They accused them of stealing the nets and checked out their car. The officer started putting a lot of pressure on them about where they stashed the nets. The officer threatened them with jail, and they folded. One guy blurted out that they were down there stashing booze. The next thing I knew an officer was knocking on my parents' door. We were all asleep. My mother got up and answered the door, and the officer walked in with those guys behind him. They were standing in our kitchen. When I got up, they questioned me about the booze. They had the bottles with them. The seals were broken on the bottles, and they had been down to the building to get the booze as evidence. They cleared themselves for stealing nets. Now they were going to hang me for getting the booze. Well, they did. They also figured out who actually bought the bottle for us, so we were all in trouble.

Because of state rules and regulations, I was out of extracurricular activities for eighteen school weeks. Because of my mistake, which I regretted very much, I was out of baseball that year and out of football the next fall. Kids make mistakes, and this was one I had to pay for. It hurt me more than anyone knew. Playing sports was my life. We lived for baseball and football in those small towns. It was something that we could excel in. Now I was out. To this day, I regret letting the team and the community down and impacting others in a negative way with my irresponsible decisions. Another lesson learned.

CHAPTER 23: ELEVENTH GRADE

I was able to play Legion and Muskie baseball that summer, so that season was not an entire waste based on my mistake. I was dating Debby Bleau. I thought she was pretty, vibrant, and smart. We got along so well. Her parents did not want her going out with me at first. So we would see each other at school and we were sneaking around and meeting at dances, games or at the movie theater. We would meet a lot behind the school, and spend time together. If it was raining we would meet in one of the buses. We liked each other and dated on and off since eighth grade.

I worked for the city that summer. I was on a federal program and was being paid minimum wage. It was nice having a paycheck. I painted, mowed, rode the garbage truck on Fridays, and did odd jobs. I bought my first car that summer. It was a 1951 four-door Plymouth, and a clutch and shift on the driving column. I bought it from Archie Moran, a mechanic at a local gas station. He said it ran okay, and I believed him. I paid sixty dollars for it and had to make two payments before I drove it away. The spare had a bent rim, but Archie said it would do if I had a flat. I was proud of that car. I walked everywhere before, or rode with someone else. It was nice to be able to get around and have the freedom. I fixed it up, put seat covers on it and fixed this and that. I also hung those fragrant Christmas trees. It was okay for a first car, and it got me around. I have some good memories of that car and the time I owned it. One time I was coming around the big curve by Marvin Windows, and as I made my way around the curve, my hood flew up and I couldn't see. I had to look through a crack to see to stop. When I got out to close the hood and wire it down, people were driving by with smiles on their faces. I used coat hangers as wire. My tires were never new. They were all used tires that I could buy for a few dollars.

One time I had a flat and had to use that old bent rim I had in the trunk. I had to put it on until I could get another tire. If you were behind me as I was driving down the road, it looked as if my tire was going to fall off. People used to catch me and yell at me that my tire was falling off. I would just smile, wave, and yell back "thanks". They would shake their heads and keep going.

Another time I was stopped for not having any brake lights. The cop came up to me and said, "Hey, do you know you don't have any brake lights?" I said, "I know, I don't have any brakes, so I didn't think I needed them." He said, "What?" Actually, I was close to being right. Sometimes I would really need to pump those brakes to stop. I always had a can of brake fluid stored under the hood, along with my cans of oil and other fluids. My muffler had holes and was wrapped with aluminum pop cans and held on with hose clamps and tape. I used the car during spring, summer, and fall. When it got cold, I could never get it started. So it was a three-season car. I was back to walking or hitching a ride in the winters. I had that car until I graduated.

I did not play football that fall due to my suspension by the Minnesota State High School League. I would be eligible just before the hockey season. I loved football and was disappointed with not playing that year. I watched the games, and it was tough not to be playing with my friends. That fall I worked at Thermo-Lite Glass Company in Warroad. They were nice enough to hire me during the football season to help me earn money and to keep busy.

Our sophomore year in hockey was a disappointing year. Our dream team faltered and did not come together. We called the troublemakers the Petition Boys and most of those guys graduated, so

BOUCHA FAMILY PICTURE.
BACK: EDDY, HENRY, JIM AND DAD (GEORGE). MIDDLE: SHIRLEY, DARLENE,
BILLY, MOM (ALICE). FRONT: LITTLE PHYLLIS, JEFF.

Figure 39

we would not have that problem this year. We needed harmony on the team to have fun and enjoy the year.

We were still trying to get to the state tournament. I had two years left to earn that right. Making it to the Minnesota State High School Hockey Tournament was still one of my goals. Maybe this was our year, with hard work and commitment. One never knows how things will turn out. We had renewed excitement like every year and hopes for a championship season.

We had good harmony all year and won some big games, but in the playoffs we were again beaten out. We just could not get over the hump. Roseau was very good, and we just could not get by them. They had more players to choose from and a better program. It seemed that they had the luck. In a close game, they would always find a way to win. Good teams do that. In close games the bounce of the puck, a timely penalty, a shorthanded goal, a goal off a skate, or a soft goal would go to the team that made it happen. In order to be a good team, we would need to change that and make things happen for us. It seemed we were a player or two short; we did not quite have it all together.

I made the WCCO Radio All-State Hockey Team again as a junior. We also played in the Coleraine Christmas Tournament that year, and it was another season highlight.

After the season, I looked back and reflected on some good wins during the year. Still, more than ever, I wanted to play in the state tournament. I had one year to go and was wondering if it was ever going to happen. Looking at all the hockey players graduating, I was wondering how this was going to work. The returning seniors were- Rodney Estling (we called him Grandpa) and I were coming back, but we had a good group of Bantams coming up.

It was spring and we concentrated on the upcoming baseball and track seasons. We prepared as usual in the gym until we could get outside. We would get outside when Mother Nature would let us. Some days we could get out in the sun and play catch even though there was snow on the ground. It seemed as if the roads thawed first, so we would stand out there and play catch.

We had a great baseball season, winning 90 percent of our games. We ended up in the regional finals against Bemidji. I was pitching, and we were leading 4–3 with two outs in the seventh inning. We played only seven innings in high school. They had runners on base, and they hit a routine fly ball to shallow left field. Our shortstop ran out and our fielder ran up to the ball and both stopped and let it drop. They scored two runs to win the game. That was a devastating way to lose. I continued to run track when I was available and when it did not interfere with baseball games. I made it to the regional by winning the long jump, 440, and by participating in the relays.

CHAPTER 24: MY SENIOR YEAR

The summer before my senior year consisted of working with the city of Warroad, painting, hauling garbage, and mowing. I played Legion and Muskie baseball all summer and had a good time. My friends were either using their parents' car or had one of their own. We spent time at the beach, park, and visited at the point in Warroad. We had routes and would do our whips around town.

On one trip to Roseau, I bought a few new pair of pants and I was wearing one that I liked a lot. I thought they fit nice and looked good. Roseau had the only traffic light in the county. Trying to be funny, we decided to do a Chinese fire drill. We all got out at the light and ran around the car like idiots. I fell and tore my new pants. It was stupid, and in those days you didn't wear your pants with holes in them. I worked hard to buy those clothes, and I was really mad at myself. When you have to buy things from the money you earned, you seem to value them more.

It seemed that in every small town, kids had their own route to take a whip (regular route). In Roseau we drove around the same loop as the locals. We were looking for girls, of course. Most times we would talk to a carloads of girls and meet at the drive-in for a while before heading back to Warroad.

On one trip to Roseau, we attended a dance. There were four of us who started for the Warroad football team who drove down in one car. We went to the dance at the municipal building where they had a live band. While at the dance one of the other guys said, "Hey, let's go for a ride with these guys out to a party." The dance was kind of boring, and I knew one of the guys although not the others. So I said "okay. "

The guy I knew was driving. It was a big sedan and all four of the Roseau guys were in the front seat, and all four of the Warroad guys in the backseat. I did not know this at the time, but these guys had been drinking. After leaving the dance, we headed out of town to the other party, and the driver was driving erratically. I was getting nervous. I told the driver to just bring us back to the dance so we could get our car. He turned around, but he was speeding. I was thinking we are going to get pulled over. Sure enough, when he turned the corner toward the dance we were stopped by a Minnesota State Trooper. We did not have anything to drink; we were just in the wrong place at the wrong time. When the trooper stepped up to the window and asked the driver if he had been drinking, he said "no." After checking his eyes, the trooper then walked around the front of the car and went to the passenger side. He asked the passenger if he had been drinking, and he said "no." Then the trooper opened up the door and looked in the car and found an open bottle of beer. He dug under the seat and found a six-pack of beer. He said, "What's this, pop?"

There were four of us in the backseat. I was in the middle of the backseat but on the left side next to a teammate. As the trooper said, "What is this, pop?" my teammate Lee Moyer opened the door and bolted and I followed. He ran down toward the river, and I headed across the bridge, running as if I was shot out of a cannon. I was halfway across the bridge when I heard someone crash into a picket fence down by the river. It was pitch-black down there, but I figured it was my friend Lee heading downriver. As we bolted from the car on the driver's and street side, the trooper came running around the front of the car, yelling, "Stop or I'll shoot." As he got over to the middle of the road, the other two guys jumped out the back seat on the other side. It was Pat O'Donnell, and Steve Stoskopf jumping out of the backseat and they took off in the other direction. The trooper went running back around again and yelled and said, "Stop or I'll shoot." The trooper was standing there and did not know what to do. He did not chase us because he had all four of the Roseau boys still in the front seat of the car. He called for backup, and they looked for us most of the night. I hid for awhile then I ran all the way down the alleys east toward Warroad and got out on the highway and managed to get a ride back home. The people that picked me up said they heard some kids ran away from a trooper. "Was that you guys?" They said they would not say anything. They were laughing about it. I was in bed when the phone rang, and I heard my mother saying that I was home and had been in bed for a while. I thought the cops called. I was worried. If I was caught, because of the beer, and with my prior charge, I was out for my senior year of hockey. It was the Minnesota High School League rules.

LEFT TO RIGHT: JON FROLANDER, BOB KRAHN,
MAYNARD NELSON, PAT O'DONNELL HENRY BOUCHA.
COURTESY OF KENNY KVARNLOV.

WARROAD HIGH SCHOOL.
COURTESY OF THE WARROAD HISTORICAL SOCIETY.

HENRY 1969
GRADUATION PICTURE.

Figure 40

I lay awake all night, praying for a miracle. After not sleeping much, I was up early the next day. I made calls to my friends, but everyone was still sleeping. I waited and called back and finally got a hold of Pat O'Donnell. He said they were all okay and had driven around Roseau looking for me. They all had hid until things calmed down and met back at the car and the dance. He said he was the one who called the house last night to find out where I was. He had not heard anything from anyone either. I was really worried. I did not know what was going to happen, if anything. If those boys from Roseau told the police who we were, we were in big trouble. I figured if they had told the police, they would have notified us by now. I thought maybe it was just a matter of time before something happened. Oh, what a mess. I went uptown to try to find out if anyone had heard anything about it. Everyone was talking about how we ran away from the State Police. It was a classic story. The trooper who stopped us was a good friend with my parents and lived in Warroad. The people I talked to that day said, they were sure he knew who we were, but he was not pushing the issue. They said he may not do anything because we were all starters on the football team. The hockey season was just around the corner. After that day, I really counted my blessings, and I walked the line. There was no mention of anything about the incident in Roseau by the law enforcement, although people in Roseau were talking about it. There were rumors around town about some kids who ran away from the police in Roseau. It was weird. No one used our names, but they all knew who we were. Nothing happened and no one said a word.

We went undefeated that football season. We finished 6-0-2 and were conference co-champions. All four of us who were in that car during the late summer incident were on the All-Conference Team.

CHAPTER 25: FINAL SEASON

The hockey season was just around the corner, and we had quite a number of Bantams who were moving up to high school hockey. We had a few underclassmen that played junior varsity the year before that would make up our team. The Bantams the year before made it to the Bantam State Tournament. I knew all of the players but we did not spend time with them as they were the younger crowd, my brother Eddy's age. There were only two seniors, and the rest would be underclassman. We figured with all the Bantams moving up, and junior varsity players, we might have a good mix and have a chance.

We started skating in late November and played our first game on December 10, as usual. We skated for two weeks in late November, and it would give us three weeks before we played our first game. We did not have any scrimmages with other teams during that time.

It was nice to have ice early that year. It was natural ice, and it was cold enough to put ice in the arena during deer season, a week earlier than usual. When you think about it, the hockey season was not very long. The season was December, January, and February, with the state tournament in early March. We played twenty games with twelve-minute periods. If we made it into the playoffs you could play a few more games. If not we were done at twenty games. That was twenty games of thirty-six minutes per game, for a total of 720 minutes of hockey. If we had three lines and played one-third of the time, we played 240 minutes of hockey for the entire season. That was four hours of game time for the entire season. That was ridiculous, when colleges, juniors and everyone else were playing twenty-minute periods.

Rodney Estling and I were the co-captains for the year. After our first few games, I was amazed we were ranked number one in the state. We had never ranked that high, ever. We took it in stride, and it was the type of team we had. We did not get overconfident and we had humility.

Our first game against Roseau was a big test for us and was great. We won 5–1. Our fans had bragging rights after we beat them. It was part of the reason why we were ranked so high. At that time, I realized we might have a chance to get to the tournament. We had not beaten Roseau in years, and it was my fifth year of playing high school hockey.

The closest we came to going to the state tournament was my freshman year when we lost to Coleraine in overtime. Could this be the year? Well, for me, it had to be. I needed to fulfill my dreams and reach my goal of playing in the state tournament.

We again played in the Coleraine Christmas Tournament. Coleraine had a good team and were high in the rankings. They were defending state champions. We played White Bear Lake first and beat them. The next night we faced Coleraine in a big matchup that everyone in the state was waiting for. The teams didn't disappoint anyone as Coleraine won it 2–1 with a late goal in the third period. It was our first loss that year. We did not hang our heads. We could have won that game just as easily. If we played again the next day, it would have had a different outcome. Our teams were that close. We were a quality team and had a shot at the state tournament.

After Christmas we were rolling with only one loss. The publicity was building, and everyone wanted to see us. Wherever we played, people came, the arenas were full, and the town was buzzing with fans and reporters.

We were scheduled for a game in Roseau. We were on a winning streak and ranked number one in the state. This was a big test. They were ready for us. They were a good team, and Roseau was always tough at home. They had the advantage of hosting the regional tournament over the years and always held home-ice advantage in the playoffs. Bemidji built a bigger arena and was hosting the Region Eight tournament that year.

The Minnesota State High School League ineligibility rules affected Dale Smedsmo and the Roseau team that year. Dale was a good player but was ineligible for eighteen school weeks. Fortunately for Roseau, he was eligible in time for our game in Roseau, his first game back. He would help them because he was an impact player.

Roseau played a tight game and was able to stick to a good strategy that night. It was a full house, and both teams were at their finest. The bands were playing, and the cheerleaders were cheering. The fans of each team were trying to outdo each other. Warroad on one side and Roseau on the other. It was amazing. The fans were filled with enthusiasm.

Roseau's plan was to drift a winger outside the blue line behind me on my defensive point. They knew that I always pinched in on that side. If I did it again, they could tip the puck out behind me and send that winger down free and clear. Well, they did on various occasions, and it did work to their advantage. They scored three goals doing that before we were able to shut it down. They also played hard and played a great game. By the middle of the third period, the score was 7–2. I scored a couple of quick goals late in the game, but they defeated us 7–4. They had their glory, as we did in the first game. It was always a sweet win in a big game like that. We were on the other side of the coin and did not like it. We knew we had to beat them in the regional tournament that year in order to make it to the state tournament. Meanwhile, we needed to finish our season strong.

We dropped out of the number-one ranking after the loss. The rest of the season went well, and we kept winning and regained the top ranking. By that time, we were getting a tremendous amount of attention, and there were news crews visiting Warroad every week. People wanted to see us play. It seemed everywhere we went the news teams and the fans were there too. We finished the season strong, winning all of our games, and we were ready for the playoffs. We were healthy with only minor bumps and bruises. Warroad had not represented our region in the state tournament since 1963. Was it our time?

My teammates that year were Richard Ellerbush, Ed Huerd, John Taylor, Bob Storey, Frank Krahn, Lyle Kvarnlov, Leo Marshall, Jerry Hodgson, Jeff Hallett, Alan Hangsleben, Mike Hanson, Mike Marvin, and my brother Ed Boucha. Student manager was Gary Pieper. Our athletics director then was Rudy Rauker. My brother Eddy did not play much that year. He had rheumatic fever. The doctor thought it was pneumonia, and treated Eddy for that, but he could not shake the illness and missed most of the season. I think Robert Marshall filled in as spare goalie during the tournament.

CHAPTER 26: THE REGION EIGHT TOURNAMENT

The Region Eight playoffs were in Bemidji at Bemidji State University. We won in the quarter finals and were in the semifinals. We were the favorites to be in the finals. We made our 2½-hour trip to Bemidji in the afternoon with great anticipation and great expectations.

It was always an exciting time of year. It was something that we looked forward to every single year. Springtime was in the air, the weather warming and the days getting longer and it was tournament time. The tournament was like waiting for Christmas. You knew it was going to happen, and the anticipation was overwhelming. It was the show of all shows. If we won the Region Tournament, we would be going to the state tournament for the first time since 1963. It was a big deal *in the land of windows, walleye's and hockey sticks*, as stated by Cal Marvin and describing Warroad (Marvin Windows which employed most of the community, and the famous Lake of the Woods walleye and of course Christian Brothers Hockey Stick factory).

We held in our hands, all of the town's hopes and dreams of Warroad returning to the state tournament. Everyone was behind us, supported us, and prayed that this was our year. To put it simply, we needed three wins to win the Region Tournament. We had one quarter final game down and needed two more wins.

1969 TOURNAMENT TEAM.
BACK ROW: MR. ROBERTS, M. MARVIN, R. ELLERBUSCH, S. HELMSETTER, M. HANSON, H. BOUCHA, F. KRAHN, J. HODGSON, L. KVARNLOV, T. STUKEL, MR. TELLE, G. PIEPER.
FRONT ROW: E. HUERD, J. TAYLOR, R. ESTLING, J. HALLET, R. MARSHALL, L. MARSHALL, A. HANGSLEBEN, R. STOREY.

Figure 41

We knew we had to play our game, focus on every shift and every situation. We could not just show up and win. We needed to be focused and play well. If we lost, we were out! Although we were ranked high at that time, we had to play our best hockey. Only the best teams would participate from here on out.

After we won our quarter final game, we came home and went to school and practiced for a few days. Then back to Bemidji for semifinals. The pressure was on as we skated onto the ice at that semifinal game. It was another packed house, standing room only again, with the bands, cheerleaders, and news crews. Every team had its own radio station that carried its games. The semifinal game was against the Bemidji Lumberjacks. They were a tough team. We had beaten them twice during the year, but they were both close games. We were in their house and in their home arena. They were a formidable team, and we had to pay attention.

As predicted, it was a close game, but we prevailed and were happy to get that one in the books. The media held up our departure from the game. It was amazing to see that much media at these games. We stopped, got our meals and bused it 2 1/2 hours back to Warroad. We got home around 1 a.m. We had school the next day. It was a fun bus trip home, knowing we were in the finals. Roseau had won its semifinal game too and they were in the finals, as was predicted. The Rams were Region Eight champions and had that experience under their belts. They were always a tough team to play against. Roseau was well coached, and they had a functional game plan and strategy. They played good position and moved the puck well.

In the past, Roseau always came up with the timely goal or a bounce of the puck to win by slimmest of margins. We had to change that. We split our series during the regular season. They beat us down in Roseau in our last meeting, and we felt the uncertainty of that loss. We knew what we needed to do in order to win. It was going to be the toughest game of the year. We knew they would be ready for us. They had the tradition, the playoff experience, and knew how to win. We had been in several regional finals but hadn't won since 1963. We were reminded of that on several occasions over the year. The pressure was on.

It was a couple of days before we played. We practiced as we always had and worked on little things that might make a difference in that final game. The butterflies were always there day in and day out, and we could not let our emotions get away from us. We had to try to stay grounded, normal and focused. Whenever we were out and about town or at the school, hockey was what everyone wanted to talk about. The big game against Roseau was on, and the finals of Region Eight were at stake. Bets were on in both Warroad and Roseau. It was the same in Roseau as it was in Warroad. There were Roseau people working at Marvin Windows in Warroad and Warroad people working at Polaris in Roseau, and the badgering was intense.

The day of the big game was finally here. We packed up and bussed back to Bemidji that afternoon, another 2½-hour ride. The team was ready. It was a quiet ride, and a million thoughts going through your head. It was hard to think of just one thing, but the thought of the game would always come back to you and you would get the butterflies. The players were intense, and wanted to win more than anything. Our pride was on the line, and everyone in Warroad was counting on us. The pressure was all part of the game, and pride for your community was at stake.

Fans were there early as we unloaded the bus with our bags in hand and made our way into the building. It felt good to get out of the bus and to walk around. Our nervousness was evident. It was hard to carry on any kind of conversation. We had been cooped up for over 2½ hours, sitting there thinking about the game and how important it was. It was all we thought about that season, and for me, since I was in eighth grade. This was my dream, my destiny. We were about to make our dreams come true. No one ever thought about losing. No one wanted that to enter our minds or thoughts. We had to win.

The building was full with standing room only and extremely loud with both bands playing their hearts out. As the game started, both teams were hesitant and did not want to make any mistakes. But as the game went on, it was back and forth and back and forth. We had scoring chances, and they had scoring chances. Both goalies made great saves while the crowd was going wild. It was a great game to watch, and the fans were into it. Both schools had their cheerleaders and their pep bands. The game was tied most of the night. Defense was the name of the game that night. In the end, Roseau managed to score late in the game, and defeated us by the score of 2–1. We were devastated. We were so close, but Roseau managed to do it again. They found a way to win by the slimmest of margins. We came close with many scoring chances but could not get that tying goal.

BOB STOREY, HENRY AND ALAN HANGSLEBEN. COURTESY OF KENNY KVARNLOV.

Figure 42

173

Luckily, we had a second chance, and we knew it before the Roseau game. We had a chance to go in through the back door. Region Three would be available to us as runner-ups to play off against the runner-ups in Region Seven. It was the same as in 1965–66 when I was a freshman and we lost to Coleraine in overtime. It was a one-game playoff that was to be played in Hibbing. The game was in a couple of days. We were emotionally and physically tired. It seemed as if we had been on the road playing in big games for a couple of weeks now. We had played late games and had to drive home and then go to school the next day. We rode the school bus back and forth 2½ hours one way. This playoff game was 3½ to 4 hours away. We absolutely needed to win this game. Our hopes were high. We had to get to the state tournament.

CHAPTER 27: REGION THREE TITLE

Needless to say it was a devastating loss to Roseau, and it was a terrible 2 1/2 hour ride home to Warroad. We all replayed the game in our minds, the game of near misses and the nightmare of losing. All the things that could have, would have, may have, and should have gone through our minds during that awful ride home, we thought about. We still had a chance after all of that. We had another game. We found out that we were to play Eveleth in Hibbing in two days. What a week of ups and downs. All the bus rides, and now Hibbing was four hours away. We needed to get re-energized and reorganized for another blockbuster of a game. We were up for it. We had another chance. We were not going to let our community of Warroad down again. It felt like we had died and were revived, and we were alive with another chance. We lived through the torment of losing. We had another shot at the title and would be ready for the day of competition. After our ride to Warroad, after our loss to Roseau, and without much sleep and rest, we had school the next day and then practiced. We were young and could bounce back quickly, and it did not take us long to re-energize. We somehow knew our destiny was about to prevail and we had to rise to the occasion. We were down but not out.

The game against Eveleth was scheduled for a 7:30 p.m. start. The fans of Warroad were making preparations to go down and support us at the game. Tickets were being sold at the school. Spectator buses were going and kids were signing up right and left. The band was coming. The whole town was in a frenzy. Excitement was in the air. It was like nothing that I ever saw before. Fans from everywhere were contacting the school wishing us success. The media called and wanted our complete schedule, with arrival times; where we were going to eat, hotels (we were going home after the game) and our every plan. It was a bonanza of excitement. For us, the pressure was building.

After a couple days at home and some much needed rest, we left the day of the game. We left early enough to stop for a pregame meal and to arrive with enough time to stretch and get our bodies going from the long bus ride. Riding in a school bus was bumpy and uncomfortable, and the heat was either too cold or too hot. Our bus driver Andy Streiff was great and was a character. He would tell story and after story and would always have "the peddle to the metal." He watched out for us and treated us well. We had our bags on the bus when we traveled, so there were a lot of bags piled up in the back. Players used to ride on top of them and try making a bed. There was always a skate or something sticking in your back. We all had our special seats and sat in the same place. Rodney Estling, the other captain, and I were always sitting in the same spot and had a seat to ourselves, and our younger players were respectful of our needs. We had a good group of kids and not one time during the year did we have any major problems. Oh, we had our times of badgering and teasing and had our share of pranks and jokes. Some players got a little mad at times, but it was all in good fun and they knew it.

We arrived at the arena two hours before the game. The arena was half full already. People were there from all over the state, and it would be standing room only. It would be a classic game of two communities with great hockey tradition. The game was broadcast on three different radio stations. TV stations from the Minneapolis area, sports shows, and a host of magazine and newspaper people were there.

We carried our bags into our locker room, got our places and waited in there. We were excited to have another chance and hoped to make the best of it. We needed time alone to mentally get ready. It was quiet. Most of us were within our own thoughts, trying to deal with the nervousness and excitement. The coaches were good about keeping everyone away from us, the last thing we needed was distractions. There were only nine teams left in the playoffs, and after tonight there would be only eight. Most high school teams at that level were very good and could beat each other on any given night. We played Eveleth a few years back when they beat us 2-1, but we had outshot and outplayed them. We just didn't score that game, the famous bounce of the puck. It was one of those games where the puck did not go in and we lost. We were told prior to going into that game that they had a very good first line. They would play two lines most of the game and use that first line on power plays and penalty killing. They were fast and you had to watch out and try to keep them wide and take away the middle of the ice with them. Doug Palazarri was the one to watch on that team. He was small but very fast. He was a good play maker and had a good shot.

Eveleth was close to Hibbing and had a great hockey history of winning the state tournament and excellent playoff experience. They had enthusiastic, knowledgeable fans, and this rink would be considered their home rink. They were familiar with the boards, the corners, and the bounces on this sheet of ice. It was their region and they played there through their youth. It was the first time that Warroad has played in this rink since I joined the high school team as an eighth-grader. The rink had wire around the board and not glass. Most rinks did at the time. Glass was expensive and would not be installed in most rinks until later. It had an Olympic sheet of ice, which meant that it was fifteen feet wider than the regular ice sheet we played on. It gave the forwards more room in the offensive zone, making it hard for the opposing team to contain them, an advantage for the forwards. The defensemen had to play their position and not chase them around and get out of position. The goalie had different angles with the larger ice surface that they needed to consider.

Both teams were in the same predicament, having lost their finals, and they wanted to go through the back door to the state tournament. It was a dream of all youngsters to play in the state tournament, for the glory of it all. Who would have the luck this time? We knew it would be a close game. Who would make the big play? Would it come down to special teams or a hot goalie? Who was going to be the hero? The tension was high.

As always, we said our prayers in the locker room before we went on to the ice. We had faith in ourselves, our team. We had the desire to win. We had traveled so far with many ups and downs, and it was our time. With the adrenalin flowing once again, we stepped onto the ice with the fans, cheerleaders and band going wild. It was a full house, and the building was booming. You could hardly hear yourself think. As we got into our rhythm of the warm-ups and into what we came here to do, the noise and crowd went away and we could concentrate on what you were supposed to do.

At the start of the game, when the puck dropped, both teams played their hearts out. The game was intense from the start. Both teams were getting scoring chances, and the game was end-to-end action. The fans were in it from the start, and it was loud in the building. Up and down we went, both teams getting chances and both goalies making excellent saves. It was tied after the first period with both teams battling each other at every turn. There was not much the coach could say. No pep talk was going to help. We were in a fast, furious and exciting game. The coach talked about situations on the ice that we needed to correct, minor things defensively and some offensive things that might work if we had the chance. Period two was the same as period one, with both teams scoring. At the end of two periods, it was tied at two goals apiece. The crowd was loud; parents were pacing when they could and wanted us to win so badly. We could hear the crowd in the locker rooms between the periods. They got what they expected, and more. It was wild in there.

The third period was like the first two, up and down, both teams battling and getting their scoring chances, and the goalies standing tall in the nets. At one point during that period, I was handling the puck and made a turnout or an escape toward the boards to get away from an opponent. As I made my quick turn, the Eveleth player swung his stick with one arm in an attempt to do something. I had beaten him and was going the other way. My head was down as I made my turn up the ice to start my rush, and his stick blade caught me on the bone above my right eye and sliced me open like a knife cutting butter and blood spurted everywhere. I threw my gloves off and covered my eye as the whistle blew and play stopped. I was on my knees trying to stop the blood with my hand. The next thing I knew a trainer and the coaches were looking at my eye and trying to stop the bleeding. They pressed a towel over it. They escorted me to the bench and determined that I needed stitches.

They took me below to the first aid room as play resumed. Mike Marvin was put out there in my place and did a good job playing the position. Coach Roberts tried to buy time until I could get back on the ice. He tried stalling, and the other coaches and everyone in the building knew what he was up to. Finally the referees had enough and told the coach that was it—let's go or they would call a delay of game penalty. The game continued. Meanwhile, I was in the first aid room. The doctor cleaned and butterflied my cut back together and taped it. He said, "It will hold well for the rest of the game." Good enough for me. I was chomping at the bit to get back out there.

Mike Marvin, one of our defensemen was skating backward and had fallen down during a 2-on-1 break, giving Eveleth a 2 on 0 going in on our goalie Jeff Hallett. This could have been the game for them, but one of the Eveleth players misplayed the puck, and sent an errant pass that went into the corner. This allowed Warroad to get it back and recover. I am sure nerves and the roar of the crowd and

BACK IN THE GAME AT HIBBING. COURTESY OF KENNY KVARNLOV.

Figure 43

the intense situation had something to do with it. Call it a bad case of nerves in a big game, or call it a choke.

When I was out of the game, it had marked the first time that I was off the ice during the entire season. I ran from the first aide room and up the stairs and I jumped right back into the play. My eye was butterflied, and had white tape over the injury. There were blood stains on my jersey. The game and the third period ended scoreless, and we were going into overtime tied at two apiece.

During the intermission, I iced down my eye, which was bruised and slowly swelling shut. The ice helped. During overtime, as in the first three periods, it was as intense as you can imagine. The crowd was going crazy. The band was playing. The cheerleaders and fans were cheering. It was an amazing game. With all that was on the line, neither team wanted to give up. Both teams had scoring chances again, and they played hard but played smart. Both goalies were strong and were not taking any chances. We ended the overtime tied at two once again.

With both teams back in the locker rooms for another break, it was intense. I iced my eye once again to try to keep the swelling down and to be able to see. We went over our strategies and talked about the first line of theirs. Then all of a sudden, it was time to go back on the ice. As we walked up the pathway to the ice, the building was going crazy, bands playing, the cheerleaders cheering, and the whole building felt like it was about to burst.

The fans were more than ready, and everyone was keyed for the second overtime. Both teams once again were playing back and forth, and the goalies were playing well. There were some near misses, but the teams were always on the defensive. Neither wanted to give up that final goal and end it. Both teams were skating their best players as much as possible. Both teams were skating two lines but mostly their first line after a short break. There were no penalties called. The refs were letting things go and leaving the outcome of the game to the players. The teams had battled for almost three hours, and it looked as if we were going into our third overtime.

I was standing inside their blue line when the puck was knocked into the right corner of the rink. Frank Krahn, our first line winger was behind the net and he raced to it first. He passed the puck out to me standing just above the circle on the right defense position. The clock was down to just a few seconds. It was as though I was suspended in time and everything moved in slow motion. The puck had just hit the tape on my stick when I heard Frank yell to shoot it, and without hesitation I did. I let a good shot go at the net. I just wanted to get it on net, because you never know if it will go in or not. Sometimes you surprise a goalie with a quick shot. As I stood there, I watched in disbelief as it went in. The red light came on, and I looked at the clock. There was no time left on it, but the red light was on. It was a goal! The building erupted.

If the green light had come on, the goal would not have counted. It was that close. If the goal judge would have been a split second slower, the goal would not have counted and we would have been in our third overtime. The goal counted, and the building erupted, and so did the bench and the players on the ice. I was being mobbed, and we were hugging and laughing. The coaches and the other players came running out on the ice to celebrate the victory. The fans were going crazy. We were going to the state tournament!

Immediately after the game in the locker room, it was a frenzy. The media and players were yelling and screaming. I was icing down my eye, which had swollen shut by then. I remember feeling as if I had just jumped out of an airplane and skydived down to earth. The pressure was off, five years of waiting and a year of great expectations. We had done what we had set out to do. We had made our town proud. We accomplished things only a few of our teams were able to do. Wow, what a moment. We had been on the road for two weeks playing in big games, traveling on school buses, eating restaurant meals, and getting home late and having to get up and go to school in the mornings. Boy, what a journey we had been on—physically, mentally, emotionally, and now definitely spiritually. We were destined for glory. It had to be.

PROUD PARENTS: ALICE WITH WINNING GAME PUCK, GEORGE IN THE BACKGROUND.
COURTESY OF KENNY KVARNLOV.

REGION THREE CHAMPIONSHIP TROPHY. HENRY HOLDING PUCK.
COURTESY OF KENNY KVARNLOV.

Figure 44

183

I was taken into the first aid room after the frenzy in the locker room had calmed down. I thanked the doctor for getting me back in the game. He gave me twelve stitches above the eye, a real souvenir of the game. After all the interviews, celebrations, attention and getting the stitches in my eyebrow, some of the boys were so excited that they carried me into the lobby area in recognition of the accomplishment. We were so proud to finally win and to show our fans how much they meant to us and how much we appreciated the support. We were all one happy family within a happy community.

It was great news when our coach told us that we were staying overnight in Hibbing and would not have to travel back to Warroad that night. It would have been a four-hour bus ride home. It was already late, and we would not have arrived home until 3 a.m., so our superintendent approved an overnight stay and travel home the next day.

I roomed with Rodney Estling, our co-captain. After getting something to eat and celebrating some more, we went to our rooms. It was late and we lay on our beds talking about going to the state tournament. We didn't know what to expect or all of the things that we were going to experience. I remember saying, "Okay, now let's get some sleep." Then after laying there in the dark for a while, one of us would say, "I cannot believe we are going to the state tournament!" We'd jump up and laugh and start talking about it again. Then we would try to sleep again.

When we arrived in Warroad the next day the whole town was there to greet us. The win was a long time coming and we stood there like celebrities with the cheers and honors coming from all the Warroad community.

CHAPTER 28: THE STATE TOURNAMENT

Warroad was in an absolute frenzy prior to our departure for the tournament. We had news crews coming in doing newspapers, radio and TV reports and interviews. We went to school, practiced, and made our preparations for a week long stay in St. Paul. One thing for sure the town would be empty and look like a ghost town once we left for the tournament. Everyone wanted to go.

We left Warroad for Saint Paul a little after 8:00 a.m. filled with excitement. After a week and a half of torment, the highs and lows of winning and losing, and then finally winning to advance to the state tournament, we were emotionally drained. The stress, the pressure, and the travel had taken a toll on all of us. We had a few days at home to rest, recuperate, and prepare for the trip.

Finally our dreams were coming true. Warroad was going to the state tournament for the first time since 1963. We were on our way, and enjoyed the all day trip on the bus. It was a happy time. Andy our bus driver contributed to keeping our morale high. He said," Hell, I knew you guys were going to win". We teased him about fighting with a bear. It's true; he shot a bear beside the road south of Warroad one time. He got out of his pickup and went to check on it. He thought the bear was dead, but to his surprise the bear jumped up and attack him. He wrestled with the bear for a while and the bear died but not before Andy suffered a few bites, claw marks, and lacerations. Andy and his friend Alfred Hangsleben were notorious for poaching deer and never getting caught.

After a few days of rest at home, our goals were set again to win it all. It was good to be on the road again. We felt we had the tools, the players, and after what we just went through; we had the experience. Could we win three games in three days? That was the big question. When in your teens, you looked for that consistency that does not come easily as you play three games in three days. Could we do it for this tournament? Did we have the stamina to take it all? Everyone who was at the tournament was in the same boat. Play three good games, and with a little luck you could win it. Was it all there for us? Could we pull it off? Could we prevail in the toughest high school tournament in the country?

The trip was over nine hours with a stop for lunch and a personal break or two. We did not have radios, CDs, or anything of the sort. We just sat there and visited, looked out the window, read, or maybe slept. Although a long and tedious bus ride, we were in good spirits, after all we were in the tournament. We were even more excited when we got to the outskirts of the city.

We arrived at the Saint Paul Hotel in the late afternoon. I roomed again with Rodney Estling, the co-captain and my friend and classmate. We had nothing scheduled that night but a team dinner. In the morning we would have a mid morning skate at the Metropolitan Sports Center in Bloomington. The Minnesota State High School Banquet was scheduled in the evening. It was a banquet that allowed the media to conduct interviews, let the coaches talk about their season, and gave an opportunity for the coaches to introduce the players and the team reps.

The tournament would start the following day with four games on the schedule as the quarterfinals were starting. There were two games in the afternoon and two games in the evening session. The winners advanced and the losers played off in the consolation bracket. All games that year would be played at the Metropolitan Sports Center, home of the NHL's Minnesota North Stars. It held fifteen thousand-plus fans, and it would be filled to standing room only each and every game of the high school tournament.

After being cooped up all day on the bus, I felt restless and nervous. Rodney and I decided to go out for a walk. It was fairly late. It was dark, but all the streetlights were on, so it looked like daylight. We never walked around a big city before, and never saw so many lights. We walked down the street looking at all the tall buildings and the traffic, passing by some closed stores, restaurants and lounges that were still open. Not much was happening in downtown Saint Paul that night. I do not know what we expected. We walked around awhile and then headed back toward the hotel. I was restless most of the night but managed to get some sleep. Staying in a hotel, with the noise of the city was foreign to us.

After our breakfast, we boarded the school bus and drove to the arena. It was interesting for us to ride the bus in the city. There was so much to see. Nobody said much, we just looked at the activity, and then on the freeway watched all the cars go by. We drove by the airport and the big planes were coming and going. We took it all in. We arrived at the arena for our skate at the Metropolitan Sports Center. It was a beautiful building, huge compared with anything that we had ever seen before. After walking inside with our equipment, I immediately notice how the sounds were so different. There was a team on the ice already and you could hear the pucks hitting the glass and the sounds of the sticks and the players on the ice. We walked down this huge corridor and an attendant showed us our dressing room. The dressing rooms were very nice and enormous compared with what we were used to. We were anxious to get dressed and on the ice. We waited for the Zamboni to finish. We were standing in the box, and they came and told us that we could go on. As we skated around the rink, we looked up at the seats, which seemed to go on forever. The seats were a mix of white, yellow, and green, and at the top there was a restaurant with black tinted glass windows. The press box was up on the north side. Across the other side and at the top was the TV area with rows of seats going to the top of the building. It was amazing. I felt as if I was standing in a hole. The glass around the rink was clear, and you could see right into the seats at eye level. Most rinks that we played in had wire safety nets. People would really have a great view sitting anywhere. The ice was smooth and easy to skate and glide on. It was warm in the building. I could tell when all the fans were in the building, the heat was going to be a problem. We were used to skating on natural ice, with the building cold and fresh, making it easy to breathe. Playing in a warm building would be hard. You seemed to run out of energy earlier and we would be gasping for air much more often.

Not only that, the ice snowed up differently. The puck would stick to the ice in a warmer building and could create problems when carrying it or passing it out of the zone. The lighting in the building was great; there were no dark spots at all. The sounds and the cheers would be different in that building, being so big. It was too large to sound anything like Hibbing or any other smaller buildings. I could not fathom filling that many seats.

The Coleraine team was at the end of the building at ice level when we started doing our final skate, and they would come on the ice after us. It always made me nervous to have someone watch me skate, but more so when it was one of the teams participating in the state tournament. They made the tournament by winning Region Seven. They had beaten Eveleth in the finals, sending Eveleth as runner-up into that game with us in Hibbing. The Greenway of Coleraine was the defending state champions.

After practice we packed our bags, carried and loaded them on the school bus, and headed back to the hotel to relax a little before the big banquet that night. We had lunch and went to our rooms to rest and relax. It was good to have a TV that was so clear, so we watched TV and tried to rest. It was the day before the start of the state tournament and we were getting nervous already and we were excited to play. It was good to see the atmosphere of the building where we were going to play. It gave us some idea of what to expect.

Our opponent in the first game of the tournament was Minneapolis Southwest, and we really didn't know much about them, other than they were well coached and had a good season. They were in the state tournament for a reason. We needed to win that game to remain in the winner's bracket and to get a shot at the championship.

At the banquet later that night, we had our "Sunday best" on. I had only one sport jacket, and I wore that as usual. Most kids that age had a sports jacket or nice sweater they would wear with a pair of dress pants and shirt and a tie.

We were nervous as we walked into the banquet, and we all stayed very close to each other as we marched in as a team. We never saw anything like this. It was all new to us. I had been at banquets before, but nothing quite this big. Everyone stared as we entered. We single-filed to our table and took our seats as everyone seemed to watch every move we made. It made us extremely nervous.

As we settled in, we saw the Roseau team, and they seemed genuinely happy for us. It was unique to have two representatives from the same region, although technically we were representing Region Three. It was a long drawn out banquet with all of the speeches and introductions of the teams and players. After the banquet ended, it was the media's turn with the players and coaches. There were several pictures taken and some interviews. By the time we returned to the hotel and our rooms, it was late, and we were tired and looking forward to a good night's rest.

We did not know much about this Southwest team—just that they had to be good to be there. We needed to play our game and try not to worry about what they would do. We felt as long as we played our game that we should come out on top. Our game wasn't until 7 p.m. so we spent time watching the other games on TV. We had lunch in the afternoon and went for a walk and then rested until game time. We left for the arena around 4:30 p.m. and expected to arrive around 5 p.m. That would give us a couple of hours to dress and get things

HENRY AT THE STATE TOURNAMENT. COURTESY OF THE MINNEAPOLIS STAR TRIBUNE.

Figure 45

ready. We would go on the ice for warm-ups at 6:30 p.m. They would flood the ice and we would come out for the game at 7 p.m. As we skated around in the warm-ups, the building filled. People mingled around the seating area and watched from the catwalk.

Our team was skating one way around in a circle, and then Southwest team was skating in the opposite direction. I collided with Southwest's spare goalie, Dennis Fermoyle, and we both fell down. We both were looking up into the stands and not paying attention.

Years later, Dennis came to Warroad as a teacher and a hockey coach. We reminisced about that when we met in Warroad some years later. I knew that I ran into someone but did not remember who it was. Dennis said, "You probably do not remember running into someone at the state tournament in 1969, do you?" I said, "Yes, I do". He said," Well, it was me." I was the spare goalie for Southwest." We both laughed and he said, "After we collided and got up, embarrassed, I apologized to him, and he said he was sorry too" and we started laughing.

Southwest's goalie was Brad Shelstad, a top-notch all-state goalie who won more than a few games for them during their season. We were determined not to let it happen to us. We had been battling good teams for the past month and put on a lot of miles. We came out on top in all but one of those games and we were ready for another battle against Minneapolis Southwest.

As predicted, the teams were close in talent. Both teams had flurries at both ends of the ice and had some good scoring chances. Both teams seemed to start slow but gained momentum as the game went along. We controlled the game heavily at times. We had our scoring chances and got enough past the all-state goalie Shelstad to move into the semifinals. Warroad was more dominant in this game, and we prevailed 4–3. Although the game looked close on paper, we felt that we had it at hand most of the night. It was good to get that first win and build our confidence for the next game. Throughout that game, I felt sluggish and I seemed to get tired easily. It was from the heat of the building, and the ice seemed slow. We were all happy to win and move on.

After the game as we sat in the locker room, I was called down to the ice for an interview for TV. I finished, and they said, "Go get that Kvarnlov kid and bring him down next". He had already taken his skates off and came running down the stairs for the interview.

We were standing in the players' box. They asked him to stand on the ice and they interviewed over the boards. He stood on the ice during the interview. When his interview was over, his sweaty sox were frozen to the ice.

Later that evening we found out that Roseau had won their game and we were to play them in the semifinals the next day. This would be the fourth time we played Roseau that year. They held the advantage with two wins and one loss. We felt relieved to win that first game. We knew what Roseau had as far as a team, and we felt confident that we could win. The stress seemed to subside, and the reality of the moment was that we had a great chance to advance to the finals if we could get by Roseau. For some reason, I felt no pressure going into that game. It was not like any other game we played that year. I was confidant and felt that we had the advantage. We just needed to play our game.

I was loose when we hit the ice for warm-ups. The building was packed with over fifteen thousand people, and the air was filled with excitement. The bands were playing, the cheerleaders were there, and the fans were loud. I felt I had the energy that I did not have against Southwest. I felt good and I wanted to play.

Roseau was tough and determined too. It didn't take long for them to create a good scoring chance. Our goalie, Jeff Hallett, made a glove save right off the bat, as one of the Roseau players got loose in front of the net, and Jeff had to reach down and grab a shot that was right on the corner. The save maybe changed the momentum of the game. We turned it up after that and seemed to control the game the rest of the way. The Roseau goalie, Mike Kvarnlov was brilliant and lucky, making save after save while we were on the attack. Mike was a first cousin to our first-line center Lyle Kvarnlov. The game was end-to-end action and entertaining. The final score was 3–2 for Warroad! We were on our way to the finals. The final win of the season over Roseau was sweet, and we got it when it counted the most.

At some point during the tournament a TV station interviewed our first line of Lyle Kvarnlov, Frank Krahn, and Leo Marshall. Dick Roberts, our coach, brought them to the studio for the interview. As they walked into the building, he was coaching them on how to act and what to say. He told them not be shy and to answer the questions with confidence and to be talkative. As the interviewer asked questions, Dick stood behind the camera waving his arm, trying to stimulate them to talk more. It was quite a distraction to the boys, who mostly said "yes" and "no" to the questions.

CHAPTER 29: CHAMPIONSHIP GAME

We played the early semifinal game Friday night against Roseau and won, but had to wait hours until the last semi final game to find out who we played in the championship on Saturday night. We were oblivious, a little shocked, and it somehow felt like the twilight zone or a dream. We could not believe we were in the finals of the Minnesota State High School Tournament. We stayed to watch the first half of the other semi final game, and when we left the game, Edina looked terrific and was dominating and leading the other team by a few goals. They were good and we knew it was going to be Edina unless they totally collapsed in the last half of the game.

Our coach wanted us back at the hotel early to rest, and we were trying to settle down after the big win. The excitement was overwhelming. It proved to be hard for us to rest and relax. Championship Saturday would be a long day. We would need to wait all day and try to stay calm for a 7:30 p.m. game.

When we awoke on Saturday morning, I thought I had slept okay but I was tired and a little foggy. I was emotionally restless and excited. My thoughts were about the long wait for the championship game. The coaching staff woke us up fairly early. They did not want us to sleep in, although we sure could have used it. We were tired but they wanted us to get up and moving around. We had a team breakfast in midmorning. It seemed my body was craving food and protein. We were young and could eat like a horse at times. The coaches talked about the game but not to the degree of getting us wound up more than we already were. We joked and talked about the others teams, players and games. We read the papers and were talking about some of the articles. It was interesting reading the media reports on the tournament. There were consolation bracket games being played. I think some of the games were on TV. The morning papers were full of the facts and figures about the upcoming championship game. They cited us as "David" and Edina as "Goliath." Warroad was a poor, blue collar community and small school of less than 200 students. Edina was a wealthy suburb of Minneapolis with over two thousand students. Edina was known for winning a lot of titles in a lot of different sports around the Twin Cities area. Statewide, people did not favor them because of it.

As it turned out, everyone who was not from Edina was on our side, and we had fans galore. The coaching staff and school kept us away from the media on game day. They wanted to us rest and focus on the task at hand—playing and winning the championship. We had no idea of the magnitude of fans and support we had until we arrived at the arena for the game. There were Warroad signs everywhere, and people were lined up at the player entrance to see us. We loved it and assumed someone had organized a pep rally out there to show support. There were a lot of people from the Warroad area living in the cities and they supported us at the game. We enjoyed the fans outside as we carried our bags into the arena and found our locker room. We slowly unpacked our bags, mingled around and got ready. My thoughts reflected back to my high school career, and how it had taken me five years to get here. I was savoring the moment. I was also thinking how I actually felt physically. I wasn't feeling that great but was not hurting. I was just plain tired. Playing three games in three days was tough. I felt physically and mentally drained. Seeing the fans and knowing how much it meant to everyone, the adrenaline and my emotions were taking over. This was the last high school game for Rodney and I. For me, it was a long road, with a lot of ups and downs throughout the seasons. I played high school hockey since eighth grade. There were times when I thought I would never have this opportunity. It wasn't easy, but this year we put ourselves in the position to win the state title, and it was simply amazing. Here we are, sitting in the locker room at the Metropolitan Sports Center before the championship game. My emotions ran high and it brought a tear to my eye. As we sat there, we could hear our band playing, and we could hear the noise and cheers of the fans. Could this be for us? It seemed too early for the fans to be there with such force. The coaches came in and told us that the fans were here early and were excited, cheering and waiting for the game. They said 90 percent of the fans out there were cheering for Warroad. If that didn't get you going nothing would. The whole situation made us all the more nervous.

As we hit the ice, the announcer shouted, "And here are your Warroad Warriors!" The building erupted, and the cheers were deafening. As we skated around the ice, the cheers continued, the band played, and the cheerleaders were cheering.

Then the announcer shouted out, "And here are your Edina Hornets!" The boos were deafening. It was unbelievable. They were being booed by the crowd, and we hadn't even started the game yet. Their cheerleaders and the school band were blocked out by the boos from the crowd. As the teams skated around during the warm-ups, the opposing players were checking each other out. I actually felt sorry for the Edina team as the crowd booed them. As I looked down the ice, it did not seem to bother them, they just went about their business, but I am sure it had to take some kind of toll on them.

We went back into the locker rooms while they cleaned the ice. Our coaches didn't say much. They didn't need to. It was our last and final game of the season. We were in the finals! We had just witnessed the emotions of the people, our people, our fans and supporters. We were running high on emotions and adrenalin.

When we came back on the ice to start the game the cheers were just as strong if not stronger. The boos were just as bad as during the warm ups for Edina. We were the away team that game and we wore our dark jerseys and were announced first. They called us out one at a time and they saved me for last. It was quiet an honor. They gave the team a standing ovation for about 5 minutes. The Edina team just stood there and looked. When they were announced, the crowd booed again and it was that way through the announcements. I can't imagine how they felt.

As the game started, we were back on our heels as Edina scored immediately with a good shot that handcuffed our goalie, Jeff Hallett. We had trailed before, and there was a lot of time left in the game. We went on the attack and scored to tie it up. Then it was back and forth, with good scoring chances by both teams. Edina was deep with four good lines, but played three, while Warroad had three lines but played two most of the time throughout the playoffs. Three games in three days and the emotional games leading up to the tournament were taking its toll They were fueling us as we skated hard and heard the crowd of thousands cheering for Warroad every time we touched the puck. Warroad scored again and the building erupted into a frenzy. The fans were going wild. The first period ended with Warroad up by one goal. We went into the locker room with the lead.

It seemed warm out there with fifteen thousand-plus fans and standing room only in the building. It was something we had to fight through and overcome. We needed to stay hydrated. With the travel and the big games of the last month, we needed to pull through this one. Amazingly we were down to two more periods of solid hockey and we could win the state tournament. It would be a first for Warroad. The first state title that Warroad won was the

1964 State Bantam Championships at Wakota Arena in South Saint Paul. Winning this tournament would be monumental for Warroad and the community.

Edina scored to tie the game early in the second period. Warroad was skating shorthanded with a penalty and a man in the box. Edina scored again to take the lead. We again took the attack to Edina. I stick handled out of our zone to find myself in a one-on-one situation with an Edina defenseman Jim Knutson. As I came down the right side of the ice, he was playing his position well. I was tired, so I shot the puck from just inside the blue line to try to use him as a screen. The Edina goalie saw it all the way and deflected the puck into the right corner. I went in to retrieve the puck and see if I could set up a play. As I got to the puck, I was trying to avoid the check, control the puck and look for someone to pass it to. The Edina defenseman, Jim Knutson, came in full stride with his elbows up over his shoulders, and one of his elbows caught me in the ear. He slammed my head into the glass, rupturing my eardrum. I fell to the ice. I was dazed but not fully knocked out. The trainers and coaches came running onto the ice as I lay there motionless on my belly, holding my head.

The coach and trainer talked to me while I was lying on the ice. They kept talking to me to see what was wrong. When I finally stood up and started to skate to the players' box, I felt as if the ice was tilted and I knew something was wrong. I told them so. I was taken to the first aid room near our locker room and examined. As the doctor looked at my left ear, he discovered that my eardrum was ruptured. He suggested that I be taken to the hospital. I thought–I can't miss this game. I always came back, I have never missed a game in my life. I thought–I can't quit. It's the state tournament! But deep down, I knew. I remembered the feeling I had when I stood up. I was dizzy. I had no chance of competing in that condition. The game resumed as soon as I was off the ice, and I could hear the crowd in the distance.

KNUTSON HIT DURING THE CHAMPIONSHIP GAME.

Figure 46

Once the extent of my injury was determined, they made the announcement for my parents to come to the first aid room. Then they called the ambulance for me. As I waited I could hear the game going on with the cheers and boos. There were more cheers than boos, so I knew Warroad was on doing well. As my parents and I left the building in the ambulance, I felt the disappointment, and I felt

I had let my teammates down. It was my first time away from the team. Whatever the outcome, I wanted to be there.

It was a long ride to the hospital across town to Saint Paul. They brought me into the ER and examined me. They cut my uniform off and it was left in a pile on the floor. (I somehow ended up with my cut up jersey, which I still have in a foot locker in storage. I plan to have it repaired and put it on display along with my other items). Then I was processed into the hospital.

My mother came in the room and told me that Warroad lost in overtime. I thought the team was outstanding. They came back and played skillfully, and we were able to push Edina to the brink. A job well done and I was proud of them. I wish I could have stayed in the game. It was not meant to be. There I was in the hospital, and I blamed myself for being in that predicament and being injured. I do not know how many times I played hurt with stitches, bumps, and bruises, but this injury was definitely different.

The next day I heard that when Bernie Burgraff was announcing our championship game for KRWB back to northern Minnesota, he said that I had died. He said he got so excited that when someone passed him a note he read it wrong and had indeed announced my death over the radio. There were people in Warroad listening to the game that night and they shut off the radio after that announcement. They went to bed thinking I had died. They did not hear the correct news until the next day. Bernie never lived it down, and we laugh about it today. Bernie has always been a good friend. Bernie 83, still has a sports radio program in the Fargo/Moorhead area.

On Sunday, the doctor came in and examined my ear. He saw the small hole in the eardrum and after some discussion with his colleagues, they decided they were going to attempt to patch the hole with a thin paper like material. The doctor explained that it would help with avoiding infection and it would enhance the healing process. I spent four days in the hospital.

My parents were there. My dad stayed with brother Dave and family, and my mother stayed with me at the hospital the whole time. I had two brothers and their families living in the Minneapolis area: David and Donna, and Jim and Laurie. The family and other relatives came to visit. There were visits from people from Warroad, Roseau and some media people.

Monday, I was going into surgery at 6 a.m. I was not looking forward to it at all. I had never been in surgery. It was a little scary. The doctor told me they were not going to put me totally under. I was lying on my side, with my injured ear up. I could hear the doctor and nurses talking quietly. Then the doctor turned around and came over holding a long needle. I was more than worried then. He said, "This might hurt a little, but please try to lay still". I could not believe he was going to stick that in my ear. I remember how much the dentist hurt when sticking a needle in my mouth, but in my ear? He poked me, and I had tears running down my face. The pain was so bad that I was about to scream. He poked me several times, and after a while the pain finally went away. He worked on my ear for an hour and put the patch on my eardrum. They brought me back to my room to recover. I was fine for a while until the numbness wore off. Then the pain set in. The whole side of my head and inside my ear was throbbing. I was in severe pain and lay there moaning and groaning. I felt sorry for my mother who watched the whole ordeal. My mother tried to comfort me but she did not know what to do. She had that look on her face of concern, worry and the frustration of not being able to comfort me. They gave me something for the pain every couple of hours, but it wasn't enough. After some time, it was better, and I survived, the pain went away by that night and I rested well. I was ready to go home as it was a long time for a young man to stay in bed.

CHAPTER 30: GOING HOME

I missed the reception the boys received in Warroad on Sunday afternoon after the tournament. I heard that it was exciting and the whole town turned out. The Warroad community was to hold a reception for me after I was released from the hospital. It was a compassionate gesture and much appreciated by my family and I, something I will always remember.

The day I was released, the plan was for Swede Carlson, a Warroad pilot, to fly his Cessna 180 to Minneapolis and bring me home. Dad and the rest of the family went back to Warroad on Sunday. Flying home and not having to make that long 7 hour drive was great. The plane was not going to arrive in St. Paul until around noon. My mother went with brother Dave and his family to lunch and would meet me at the airport later. A University of Minnesota alumni promised he would buy me "the biggest steak there was, when I was released." He took me to a steak house for lunch and he ordered the biggest steak on the menu. It was huge. I could not finish it. My stomach must have shrunk after being in the hospital for a few days. After lunch, he drove me to Midway Airport in downtown Saint Paul. Swede Carlson, the pilot and my mother were already waiting.

LEFT TO RIGHT: DAD- GEORGE BOUCHA, MARTY ROBERTS, MOM- ALICE BOUCHA, AND SISTER SHIRLEY. COURTESY OF KENNY KVARNLOV.

WARROAD WARRIORS AFTER THE '69 STATE TOURNAMENT. KENNY KVARNLOV PHOTO.

Figure 47

It was a 350-mile flight to Warroad, and it took us over three hours. We landed on the Warroad River just before dark. Swede had skis/wheels and we bounced around as we landed. A car was waiting to bring us home. The reception was to be held in a matter of minutes and we had very little time to get to the school. We just had time to change and freshen up. The reception was amazing. There was a short program in the gym, and I was seated on the stage, along with the MC, and coaches. When I saw the microphone and podium, it made me nervous to think that I might have to get up and talk, but they had it figured out. The MC asked me questions and I answered them. It went smoothly and everyone seemed to enjoy it. We move into the cafeteria and had dinner. We got to visit with people and had a nice time. The event was filled with our entire community— the parents, players, band, cheerleaders, students, and even some of the Roseau hockey players and fans from the surrounding area.

Warroad was the darling of the state tournament. The media— the TV stations, newspapers, and magazines—could not get enough of Warroad. Everyone wanted to celebrate our success, even though we lost the title game. It was a glorious time for Warroad Hockey. The 1969 tournament with all of the attention and media put Warroad on the map.

Cards and letters congratulating the team and the community were pouring into Warroad. There were also cards coming in with donations to help pay my hospital expenses. The director of the Minnesota High School Insurance Program stuck his foot in his mouth and had to resign after making a comment about me being a minority, and the MSHSL not being able to cover 100% of my hospital bill. So it seemed, The Minnesota High School League would cover only part of the bill, and I would have to pay the rest. People were outraged and upset, and besides that, he called me a minority. Support from all over the state poured in and many sent donations.

CHAPTER 31: SPRINGTIME & GRADUATION

It was fast and furious in the months of February and March. It was like a blur. We had a lot of drama in a short time. Could things get any better? We were heading into spring and looking back at the events and were in awe of what we accomplished. What a ride. We had baseball and track to look forward to, and of course graduation.

The school and community were still getting a tremendous amount of fan mail from all over the state. It was nice to hear from all those people who cared and were proud of what we accomplished. We were getting calls at the school requesting that I give talks at the surrounding schools. I was totally amazed—and scared. I was not a trained speaker. I was too shy, but Coach Roberts suggested that maybe it would be good for me to do that and that I needed to get used to being in front of people. He said it would help me gain confidence. We worked out a plan and visited the schools. After being introduced, I had a question and answer programs.

While in the Twin Cities for another banquet, I was invited to a sports luncheon. It was the first luncheon I attend with well known people like Billy Martin, then manager of the Twins, several other baseball players, and other celebrities. I sat at the head table with the celebrities. I felt out of place. After listening to the speeches, I was introduced and asked a few questions.

LEFT TO RIGHT: BOB KRAHN, ALAN HANGSLEBEN,
LES BALDWIN, FRANK KRAHN, LEO MARSHALL.
COURTESY OF KENNY KVARNLOV.

HENRY SENIOR YEAR.

1969 WARROAD BASEBALL TEAM. COURTESY OF KENNY KVARNLOV.

1969 GRADUATION WALK WITH MY GOOD FRIEND, TEAMMATE, AND
CLASSMATE PATRICK O'DONNELL (RIP). COURTESY OF ALVERA AND KENNY KVARNLOV.

Figure 48

At that time, the WCCO All-State Hockey Banquet was being held in Minneapolis. I was chosen along with Alan Hangsleben, a sophomore for the All State Team. Coach Roberts drove us down to the Cities. Coach Roberts was a great friend and father figure/mentor for me throughout my youth. He gave me a good talking to more than once when I strayed off the right path. It is something that I will never forget and always appreciate.

That spring, the University of Minnesota (UofM) announced that five of the state's top hockey players had signed a letter of intent to play for the university. I was one of them. Coach Roberts was an alumni from the U of M. He was very happy to see me sign that letter, as was the school and community. I was proud to be going to the U of M too. The U of M alumni made arrangements for me to go to Minneapolis to work and play summer hockey. So, I had plans for the summer. After all of the talk about me going to college for the past few years, it was good to finally sign the letter of intent, and make a decision. I was highly recruited in baseball, football and hockey. I did not do well in school, although I could have. I was not slow, although some people may beg to differ. I did not put in the time or have the support and discipline at home. I loved to play sports and kept my grades just above the eligibility mark so that I could play. Looking back, we did not have the family values that supported educational success or personal goal setting. My parents did not have a formal education so it made it tough for them to help us with our school work. Although they loved us, they thought as long as we went to school, that was enough.

In Warroad that spring, we were throwing baseballs in the gym again. We had great success as juniors in baseball and made it to the regional tournament before losing in the last inning to Bemidji. We were a year older, had most of our team back and thought we could take it all that year. We were excited to get the season under way. We had a great team, and we did not lose a game throughout the high school season. I was the top pitcher but developed a sore arm and elbow while pitching. I did not tell anyone or complain. During a regular game in Thief River Falls, my arm was sore and I should not have thrown at all. It was not a must win game. I pitched anyway. The pain was getting worse and I stayed in too long. My coach and players knew something had happened. The coach should have taken me out but I talked him out of it and said I was okay. My velocity was not there as I was not throwing as hard as usual. After that game, and for the rest of the season, I played first base. Coach Stukel wanted me to save my arm, and let it heal as much as possible before the play-offs. My arm hurt as if I tore or detached something in my elbow. I lost strength in my arm. I was disappointed and mad at myself for doing that. I knew it would take a miracle, and knew that it was not going to be better in a short time. I went to the doctor and he examined it but in those days, after giving me some pain meds, he only told me to rest it.

Tragedy struck our baseball team and class just before graduation. Our good friend and teammate Ted Schnurr was killed in a car accident along with another friend, Gary Thompson. Gary graduated a year or two before us; it was a situation that jolted us right down to our socks. He was our teammate, classmate, and close friend. The funeral was just weeks before our graduation, and we were still playing in the baseball playoffs when it happened. It was a hard time for all of us and a horrible way to end our high school days.

When thinking about Ted Schnurr, I remember him with a few stories and how much fun we had off the field. Ted Schnurr, Richard Kruger, Don Toulouse and I would skip school together, and we always had a blast. We skipped school to go hunting partridge, ducks and geese. Sometimes we went south of Warroad in the massive Beltrami Island State Forest. No one could find us out there. There were roads all over the place. One time, I had a shotgun that didn't fire right. The firing pin was stuck, and it delayed; so if you pulled the trigger, it wouldn't fire right away. When you brought it down to take a look, it would go off. It was dangerous. We gave it to Richard Kruger who was our comedian in the group, so he would shoot it. When he pulled the trigger, we all knew the problem and hit the ditch. We did not tell him about the trigger. So when he brought it down, he said, "Hey what's wrong?" Just then it went off. It scared the heck out of him and it was a good thing he did not point it at anyone or shoot himself. When I think about that now, I shiver at the thought of what could have happened.

Another time when all of us went to Roseau for a festival, Richard was driving his car. He was older than us, so he was the only one with a car. It was crazy days shopping in Roseau. Displays were up and down the sidewalks. The streets were filled with people and cars had to drive slowly through the crowds. While Richard was maneuvering through it all, we rolled down the windows and hung our heads out and held our noses as if he had farted saying "Jeez, Richard!" He was so embarrassed and so mad at us that he kicked us out of the car and left us in Roseau. We had to hitchhike back to Warroad.

We also talked Richard into driving his car to Winnipeg, skipping school for the day. We had a blast. We tried to time it so that we got back to Warroad as school was getting out. On the way back from the border, his car broke down just outside Warroad. There was antifreeze all over the place and he had a cracked block. The car was done. As we were standing there, one of our teachers stopped to help us. Needless to say, we all got caught that time and had to complete detention. We had many good times with Ted Schnurr, in school, out in public, and on the playing field. He was a good friend and classmate. I still think of him often and from time to time remember our antics as kids.

In baseball we made it to the finals again. I pitched the final game in the regional tournament. It was the first time I pitched in a game since I hurt my arm. My arm was sore, and I had pain killers left over and I took one before the game to help with the pain. I threw the best I could but I didn't have the velocity. I used the curve ball more than normal, and tried to pitch around the batters more. We came close that year once again. We lost to Bemidji in extra innings in the final game. We couldn't believe it happened again. We were leading in the seventh and final inning when they tied it up. In extra innings they managed to score the final run to beat us again. We were not destined to win and play in the State Baseball Tournament. My high school sports days were over.

Graduation was finally here, and we walked down the aisle. It would not be the same without our classmate Ted Schnurr or our friend Gary Thompson. There would be no wild parties or celebrations that year. Although we celebrated with our family and friends, our thoughts of the tragedy was still fresh on our minds.

All in all, it was a great senior high school season. I could not have asked for more. We won the football conference title. We played in the finals of the Minnesota State High School Hockey Tournament, and we were in the finals in the High School Regional Baseball Championships in Thief River Falls. What a year to remember. There was a lot of victories, very few losses, and a lot of drama and memories.

CHAPTER 32: SUMMER HOCKEY

It was just after graduation, and my eighteenth birthday, I left for Minneapolis. I said my good-byes to Debby, and to my friends and family. I was packed the night before and it was hard to sleep with all of the excitement of leaving home. It was only for the summer but it felt more permanent. I graduated from high school, and the big wide world was out there waiting for me and I was a little scared of the uncertainty.

It was nearly 6 a.m. when a car pulled up to give me a ride to the Cities. One of my teachers, Miss Henke, a good friend, had offered me a ride. She was a young teacher from North Dakota and was in Warroad the past year. She was on her way to North Dakota but wanted to visit friends in Minneapolis for a couple of weeks. I called my brother David and his wife to let them know that I was coming to stay with them for a short time until I could get situated with my host family for the summer.

The university arranged for me to stay with the Kroska family. They lived in Newport, a suburb of Saint Paul. The family owned an electrical company, where I was to work. I met the family after about a week. They made me feel comfortable and were wonderful, down-to-earth people. Their kids were great too. Kevin, their son, and I hit it off well. The university set up a thirty-game summer league. All of the university players and some other college players made up the teams.

They made arrangements to have Kevin Kroska play hockey too. So I was to work and ride with him on a daily basis and we were on the same team. It was the first time I had been away from home for any length of time. I occasionally got homesick and spent time with my brother and his family. I still missed the Warroad area and my girlfriend, Debby. I sometimes would hitchhike home on weekends. We played three times a week, on Tuesday, Wednesday, and Thursday nights, so the weekends were long and lonely. We only worked 5 days a week. With no car, I relied on Kevin to get where I wanted to go. Sometimes brother David would pick me up and bring me to his house.

Summer hockey was totally different from playing high school hockey. There was no emotion to the games. We had more emotion playing road hockey or pick up hockey at the Warroad Arena. They were basically like scrimmages. It seemed no one wanted to be there. Although we had teams, we were not close to most of the players. We hardly ever talked and never practiced or hung out together. I felt like it was a waste time. There were times when we got mad or emotionally charged, but basically it meant nothing. It was hard for me. I felt out of my element and comfort zone the whole time I was there.

On the bright side of things, we made some friends with players like Mike Antonivich, Dean Blais and a few others. We would sometimes fly up to Hibbing for the weekend. The university staff never knew about the trips, and I do not know if they would have approved, but we didn't care. We went anyway, and had a good time. Ginny and Emma Christian, from Warroad were living in Hibbing and were involved in hockey. They, along with others decided to have a few summer hockey games over the weekend and invited us to play. The teams were divided equally and we played Friday and Saturday nights, and flew home on Sunday. The fans came out and enjoyed it very much. We did it on several weekends over the summer. The games were fun and it broke the monotony of living and working in the city during the summer.

During a summer hockey league game, I got my teeth knocked out. I was not wearing a mouth guard, although I had one in my bag. John Roberts, Coach Dick Roberts's son from War-road, accidentally knocked them out. He was attending West Point and was on leave. He made arrangements to play a few games while in Minneapolis. He was a defenseman on the other team. He was always a bit clumsy, and things had not changed since I played with him in high school. I was going up the left side, coming fast, and I made a couple of moves on him. I faked outside and then inside and back to the outside. He could not handle it. His feet were tangled up, and he was falling over. He swung his stick around while falling and caught me square in the mouth with his stick. The shaft of the stick cut my upper lip and hit with such force that it broke both my front teeth out at the gums.

I immediately went down and dropped my gloves and covered my mouth and discovered my teeth were gone. In my moment of rage, I felt like going after him but did not. I was mad and upset, and I charged off the ice to the locker room. I could not believe it. Our hometown doctor came into the locker room to see if he could help. I was rude to him while I was upset, and he left after the remark I made. I felt bad for the way I acted. I never had a chance to apologize to him. The university staff trainer came to take a look, but there was nothing anyone could do. The teeth were gone. They called the dentist the next day and made an appointment for me to see him.

In my senior year in high school, and after the hockey tournament, I had my teeth fixed and they were near perfect. There was a lot of pain that I went through to get them fixed. I can't tell you how disappointed I was that I had not worn my mouth guard that day.

When I arrived at Dr. Bob May's dentist office in a suburb in Minneapolis, I learned he was a former University of North Dakota hockey player and a former Warroad Laker. He played with Cal Marvin among others. It was a small world. He wanted to know all about Warroad. So I told him as much as I could. It had been a few years since he was in Warroad to visit. He was a very nice fellow and a skilled dentist.

He gave me a few shots of Novocain and let it set in before he started. He said it might hurt a little as he started to pull on the roots of my front teeth. They were hard to get out. He pulled and was yanking on them, and yes, it hurt like heck. I had tears running down my face, and I was trying to bear the pain as much as I could. I could feel and hear the roots tearing under my nose, and it was painful even with the Novocain. It felt as if my eyes were going to come out of the sockets. It is something that I will never forget. It hurt almost as much as the needles in the ear. He finally extracted the roots. My face was swollen but finally, in a few days it went down. Later on, I was fit for my two, new front teeth. They were bridged with wires connected to my back teeth. It took a while to get used to them.

My busy schedule of working and hockey continued, and I was also taking some summer classes to boost my ACT scores. It was frustrating without a car. I relied on others to get around. There was a lot of pressure from the university and alumni to get that ACT score up. I was only a point off where I needed to be. So I was close but as time went on, I felt more frustrated, trapped and I was not sure I wanted to be there. Things seemed to be closing in. I needed time to think things through.

JIM, HENRY AND EDDY.

DEBBY'S PROM PICTURE.

HENRY AND DEBBY.

WARROAD SIGN.
COURTESY OF THE WARROAD HISTORICAL SOCIETY.

Figure 49

217

While back in Warroad one weekend in early August, Eddy Dorohoy, coach of the Winnipeg Jets Junior Hockey Team came to Warroad. He wanted me to play for Winnipeg in Western Canada. On another weekend, I had the GM of the Montreal Junior Canadians sitting at our table. He told me how much they wanted me in Montreal, and he left an airline ticket for me to report to camp. The university was calling and telling me to come back and take that ACT test so we could get things settled and get me enrolled. There was a lot of pressure, and things were happening fast. I needed a mentor or a career manager. I did not have an adult helping me assess the options and make the right life choices. I did not have the tools to do it by myself.

Meanwhile, Debby and I were in a deep relationship and talked about our options. She had another year of high school. I was going off somewhere, but I really didn't know what I was going to do at that time. I was having second thoughts about the university and was thinking of junior hockey. Debby and I were young and in love. We took our relationship to another level that summer and wanted to be together no matter what happened. I felt that it was us against the world. She feared she might be pregnant. I was in a real fix and didn't know what to do or who to talk to. We had gone together on and off since 8th grade. Debby was a twin and Donna was her sister. Debby had undiagnosed emotional and mental illness. Donna was healthy and more stable. Debby would have crying binges and emotional tantrums. June, her mother did not know what to do and like any good parent, she took Debby to see a physiatrist and other professional people. We all stood behind her and tried to help. We all thought it would pass. Nothing was determined and she was always brought back home. She was fine around me but she felt the world was against her. I personally never experienced anything similar to what Debby was going through. I had no idea what they were talking about. Her mother was the only one that seemed to be able to calm Debby down when she was having a bad day or going through

a crisis. Now she thought she was pregnant and we both were dealing with that.

While sitting with Debby in her parent's yard one day, the guilt she
was feeling about possibly being pregnant was overwhelming and it was
getting to her. She was emotional, and wanted to talk to her mother.
She was waiting for her mother to come home from work. She said that
she was going to tell her mother she was pregnant. She had not been
to the doctor so there was no proof that she was pregnant. I said, "Let's
wait and go to the doctor first. He will tell you if you are pregnant,
and then we can plan from there." So, I thought it was settled. When
her mother came home from work, we were sitting in the yard talking.
When her mother got out of the car and started walking toward the
house, to my surprise Debby blurted out that she was pregnant. I just
about died. Her mother stopped, look at us very calmly. She said that
she knew something was going to happen because we were spending
too much time together. She threw it back on us, asking, "What are
your plans?" At that moment, I was in shock and surprised. We did not
have any plans. Debby was crying and in hysterics and was no help. We
needed to settle things down, think things through. Debby and June
went into the house and I left. We did not see each other for a couple of
days, although we talked on the phone. We were thinking through our
options and trying to come up with some answers.

It was August, time was running out. I needed to make some
decisions. I was working in Minneapolis and playing summer
hockey which was just about over. When I went back, I turned in
my equipment, and moved home to Warroad. It was all too much.
It was stressful, and I had no time to think about things. I felt that if
I told the university about Debby possibly being pregnant, it would
ruin everything. I had people pressuring me from every direction.
Everyone had their opinion. I was confused and I needed to separate
from everything and try to sort things out.

I thought I needed to include Debby in my plans. Debby found
out she was not pregnant. June suggested that we get married. If

marriage was what we wanted, she would support it. I had no idea what emotional problems Debby was going through, and to the extent of her illness. The family kept it quiet. They thought getting married might help Debby stabilize her emotions. The doctors could not find anything physically wrong, but she continued to seek out doctors when she was not feeling well. She would go to a different doctor each time.

Personally, I felt I did not have a good mentor, so therefore, no adult to talk to. I was shy, and did not seek out any advice. I had Dick Roberts but I was often afraid to talk to him. I am sure he was disappointed when I was about to give up that full scholarship, let alone thinking about getting married. I did not want to discuss those decisions with him. I was getting bits of advice from everyone, some good and some bad, and I was confused. I thought Debby would be the one to help me make some of these decisions. Isn't that what a relationship is all about—collaborative decision making? I needed a good partner to stand by me and help make some of life's decisions and to be there in support. I thought after we were together, she would be more grown up, stable and understanding.

When June suggested marriage, it was an option that I had not considered. I thought it might work. After all, it would be nice starting out being with the one you love. I would have support at home. She could work and help me make decisions. Before, it seemed as if I had everyone making my decisions for me. Sometimes, people didn't ask what I wanted, they made the decisions and I would just go along with it.

So in the end, after considering all of our options, we decided to get married and I would go to Winnipeg to play for the Jets. I thought we could work through Debby's problems or maybe she would grow out of them. It was worth the chance. Winnipeg was close, only 2½ hours from home. Debby could come home anytime. They had bus service to and from Warroad. Debby did not drive, so it was nice to have that option. In the end, hopefully, we would be happy. I thought I would build my hockey career playing juniors in Canada, and not attend the university that year. I made my choice thinking that I had my partner who would love and support me. I hoped Debby would energize me through my hockey career. In turn I would love and support her and we would live our lives together. It was a nice thought...

CHAPTER 33: WINNIPEG, MANITOBA

I notified the University of Minnesota of my decision not to attend school and play for the Gophers. I thanked them for their offer and opportunity. Then, I notified Winnipeg Jets coach Eddy "Pistol Pete" Dorohoy that I would be attending the rookie camp in a couple of weeks. I was relieved. The pressure was off and I had a positive plan, just to play hockey.

Coach Dorohoy drove right down to Warroad the next day. He brought a player contract, and we got down to the business of me playing in Winnipeg. First, the Flin Flon Bombers in Flin Flon, Manitoba, owned my player rights, so the Jets needed to get my player rights through a trade. (In Canada, a team can place a player's name on their "potential list", then they submit the list to the WCHL, and then they own the player's rights.) Secondly, I told him that Debby and I were getting married. He said, "No problem." They would provide us with an apartment and per diem for living expenses. Thirdly, I mentioned that I did not have a car and I asked for a car allowance and they agreed. Finally, they also agreed to pay for all of my tuition, should I decide that I wanted to go to college.

Everything seemed to be working out for us. With everything agreed and written in the contract, I signed it. It was settled. We were going to Winnipeg. I still had to make the team.

They came to Warroad to pick me up and bring me to Winnipeg. I was to attend the rookie camp. They put me up at a hotel and drove me to and from practice each day. They were satisfied with my performance and gave us a couple of days off. As agreed, they gave me an allowance for the car and gave me a ride home to Warroad. The next day, I found a car in Roseau, a 1964 Dodge push-button car. The car was in good condition and ran well. I had been without a car that whole summer. I drove it back to Warroad to show it to everyone. Preparations were being made for our wedding in October. We were being married in the Catholic Church, so as required, I converted from the Lutheran faith.

Our training camp would start soon, and we needed to find a furnished apartment. After looking at several apartments around Winnipeg, we finally found one that was near downtown, close to the arena and the bus station. The team paid the deposit, the first month's rent, and the rent directly each month after. We had to wait a few of weeks until we could move in.

After a stressful summer, everything seemed to be going well. We had planned carefully and had everything scheduled. We were happy that we were getting married and were going to be together. I was relived and glad to have a partner who would share the joys and help me climb the ladder. It all seemed right.

I left for camp and stayed at the hotel with the others. Our training camp went well. We had a lot of talent trying out for the team. I was excited to be on the ice again and to play at that level and to see how I measured up. Most of the NHL players were from the Canadian junior leagues. There were many from this league, the WCHL. There were also a number of players attending pro camps that would return and join us.

HENRY BOUCHA, WINNIPEG JETS IN ACTION.
COURTESY OF THE MINNEAPOLIS STAR TRIBUNE.

HENRY BOUCHA, WINNIPEG JETS.
COURTESY OF THE MINNEAPOLIS STAR TRIBUNE.

Figure 50

Our training camp was at the Winnipeg Arena, our home rink. I remembered the first time I was in the building, years before, to watch a Toronto Maple Leafs and Detroit Red Wings exhibition game. I was a kid, and I sold candy to win that trip. I was there again to attend my first concert, Paul Revere & the Raiders. It seemed like ages ago, but there I was, now skating in Winnipeg.

There was no turning back for me now. Once I signed that contract to play in Western Canada, I was no longer eligible for college hockey under the NCAA rules. I know I disappointed some people with my decision, but for Debby and I, it seemed to be working out like a fairy tale.

We played a few exhibition games, and we did well. I thought we had a good team. We drew a lot of fans, and we were still getting players in from the pro camps as they made their cuts. The Winnipeg Arena held about twelve thousand fans. We drew four thousand a game on average and sometimes as much as six thousand. The other teams in the league had smaller venues and drew fewer than three thousand fans per game.

I felt fortunate that I signed with Winnipeg. It was a city with plenty to do and see, compared to the small town of Warroad. Although we had per diem, we did not have any extra money. We were just getting by. Most teams and communities hated Winnipeg, probably because of Winnipeg's size. They all wanted to beat us. Our uniforms were like the New York Rangers' uniforms—red, white, and blue, like our youth hockey program in Warroad. I always liked the colors. They were also the colors of USA Hockey.

Our exhibition schedule progressed and soon it was October and time for our wedding. I left Winnipeg and drove to Warroad the day before the wedding. It was a small, simple, church wedding. Our families and a few close friends attended. After we were married, we opened our gifts and had a small reception. After the reception, we said our good-byes and traveled to Winnipeg.

We checked in at the hotel in Winnipeg. It was the same hotel where the team was staying for camp. The management gave me a few days off, but I did not take it. I was anxious to get going and play. I decided to play in an exhibition game the next night in Winnipeg. We did not have money for a honeymoon. We were staying next to the arena. I played and Debby went to the game. We went out for pizza after with some of the team. We stayed at the hotel for a week and then moved into our apartment. We thought we were living the dream.

The apartment was a one bedroom and furnished. It had everything we needed: dishes, silverware, pots, and pans, bed, bedding, furniture and a TV. Debby liked it and thought I made a good choice. We moved our clothes in and unpacked. We grocery shopped and set up house. During our time away from the team, we explored the city as if we were tourists on vacation. We discovered areas where we could go and not spend much money. We found a great place to get pizza and we ate out when we could afford too.

Whenever the team went on a road trip, Debby would pack a bag and jump on a bus and head down to Warroad to stay with her parents. Her dad, Leo Bleau, was a well driller and was gone most of the time. She would stay with her mom. She was close to all of her relatives. Both Donna and Dale were in college. Terry was married and in the Air Force. June was there by herself most of the time. The bus route was convenient both ways. The bus station was only four blocks from our apartment, and the bus stopped at a gas station in Warroad about three blocks from their home.

We settled into life in Wnnipeg. Debby enjoyed the home games, and they gave us a sense of belonging. We were getting used to the city. We would sometimes go out with the team for a while after the games. Relatives or someone from our hometown would come for the games. We would visit for a while after the games, and usually they drove home that same night. We ran into my Uncle Fred Boucha and his wife, Elsie, from Kenora, Ontario. They were staying overnight, and they invited us to dinner. We enjoyed that very much.

Neither of us were very sociable. We were so young. I was shy, and Debby did not like meeting new people. We really did not make any friends there other than the players and their friends. Most of the players were single and were billeted out with families from all over the city. Some were going to college part-time. Some of the other players were from Winnipeg and lived at home. Some worked odd jobs. The hockey schedule was demanding. When at home we were all right, but we played 2 to 3 times a week. Our road trips were up to 10 days long. The players that were in school had to bring their homework with them and study on the bus.

I asked Debby if she would like to get a job, but she was shy and she did not want to work. She did not want to stay in Winnipeg when I was on the road. The city could be overwhelming when you come from a small town. We did not know what to do with our downtime. We certainly could have been more constructive and creative. We could have done a lot of things, like education, jobs or even volunteered. We went swimming in the Pan Am pool a few times. We walked around the mall and took other short walks, and we went out to eat. Game nights were good, with a lot to do. We had a sixty-game schedule, so we had plenty of home games. We ran out of gas one time, a few blocks from home. We were broke. I had no money and had to scrape a few coins together to pay a guy back for some gas. I gave him some Jets tickets to keep him happy. We attended most of the free events at the Winnipeg Arena: the car shows and the Canadian National Team playing Russia and the Czechs. Most of the time we could get free tickets through the Jets office if we wanted to attend an event at the arena.

As time went on, it was more evident that Debby was depressed as she became more moody. She had been stable most of the time with only a few outbreaks. We did not do much during those times and she did not want to talk about it. We tried to do more outside the apartment, and we talked about hobbies but she wanted to be in Warroad most of the time. She did not mind leaving me alone in Winnipeg. It was understandable when I was on the road. She wanted to be home in Warroad with her mother, even when I was in Winnipeg.

I received a call one night after a hockey game in Winnipeg from Murray Williamson. He introduced himself as the head coach for the United States National Hockey Team. He said he had been at the game that night and asked me how I thought I played. I told him I had bruised, sore ribs and that I didn't play that well. He said that they had been scouting me these past few months and wanted to know if I would be interested in trying out for the United States National Hockey Team. He went on to say that he was putting together a team that would represent the United States in the World B Qualifying Championships in Bucharest, Romania. He said the United States team needed to win that tournament to qualify for the A Pool in 1971 and the Olympics in 1972. He said that if I was interested, they were having a tryout during the Christmas holidays, during our break in Winnipeg. He said the timing would work out for me to be there. The tryouts were to be held at the Metropolitan Ice Center in Minneapolis. He also said he had already talked to Ben Haskins, Winnipeg Jets owner. He said that Mr. Haskins agreed for me to make the trip to Bucharest in February for three weeks, if I made the team. After the tournament, I would need to come back to Winnipeg and finish the season. I could not say "YES" fast enough. I was interested in the tryout. It would be a real blessing for me to play on a US National Team.

It was one of my life's goals. I always wanted to play on the United States Hockey Team. The Christian brothers won a gold medal in Squaw Valley in 1960, and their brother Ginny won a silver in 1956 in Cortina, Italy. As a youngster I watched the US National and the US Olympic teams play in Warroad. This was great, and an opportunity of a lifetime. I called my family and told them about the call. I was proud that I was selected to try out. I was not sure if I would make the team.

Playing junior hockey in Western Canada was turning out to be good for me, but hard at times. There was not a game that there was not a NHL scout present. It was hard-core hockey, brutally dirty at times. It was hard hitting, and there was plenty of fighting and intimidation. Name-calling was relentless. It was the first time I was called derogatory Indian names to my face that were degrading and discriminating. It hurt badly and it was emotionally draining. Being a Native American left you open for those types of derogatory statements. They saw the same movies as I did. So a lot of the remarks were the same as in the movies. The comments hurt, but I could not and I would not let them get to me. Only after the game and when I was alone, I would let my feelings go, and cry. I was alone most of the time, while Debby was home in Warroad. I had no one to talk to about these things. I do not know if she would have helped anyway. I had to get it out and I cried about it, alone. Carrying those severely sad feelings around did more damage than good. Some players on your team would come up and try console me after an incident. Others just went about their business. Some players, and fans did not like Indians at all, and they did not like US-born players either. So I got it from both directions.

It was constant harassments, cheap shots, hacking, spearing and endless, degrading comments in every rink and building in the league, by fans, the players, and even the other coaches. The referees just turned their heads and acted as if they did not hear or see anything. There was no governance in Hockey Canada regarding these senseless attacks. This would all change years later when African/Americans came into the leagues. For now, you just had to take it and act as if it did not bother you. There were times on the bus when I just wanted to break down and cry, but I did not. Sometimes though, I would go into the bathroom on the bus and try to deal with it for a few minutes. There were also times that I wanted to quit, but I did not. When I thought about quitting, it seemed something positive would happen, just when I wanted to give up. I came to the conclusion that the players doing this were uneducated morons with little self-discipline. They were brought up through the midget or junior systems, did not attend the university or a training program, they lived in billets and were idiots. They were ignorant kids without any morals, being trained by coaches who themselves were the same way. These coaches were leading these kids up the ladder to professional hockey. I could see it on our team too; some of the players fit that mold.

We had a nine-day, seven-game road trip out west from Winnipeg. We played Brandon, Manitoba, Estevan, Saskatchewan, Swift Current, and two games in Calgary and Edmonton, Alberta, and then played in Saskatoon, Saskatchewan. We rode a Greyhound bus, miles and miles and when it was time to eat they stopped at a restaurant and picked up box lunches. Once in a while we would stop to get a hot meal. The ride was so long that we read the whole *Winnipeg Free Press* a time or two during the trip. We slept as long as we could, played cards as long as we could, look out the window as long as we could, and sometimes we still weren't there. Talk about paying your dues.

Our coach was Eddy "Pistol Pete" Dorohoy. He was a vitamin with legs. When he recruited me in Warroad, he sat outside with me in his car for three hours, talking steadily. Whenever I looked away or he thought I was not paying attention, he would tap me on the arm. He talked and talked and talked some more. He definitely had attention deficit disorder. To get rid of him when he was talking with me in Warroad, I said that I would come to Winnipeg. I wasn't sure at that point, but it worked out that I went anyway. Eddy was a good hockey player in the old Western League and was quite successful. He never made it to the NHL but he was a good minor leaguer. Dorohoy was fired after that trip out west. We went 0–7 and Jets owner Ben Haskins said it was enough. He hired another coach, Nick Mickowski, who had played for the New York Rangers. He would take Eddy's job and finish out the season.

At Christmas break, Debby and I drove to Warroad and stayed with the Bleau family. We were going to leave for Minneapolis the next day. Cal Marvin called me before we left Winnipeg and asked if I would stop in Warroad. He wanted me to suit up and play a game with the Warroad Lakers and I said that I would. I was excited to be home and play for the Lakers. We won the game, and it was good to see everyone. I got to play with Billy and Roger Christian, gold medalists from the 1960 US team, among some other great players.

The next day Debby and I left for Minneapolis. It was an all-day trip. We had made arrangements to stay at Debby's cousin, Bonnie Hokanson's in South Minneapolis. She was away and let us use her apartment. I was to report to the Metropolitan Sports Center for the tryouts the next day. I played in the Minnesota State High School Hockey Tournament in that same building. It was different skating there now. It was quiet and empty compared with the exciting night at the high school state championship game when I was hurt.

The tryouts were not difficult, but I had been playing regular and was in good shape. The drills were easy for me, and we played a couple of exhibition games with teams from the United States Hockey League. Green Bay, Des Moines, and Waterloo were some of the teams in that league. I was surprised that I had no problem skating with them. For some reason, I thought these guys would be superior. There were several players from all over the United States that tried out for the team. Not all players played in every game. We won all of our games, and after our final game the coach said that he would make the announcement and be in touch with those players who made the cut.

It was the first time I saw Debby totally out of control during our short marriage. Darlene and Jim, and family were visiting my mother and dad in Warroad. They decided to visit brother David and family in Minneapolis, and wanted to see some of the US Team hockey games at the Met. It somehow set Debby off. She was unhappy about visiting with my family and having them around. I thought it was great to have them all there, together. We were invited to Dave's place for dinner, but Debby would not go. I tried to talk and reason with her about going for dinner. She absolutely said "no". I went despite what she said and paid for it. Debby attended one game out of four. She was out of control and I did not know why. She would rant and rave at me for no apparent reason. The only reason I could think of was because I went to see my family at David's or I was gone too long. I was trying out for the US National team and I would stop in to say "hi" to the family at David's. She behaved as if she was possessed. Throwing a fit, she ranted, raved and cursed at me about my family and would not let me sleep. I was so exhausted when I went to practice that Murray Williamson noticed and asked me what was going on. He told me to get some rest. I was too embarrassed to tell him. Debby would sleep when I was gone and when I got back to the apartment she would start in on me again and again. She would not leave me alone and let me rest or sleep. By the last game, I was so exhausted that I did not think I made the team. The next day, and without much rest again, I drove to Warroad. I was so exhausted that I thought about stopping to sleep along the way, so I drank coffee and kept going. We got to Warroad at 4 p.m. and I went right to bed and didn't wake up until 9 a.m. the next morning. Debby acted like nothing happened. She did not say a word about what she had put me through or how she acted. She was a different person, all happy and cheery. I packed up my stuff and went back to Winnipeg alone. I was emotionally drained, hurt, a bit shocked from what I had experienced. I was worried about her condition, and now I knew what her parents went through when she lost control. Debby was supposed to go back with me but wanted to stay. She was insecure. She felt comfortable, secure and safe at home with her parents. June would put up with her, comfort her, and at times argue with her. She was a saint to do it.

It was not long after I received a phone call from Murray, announcing that I made the team. I was stunned, and overwhelmed.

He congratulated me and welcomed me as a member of the team that was going to Bucharest. I was absolutely thrilled and called everyone to share the good news.

Although my trip was weeks away, when I thought about it, I was excited. I could not believe I was going to the world championships in Bucharest, Romania. The trip would take us behind the Iron Curtain in the Soviet Block of Communist Countries.

CHAPTER 34: BUCHAREST, ROMANIA

After waiting patiently for the trip abroad, I was more than ready to go. My Winnipeg teammates wished me well as I left the arena. I had my skates, sticks, equipment, and all the important papers; passport, shot records, visa, etc. with me. I spent the last few weeks gathering all my documents in Winnipeg through the US Consulate. It felt good to get away from the grind of junior hockey for a while. There was a lot of stress maintaining a position in the league during the physical battles and daily grind of the regular season. I was looking forward to the break and to travel to Europe. This tournament would be new and exciting. The tournament was short, and very competitive. It would be easier getting up for games like this. The United States had to win this tournament to qualify and advance to the Pool A Tournament in the 1971 World Championships and the 1972 Olympics. If not, the United States would not be able to qualify for a medal in the Olympics. We had our backs to the wall. It was up to the 1970 Team to win this tournament and get the United States back in good standing in World Hockey. It was a lot of pressure, but the players felt we could win it all. I was anxious to play against the other countries represented in the tournament. There would be no easy games.

I made my way to Warroad to stay overnight at the in-laws and with Debby. I wanted to see her before I left on my dream trip with the US National Team. Debby and I had not seen each other much since the torment she put me through while trying out for the US team in Minneapolis. She was in Warroad most of the time. Although she would come to Winnipeg for a day or two, Debby always found an excuse to go back to her mother in Warroad. I just let her go. I didn't want to argue with her any more. So, I was in Winnipeg alone most of the time.

I left Warroad the next day and traveled to Minneapolis. When I arrived, I checked in at a hotel near the Metropolitan Sports Center. The hotel is where the team met and would stay until we left for Europe. We practice for a few days before our departure to Europe. We also would receive our travel gear, uniforms, jackets, etc. There were some older players whom I knew from high school games. I played high school hockey in 8th grade when I was 13, so there were a lot of players who I remembered. Now I was eighteen years old, and the youngest on the team. Compared to these guys, I was about as green as one could be. The guys were helpful as we packed for a three week trip, and we tried to pack light and take only what we really needed.

A bus transported us to the airport. We flew to Kennedy in New York. We changed planes there and flew to Heathrow in London. We arrived in London in the morning, and our plane did not leave for Zurich, Switzerland, until late in the afternoon. Coach Williamson said we could stay together in small groups and look around the city. At eighteen years old, I just tagged along with some of the other guys. We took a cab into downtown London. I did not have a lot of money but we were given per diem each day for incidentals. Being in London was different. The cars drove on the left side of the street and it was interesting to see how the British talked and lived. I noticed how polite and proper they were. We walked the streets and looked at the shops. We visited with the locals and stayed for few hours before returning to the airport. It was an education for me to be there.

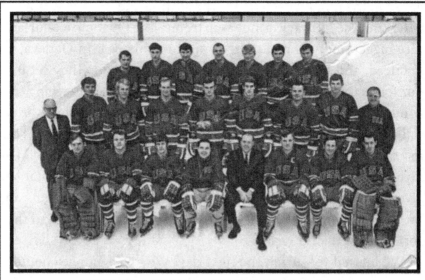

1970 WORLD CHAMPIONSHIPS BUCHAREST, ROMANIA.

— LEFT TO RIGHT, FIRST ROW: GARY JOHNSON, LARRY STORDAHL, LEN LILYHOHL, MURRAY WILLIAMSON, COACH, HAL TRUMBLE, MANAGER, DON ROSS, DOUG WOOG, CARL WETZEL. SECOND ROW: DR. V. GEORGE NAGABODS, HENRY BOUCHA, BOB LINDBERG, CRAIG PATRICK, JIM MCELMURY, CHARLIE BROWN, GEORGE KONICK, WALLY OLDS, DOC ROSE TRAINER. THIRD ROW: KEITH CHRISTIANSON, OZZIE O'NEIL, MIKE GREENLEAF, GARY GAMBUCCI, BRAYN GRAND, CHUCK TOOMY, GARY SCHMAIZBOUER. NOT PICTURED: HERB BROOKS, BRUCE RIUTTA, PETE FITCUK, AND PETE MARKLE. NOTE: SOME OF THESE PLAYERS DID NOT TRAVEL WITH US TO BUCHAREST, ROMANIA.

Figure 51

When everyone returned, we boarded our flight to Zurich. The staff wanted us to stay up and try not to sleep to adjust to the time zone change. We scheduled games with the Swiss National Team and another all-star teams in the area over the next few days before traveling to the World Championships in Romania.

After staying the night in Zurich, we traveled by bus to Geneva. We checked into the Hotel Metropol in Geneva and settled in. Later that day we skated and got the kinks out. The next day we played a tough Swiss National Team and won. We played them the following night also, and we played better and we won again. They were a very formidable hockey team. They were better and more accomplished than I thought. The games were tight and we had to play hard to beat them. The talent and competition was definitely better than I played in the juniors in Canada. The skating and passing was much better, and the hitting was not as extreme. The Olympic ice surfaces were bigger and you had more room to maneuver. In Geneva, we practiced, and had a couple of days to look around. They set up a tour for us to see sites around Geneva, as well as a sight-seeing tour by bus to Mount Blanc. I was in awe of almost everything, especially the old buildings and architecture. For most of us, it was our first trip to Europe. Herb Brooks, George Konic, Carl Wetzel, Len Lilyholm, and a few of the others, played for the US National and Olympic teams in Europe in the past. We had some veterans and they informed us on what to expect. It was great listening to their stories about their travels.

We bussed to Zurich the next day. We had a game scheduled on the way. After leaving Geneva, we traveled to a ski community. We played that night against an all-star team that was made up of players that played in the Swiss League. The team was made up of the locals as well as some American and Canadian players. It was a good and competitive team. They were loaded up on talent. We played on an outdoor rink, and seating was all on one side of the ice with bleachers that rose well above fifty feet in back of our team benches. The game got a little chippy toward the end, and the fans were into it and seemed to enjoy the roughness that was happening on the ice. When a penalty was called on the home team, an array of wine bottles hit just in front of our team bench, smashing all over the ice. Time was called to clean the ice, and the crowd seemed to be getting out of hand. I thought they were going to riot. It was like playing in Flin Flon in juniors. Once everything settled down and the ice was cleared, we resumed the game. We scored late in the game and came away with another win. During the time of the wine bottles hitting the ice, I have to admit I was a little scared. Being eighteen years old, in a foreign country and far away from home, was stressful for me. As a team, we started to blend.

238

After the game we stayed in a local hotel and then continued to Zurich the next day. We left Zurich to fly to Bucharest, Romania for the tournament. We were getting to know each other a little more each day. Only a few of us had played together before. We arrived at the airport early, giving us enough time to get our gear and luggage checked in and our papers in order to leave Switzerland and enter Romania. Although Romania was hosting the world tournament, the communists were leery of all westerners.

While at the airport in Zurich, we waited and took pictures, talked and joked around. Once we boarded the plane, we found our seats and were ready for our flight. Then an announcement came. There was a security warning and we all had to disembark. We waited back in the airport. We found out later that there was a bomb threat. We had to wait until they cleared the airplane. Terrorism was a threat then as it is now. There was a possibility that if they knew that we were a United States team traveling together; they would want to harm us. Once cleared, we boarded the plane. They hurried to get us out of there. We were finally on our way to Bucharest, Romania. Everyone was excited, because we ordinarily did not travel into communist countries to play in tournaments. It was a long flight, and as usual the older guys who thought they were comedians were up to no good. They loved picking on us young, green kids.

Of course, being a rookie, I had to sit in the middle seat. I sat between Carl Wetzel and Don Ross. They were talking about their papers being in order to enter the communist country. They were taking some papers out of their sports jacket pockets and looking at them, as if they had something important that I didn't have. Yes, it made me uneasy. My passport and other documents were with the team manager. He carried all the paperwork for the team. The way these guys were talking, they led me to believe that I missed getting my papers back from the manager and maybe I wouldn't get into the country. Well, I sat there not saying a word, and I did not look in my pockets. They had me going with a million thoughts running through my head. At one point I was going to get up and go talk to the manager and ask him if I needed those papers back. I held my cool and sat there. It was not the first time or the last time they would pull some of these jokes on me, as a rookie.

We were still getting used to the time change. We started our descent into Bucharest. It was rough coming through the clouds and the winds were crossways and it was bumpy. We landed in Bucharest at dusk. It was cloudy, cold, and rainy. It all looked so gray. As we disembarked the plane, military guards were everywhere. Not one of the guards or immigration people had a smile on their face or made any welcoming gesture. They seemed to be stone-cold people and so serious. I was scared. I was like a shadow to the other players. I did not stray one inch away from them as we went through customs and got on our bus.

We traveled through the streets of Bucharest. I was taking it all in. I was amazed at the big sidewalks and small streets. Then I realized that there was no traffic to speak of. There were no cars on the streets as there were in other large cities. People were walking everywhere or traveling on old, broken-down electric trolleys.

We arrived at the International Hotel; a huge, old-style building that was well kept. We retrieved our belongings from the bus. We had to take our own hockey equipment and baggage into our hotel. We kept our equipment in our rooms. I was rooming with Ozzie O'Neil from Marquette, Michigan. He was playing with Marquette in the United States Hockey League at the time. He was only nineteen years old, so we were tagged as Ozzie and Harriet from that time on. The older players loved to pick on us, and we were the brunt of most of the jokes and pranks. We were culture shocked by the time we left Bucharest.

THE 1970 U.S. NATIONAL TEAM IN AN AIRPORT.
LEFT TO RIGHT: HUFFER CHRISTIANSON, COACH MURRAY WILLIAMSON, LENNY LILLYHOM,
GARY GAMBUCCI, PETE MARKLE, OZZIE O'NEILL, GARY JOHNSON,
TRAINER DOC ROSE, GENERAL MANAGER HAL TRUMBLE, GEORGE KONIK, JIM
MCELMURY, BRUCE RIUTTA, HENRY BOUCHA, CARL WETZEL, LARRY STORDAHL,
CHARLIE BROWN, CRAIG PATRICK, BOB FLEMING (CHAIRMAN OF AHAUS), DON ROSS,
BOB LINDBERG, HERB BROOKS, PUBLIC RELATIONS G. ANDERSON,
BRIAN GRAND, AND TEAM DOCTOR DOC NAGOBADS.
COURTESY OF DR. GEORGE NAGOBADS COLLECTION.

ROMANIAN OFFICERS WATCHING THE U.S. TEAM. 1970.
COURTESY OF DR. GEORGE NAGOBADS COLLECTION.

Figure 52

The lobby of the hotel was huge, with nice plants and furniture spread out like in the old movies. We checked in and made our way to the elevators. It was the first time I had experienced an elevator attendant. You would hold up your fingers to signal the floor you wanted, or point to the number and he would bring you there. The rooms were old but large and elegant. The bathroom had a bath but no shower. Our room looked out over the front of the building onto the wide sidewalks and small streets. It seemed everyone wore gray, black, or brown coats. Nothing bright stood out. No one drew attention to themselves. It seemed colorless, like a black-and-white film, and it was very smoky and smoggy.

It was late when we went to bed. We were awakened by a knock on the door. It was our team doctor, and he said we were having breakfast in a few minutes in the dining room. We were still getting use to the time change. We got ready and went down to eat. It always amazed me how slow people ate in Europe. I was not accustomed to eating slow. We experienced about ten to fifteen minutes between courses. In Switzerland, we would start off with mineral water and then bread. Then they would bring the soup. When everyone was finished, they would bring a salad. Then they would bring the main entrée, then coffee and dessert. It took us an hour and a half to eat each meal.

For breakfast we had mineral water, one fried egg, a few ounces of potatoes, and bread. They would not allow us to have seconds. I am sure they thought we were rude to ask for more. Most of us walked away from the table still hungry. The lunches and dinners were the same way, with small portions and no seconds. There was nowhere to buy anything else to eat. We were athletes competing for the world championships. We would burn up a few thousand calories a day or more. We were scheduled to play every other day for twelve days. On the days that we were not playing, we would practice and sometimes go on sightseeing tours. The coach and manager said they would look into getting us more food at our meals and would work something out about some nutritional snacks. Behind the Iron Curtain, they did not allow Pepsi or Coke or any foreign foods that came from the West. We ate what they ate, and that was it. Their soda was made in Romania and it tasted horrible. The only water we were allowed to drink was the bottled mineral water. At the hotel, the tap water had a foul taste to it, so we did not drink it. It was a dilemma for us Americans, and I guess for most western-ers. As time went on, our staff worked on the food shortage, and the food was getting better. They allowed us to fly in Coke from France. We never ate in restaurants that I remember, although we had beer at the night clubs. I don't remember them offering food.

The opening ceremonies were wonderful and memorable. I was proud to be representing America in the tournament. We were one of the favorites to win the tournament. We needed to win all the games. The other participants were Norway, Bulgaria, Romania, West Germany, Yugoslavia, Japan, and Switzerland.

This World B Tournament was significant for the United States. If the United States did not win this tournament, the United States would miss the 1972 Olympics in Sapporo, Japan and a chance at a medal. The United States was dropped from the A Pool in the Inter-national Hockey Federation because of poor showings in the world tournaments and the Olympics. The International Ice Hockey Fed-eration determined that the United States had to earn its way back to the A Pool. The only way back in was to win this tournament. It was an absolute must that the United States win. It was a cross roads for USA Hockey and tremendous pressure on the team.

Murray Williamson and Hal Trumble asked for and received a three-year commitment to coach and manage the United States team for USA Hockey. They gathered this team together by scout-ing and producing the best available amateur players in the country. Remember, only amateurs were allowed to play.

It was hard for the free-world or noncommunist countries to cheat because everything was transparent. People could track your movements, and knew if you played for money. If you did you were considered a professional player, paid for your services, and you were not eligible for world competition in the World Championships or Olympics.

Some former professional players could regain their amateur status by petitioning the International Ice Hockey Federation and obtaining amateur status. On the other hand, all communist countries did everything in secret, and the International Ice Hockey Federation was not allowed to investigate any of the players, so they could not determine their true status. For instance, all of the Russians were in the Red Army and were paid to play for their country. They all lived together and practiced eleven months a year, six hours a day. They were given all of their living expenses, including apartments, cars to drive, and money from the government. Yet they were considered amateurs. See the difference? In the west, we all had jobs or played college, senior, or some other form of amateur hockey. So in our way of life, if you were good, you played professional, made a living, and were out of the world tournaments and Olympics. However, if you played without pay, and had a regular job or were a student you could play for your country. In reality, we could not compete with the likes of the Russians on a regular basis. Sometimes we were able to beat them, but it was rare.

Canada petitioned and argued with the International Ice Hockey Confederation to be able to use its professional players, but their request was denied. As a result, Canada withdrew from the world competition.

For me, playing for the United States in the World Championships in Romania was my most signification role and highlight to date. Playing in the Minnesota State High School Hockey Tournament was high on my list of experiences to be proud of, and it will remain so.

The hockey skill and the competition in the tournament was very good. I had not experienced anything like it before. The players were older, more polished, mature and stronger. There was very little hitting or body contact. The skating, passing, and shooting were excellent. It was faster, better puck movement and the large ice surfaces were interesting. The goalies were very skilled and hard to score on. I was experiencing international hockey and it was better hockey. This is what I needed, in my young career, to grow and learn the game.

On our days off from the tournament or after a morning practice, we would explore the city. We were restricted to certain areas of the city. Even when we had tours, the communists would regulate and include only places they wanted us to see. We knew what was happening.

One day the guys pulled a good one on Ozzie and me. We were resting in our room, and we got a call from a Swedish sports writer. We thought he was authentic as he had a good accent. He said he was doing a story on the differences between hockey equipment. He asked if we could meet him in the lobby and bring some of our equipment like a shin pad, a skate, elbow pad, etc. We said, "sure". Ozzie and I grabbed our stuff and went down to the lobby and waited for the writer to show up. As we sat there one of our players would come by and say, "Hey what are you guys up to?" We would say we were waiting on this Swedish sports writer, and that he was going to do a story about us and the equipment. After the third or fourth team mate came by, it finally dawned on us that we been had. It was either Herbie Brooks, Don Ross, or maybe Carl Wetzel, and probably some others, all in on it.

Gary Gambucci bought a new watch from Switzerland and brought it to Bucharest. In the locker room and everyday for a week, George Konic would change the time on his watch to show it was losing 10 minutes a day. It was driving Gary nuts, and he would get angry thinking he had bought a lemon. After a while the first thing Gary would do was come in off the ice and checks his watch. He would see it was losing time and would hold it up to his ear and listen and shake it and set the time. No one ever told him the difference.

I didn't have much money to spend, but I bought souvenirs to take home for the family. As a team, we players were given several souvenirs. We were always looking for a deal. While in the hotel, some of us were approached by some black market people. They were looking for US dollars and wanted to exchange money with us. It was illegal. They dressed in a long black coats and hats, and they were always looking around to see if anyone was watching them. It was as if they came right out of central casting from a movie. It was actually kind of funny to see these people but they were dead serious. They were willing to give us a 32-to-1 exchange on the black market. The going rate at the bank was only 16-to-1.

After talking it over with some of the other players, some of us met with our team captain, George Konik. George was older and more experienced, and said he would collect all our money, and meet with these guys to exchange the money. They wanted to meet somewhere else and do it away from the hotel. We went along with it but were a little leery. You would see people hanging out in the lobby and it seemed that the communists always had an eye on us. One day at the hotel, Murray Williamson went to his room and found our tournament guide and interpreter going through his stuff. Murray asked him what he was doing, and the guy just walked out of the room without saying anything. So we were leery of the people around us, therefore, we stayed close together.

George collected our money. I think I had forty dollars in the pool to be exchanged. We were sitting in the lobby when George left to make the exchange. We thought it should not take much time to complete the exchange. We waited a long time, and he did not come back. We were concerned for him and were thinking about telling our coach and manager about the situation. Then, we saw George, our coach, and manager walk into the hotel lobby. They all looked distressed and shaken. The police had arrested George and the other two guys making the exchange. They had been taken to the police station. George was terrified because the police were beating up and slapping the other two guys. George kept blurting out that he was an American playing hockey in the tournament. The police called the hotel and talked to the coach and manager, and they had to go down and bail George out. We lost all of our money on that deal, and I stayed out of trouble from then on.

On our days off, we had some time on our own. We would frequent a nightclub within easy walking distance from the hotel. It had live music, and the bandleader could speak a little English so we got to know him. Walking into that nightclub was like walking into a nightclub in the 1950s. The music the band played was all old 1950s music that was easy to sing. The lead singer learned English from the songs. We became friends during that time. I gave him some blue jeans that the Romanians cherished and could not get in those days. We also exchanged some other clothes and gifts.

During another side trip on a day off, the team went to a castle in the country. I think it was in Transylvania. There was talk about Count Dracula. It was not his castle but it was one like it. It was an all-day trip. We stopped for lunch somewhere along the way. The castle was amazing with old swords, shields, and armor hanging on the halls. We were down in the dungeons and rooms below. We spent a few hours going from room to room. It was a beautiful day with sunshine. We looked at the countryside with mountains, streams and trees.

The United States won the World B Championship and Qualifying Tournament. With a great team effort and some luck, we ended the tournament undefeated. Our coaches and managers were so happy and impressed that they gave us a three-day, all-expense-paid holiday in Rome on the way home.

1970 GOLD MEDAL, AND THE PARTICIPATION MEDAL.

Figure 53

At the closing banquet, Neil Armstrong and the other US astronauts who landed on the moon were there. They were in Bucharest as part of their goodwill tour and visits to various countries. They were seated at the head table and were about to be introduced, when suddenly they were whisked away. We heard there was a terroristic threat, and before they gave their talk and we had a chance to meet them, they were gone. They intended to come to our table and meet us and congratulate us on the tournament. We received the first-place trophy and our medals that night. The United States had regained entry to the A Pool. We accomplished our goal and regained our status in the International Ice Hockey Federation and in World Hockey. We were able to complete in the 1971 World Championships, and in the 1972 Olympics in Sapporo, Japan.

248

Experiencing life behind the Iron Curtain was amazing for me. We learned about communism in school and the Cold War was in the news on a daily basis. Coming from a small town in northern Minnesota, traveling to Romania was certainly a highlight in my career. It was also a dream and goal of mine coming true; playing for the United States and wearing the red, white, and blue.

CHAPTER 35: ROME AND BACK TO WINNIPEG

With our mission accomplished, we packed and left Romania the next day. As promised, we flew to Rome for much-needed rest and relaxation. We planned to sightsee for a few days and just have fun. Having played in Bucharest for over two weeks, we were all looking forward to some good food and relaxation. Most players lost weight. Some, up to 15 pounds during our stay in Romania. The food rationing, the poor quality of the food and playing in a two week tournament leaned us out. It took a toll on all of us.

It was glorious time when we were approaching Rome. It was clear, bright and sunny. The green grass, trees and shrubs looked like they were right out of a book. Bucharest did not look this good. Maybe it was the smog of the factories in the city that made Bucharest so dreary. Nonetheless, the Romanian trip was over and we were eager to see Italy.

It was late afternoon when we arrived at the hotel. Before going to my room, I set my bags down in the lobby and went into the café. I quickly looked at a menu and saw that they had ice cream. So I ordered a strawberry malt and drank it down as if I had not eaten in weeks. The waiter was watching me as I drank it down in a few gulps. It was wonderful to have ice cream. We had not been served milk in a month.

The next day we gathered in the lobby and we were assigned to different groups, and took tours around the city. We stopped for meals and ate like there was no tomorrow. The food was extraordinary. We went to the Vatican City and spent most of the day looking at the beautiful works of art. We saw the Coliseum, ancient fountains, and we explored the city. We ate at several restaurants where the food was absolutely wonderful. We visited with the locals and took a thousand pictures. It was a tremendous gift to the team and a reward for this kid from Minnesota.

It was a long flight home. I missed my wife and family. I was anxious to get home and get back to normal. I felt worldly. The experiences broadened my mind. The trip was priceless. We landed in New York and it felt good to be back on US soil. We were proud of our accomplishments and could not wait to share stories with our friends and loved ones. We changed planes and said our goodbyes to those teammates on the east coast. Those of us from the Midwest flew to Minneapolis and after our goodbyes; we all went our separate ways.

I stayed overnight in Minneapolis and then drove home to Warroad the next day. It was a wonderful reunion with Debby. I rested and visited in Warroad for a couple of days. I brought gifts from the trip for Debby and the family. I notified the Jets office that I would be there in a few days and just in time for another road trip. Debby decided to stay in Warroad until I came back off the road.

Back in Winnipeg, it was good to see the guys. I shared my stories and experiences. They enjoyed my stories of the journey. They maintained our rankings in the league, and they were going into the last part of our season. The playoffs were just around the corner. On our road trip, it was noticeable to the players and coaches that I had learned something. I was playing better. Playing with the older and more experienced players in the international competition helped me a lot. I was more aware of my surroundings on the ice and where my players were in different situations. The Canadian Junior game was slower. The Europeans played on bigger ice surfaces with not as much hitting. The international games were more open and faster.

During the East Division Playoffs, we won our series over the Estevan Bruins in five games. The next series was a best of nine series. In the semi finals we were to play the Flin Flon Bombers, our big rivals in the Eastern Conference. We hated each other, and it showed. There would be a lot of fighting and intimidation in these games. This was a dog-eat-dog playoff series.

Every time we played in Flin Flon, we had a police escort to the hotel where we stayed. If we went by bus or to the airport, we also needed a police escort. It was scary to have the fans come after you during the game, over the glass, on the ice and on the bench. They tried to pick a fight every time you turned around. The winner of the East and West Divisions would play off in the final series. Flin Flon was five hundred miles north of Winnipeg and a 12 hours bus ride one way. We traveled there by bus during the season. We were flying there during the playoff series. It was nice not to have to sit for hours on end riding on the bus.

The series went all nine games, and the final game was to be played in Flin Flon, who finished ahead of us by a slim margin in the standings. They had home-ice advantage. The final game was in Flin Flon and it was end to end action throughout the whole game. The seventh and final game was tied in regulation and the game was going into overtime. Neither team wanted to be in the penalty box, although we hit each other, there were no fights in that game. It was a hard fought and a terrific game for the spectators to watch. We had a chance to win it in overtime. I hit the post right off the bat, and the puck stayed out of the net. With time winding down, they scored to end the game and series. They would move on to play Edmonton in the finals. Edmonton would go on to win the league championship that year.

It was a good year for me. I finished second in scoring on our team, even being gone for a month. The experience was excellent. I learned a lot from playing the WCHL and playing for the US Team. Now, I was tired. It had been a long grueling season.

I was ready for summer and a rest. Thinking back about the past year, I had played twenty-five games with Warroad High School, played in the crazy regional tournaments, and played in the Minnesota High School Hockey Tournament. In the summer, I played another thirty games in the summer league, plus games in Hibbing. I played in the Jets' ten-game exhibition season, played a sixty-game Jets schedule, took a leave of absence, and played another twenty games with the US National Team. Then I came back and played in another ten-game regular season with the Jets and then I played a fourteen-game playoff schedule. I was exhausted and needed to take some time off. Thank God, the season was over.

Debby was in Warroad when the season ended. We flew back to Winnipeg after the final game in Flin Flon. I had some of the players over the next afternoon. I made sandwiches, and some of the boys brought over some beer and we sat around and talked about the season. We talked about our plans for the summer, and the next year. Most of us would come back to Winnipeg. The party lasted for a few hours, and then everyone wanted to go out to the bars. I stayed and cleaned the apartment, packed my bags, left the keys on the counter, and headed to Warroad.

CHAPTER 36: HOME FOR THE SUMMER

With Debby in Warroad at her parents' house, I moved there also. It was late April, and her twin sister, Donna, and her brother, Dale, were still away at college. They had room for us until we could make arrangements to rent our own place for the summer.

June Huerd Bleau (Debby's mother) was a fine woman. She was born and raised in Warroad. The Huerds were a large and a long-time family in the Warroad area. Our families go back a long way. June married a Canadian by the name of Leon Bleau, who grew up just over the Ontario Canadian border in Pinewood. He was a well driller by trade. His dad was a well driller too. Over the years they drilled water wells on both sides of the border and up and down the Rainy River. The Rainy River divided Ontario and Minnesota. Leon was working a lot and was not home that much during the drilling time from April until late October. June was working at the Thermo-Lite Glass Company and was a hard worker. June and her sister, Rhoda Hokanson, worked there together. Terry, the oldest boy, was in the Air Force. When Dale and Donna came home for the summer, there was no room for us and we needed to find a place of our own. I applied for work at Marvin Windows.

It was so nice being home. The stress was leaving my body. It was nice to do nothing for a while. I needed money and that was a great motivator. I started working on the swing shift at Marvin Windows after about a week. I worked the day shift for two weeks and nights for two weeks. Debby and I found a nice little apartment across the Warroad River and down past my parents' house. It was a small, one-bedroom unit with a kitchen and a living room and the bedroom upstairs. It was furnished, and it was only fifty dollars a month, utilities included. When I worked, Debby was at her mother's most of the time.

Debby became pregnant that spring. We celebrated the news with family. She was tired, moody and depressed most of the time. It became a hard time for us. We were still newly married and spending extended time together for the first time. We really did not know each other well because, I was on the road so much and we would only see each other for a week at a time during the season. It seemed we did not have much in common. We went to the movies or an event here and there. I worked as much as I could. We did not communicate very well. Debby did not work or have hobbies and she did not have anything to talk about. She did not want to hear my hockey news or work related things. We only visited her parents and Rhoda and Alvin Hokanson (Debby's aunt and uncle) and never went to see my parents. She would not participate with my family. That was our life. Debby went home to her parent's house when I was working. I do not know why Debby resented my family so much. This was confusing to me. They were always nice to her. That really bothered me.

I took up golf that summer. I would play with Alvin Hokanson, Rhoda's husband, on the old golf course south of Warroad. It was primitive, a short nine-hole course with sand greens. Alvin worked at Marvin Windows too, but on a straight day shift. When I was on the same shift, we would play golf in the evenings. I bought a club here and there. I could not afford to buy the whole set, so I bought one at a time. I bought a seven iron first, then a five iron, and then a pitching wedge, and so on. I spent a lot of time there. I rode my bike back and forth and walked around to find golf balls. It was a good exercise and a good pastime. Debby would be at her mother's while I was working or golfing. I enjoyed my time at Marvin Windows and I appreciated the work. I worked

CHRISTIAN BROS. HOCKEY STICKS, BILLY CHRISTIAN, HAL BAKKE
AND ROGER CHRISTIAN. COURTESY OF THE WARROAD MUSEUM.

MARVIN'S WARROAD. COURTESY OF THE WARROAD MUSEUM.

Figure 54

overtime as much as I could. I was paying the bills and I had
started a little savings. I was looking forward to going back to
Winnipeg in the fall.One fine summer day, I received a letter in the

mail from the military draft board. At first, I had trouble compre-
hending what it meant and what consequences this would have for
me. Then I realized that it said my lottery number was thirty-two
and that I should expect to be drafted that year because they were
drafting numbers up to three-hundred and fifty! When I thought
about it, I was stunned. I sat down and read it again and again. I
took the letter to someone else who read it and said it meant the
same thing to them. I was going to be drafted in the US Army that
year. I thought this was going to ruin my hockey career. It took me
a while to process it all. The US military was drafting all eligible
young males as the US was actively participating in the war in Vietnam. Then I thought I better call the US National Hockey Team's
coach, Murray Williamson to see what he would say. Murray was
not surprised. He said, "Let me call the Pentagon and see what I can
find out." I thought wow, ok. He had other players dealing with the
Army also, so I was not the only one with that problem. It would be
to his advantage to have us on the team and in the Army. He would
have total control over us. The Army would pay us, and put us on
temporary duty to the US team. He would not have to pay us either.
I could hear it in his voice and I understood the way his mind was
working. He said he would call me back in a few days.

I could hardly stand it because I was worried. He finally called
and said that he had talked to the Pentagon. He was told that I
would be called by December 1970 and no later than February 1971.
He had it all worked out for me and I am sure for the other players.
I would volunteer draft in August and attend boot camp and finish by the first of November. The Army would assign me to TDY
(Temporary Duty) to the US Team. I would play a 55 game schedule
with the US National Team and I would play in the World Championships in Europe. Then, the next spring I would go back into the
Army and take up where I left off. In the 1971-72, season we would
do it again and I would play in the Olympics. I thought the plan was

okay, so I said go for it and let me know when you hear something. I really didn't have much choice.

The time I would spend with the US National Team would count as Army time; I would be on TDY with no expense to the government other than my regular Army pay. Then the next year in 1971-72 we could do the same thing and I could play on the US Olympic Team on Army time and then go back in the summers to fulfill my military obligations.

It was the only way I could continue my hockey career. I was thrilled and also counting my blessings. I had to make sure I made the teams and kept out of trouble and worked hard. It really couldn't have worked out any better. The competition was going to be great. I was playing against the best in the world. How could I lose? The experience would be fantastic.

Once I agreed, Murray was going to work out the details with the Pentagon, the US Army and get back to me as soon as he could. So the tentative plan was set. I would be volunteering for an early draft, but the dates were not set yet. It would be soon. It was already July, and he mentioned August. While waiting for Murray to call, I carried on working at Marvin's, and playing golf. The new coach from the Winnipeg Jets called, and wanted to check in with me, and to see if everything was going okay. He said they were looking forward to having me back and wanted to know if I needed anything. I told him about the US Army draft and that I was waiting on the army to contact me. I told him I may be able to play with the US team. He was sorry to hear about the draft, but understood the situation. I told him I would not be going back to Winnipeg that year. He wished me luck and I thanked him.

Murray called me in July and time was getting short. I kept working and waiting. He said I was to report to Minneapolis to the US Army Induction Center on August 20, 1970. I would get a letter stating when to report from the draft board. I would volunteer draft on that date in Minneapolis and be sent to Fort Knox, Kentucky, for basic training. When I finished basic training, they would send me to the US National Hockey Team, based at the Metropolitan Sports Center in Bloomington, Minnesota. I was volunteering on his word and I had to believe him. I would be able to collect the regular Army pay each month at Fort Snelling. I would receive some per diem by the team for living expenses. Hopefully, it would work out as planned. I was lucky, and I was counting my blessings. It could have been much worse.

I continued to work at Marvin Windows until it was time to go. We gave up our apartment and Debby moved back in with her family. I went to Minneapolis a couple of days early and stayed with my brother Dave and his family. I was nervous about reporting to the Army. I was worried and I wasn't sure if it was going to work out like Murray said. Once I was in the Army, I was in and had no control of what happened after that.

Dave assured me that it was going to be alright. He served in the Navy. Unknowns always make me nervous, because I just do not know what I am getting into. Brother Dave hosted a going-away party. Jim and his wife, Lori, Richard Oshie, wife Carol, and a few others came to celebrate. We ate, drank and danced the night away listening to music. It was a good send-off.

CHAPTER 37: US ARMY

The next day I reported to the induction center in Minneapolis. Quite a few people were going in at the same time. There were people from Iowa, Wisconsin, and Minnesota. We had our physicals and went through the process of joining the US military. After the daylong event, we were on a bus and off to the airport.

We flew to Louisville, Kentucky, and then we traveled to Fort Knox by military bus arriving in the middle of the night. We were put into barracks, given pillows and blankets and were told to get some sleep—they would come for us in the morning.

We all hit the beds for a few hours of sleep. We were abruptly awakened at 5 a.m. by someone yelling and screaming. It was our drill sergeant telling us to get up and stand at attention. We were told to leave and lock our bags in the footlocker but no one had locks. We put our stuff in the footlocker and quickly made our beds, and assembled outside. After roll call, we marched to the mess hall to eat breakfast. Once we finished our breakfast, we assembled outside and started our reception process and orientation into the Army. Over the next week, we would be given our summer and winter uniforms and everything else we needed. We stood in line for everything from eating to going to the bathroom. We received haircuts. I kept my hair cut one inch long on top, Army regulations. We were given physicals, hearing, vision, aptitude tests and more orientation to the rules and regulations. We spent half of the time waiting in line. It took a long time to go through each line. It was Army life and it was miserable—hurry up and wait.

We were tired from not much sleep and all the standing around waiting in lines. There were fifty of us in our barracks. On the first day at the barracks, we had only a minute to put things away before we ate dinner. When I went through my foot-locker, someone had already stolen my new electric razor and a few other things of value. I was not the only one with missing belongings. After reporting it to the drill sergeant, he said, "Too bad, you should have locked it."

The drill sergeant noticed my haircut right away. I was the only one who did not get his hair cut all the way off. He immedi-ately called me to attention. He was face-to-face with me, yelling at me and asking me questions about not getting my hair cut all the way off. He asked me if I was some kind of rebel or radical. He asked me if I was special. He kept it up for five minutes or so. I told him that I was going to play on the US National Hockey Team right after boot camp. He did not believe me, called me a liar and went on and on. He told me to report to the mess hall in the morning for KP (kitchen patrol). I reported to the mess hall at 4:30 a.m. I was washing pots, pans, dishes and cleaning. I was there from 4:30 a.m. to 9 a.m, before I could join the group.

We were in the reception center for about ten days before we were put into a boot camp cycle. They kept us busy and each time I ran into a drill sergeant the same thing happened. I would be called to attention, yelled at, and asked if I was willing to get my hair cut now to be like everyone else. When I said "no, thank you Drill Sar-gent". I was given KP duty again. I had KP duty every day while I was in the reception center. They thought I would break sooner or later. By then my buddies were saying, "Boo-shay don't give in. We're all behind you."

US ARMY, 1970-72.

Figure 55

When the reception cycle ended, we were assigned to a squad in the barracks of the new company. We had our own drill sergeant, our own floor of the barracks, our own beds and footlockers to take care of. We were trained the Army way. They had their way of doing things and we had to learn to do everything the Army way. We drilled, went to class and did everything with the squad, including competing with the other squads over the 8 weeks.

The first two weeks our drill sergeant was on my back about my hair. He sent me down to the PX several times to get my hair cut. I would walk down there, have a beer and come back without getting it cut. He would give me KP or police call duty (picking up cigarette butts) after the day of drilling. It went on for a while, and then one day it stopped.

After ten weeks of marching, drills, classes, hiking, regulations, shooting, and camping, we were getting down to the end. It was not as bad then as we were use to the daily routine. Around week number six, some of the drill sergeants started believing me about playing for the United States Hockey Team. I scored nearly a perfect score in the PT test. Murray Williamson called the company officer (CO) and talked with him about me running extra at night after our duties. They called me into the office, and the young captains and lieutenants were interested in visiting with me about the US team. As I was leaving, I was stopped by the master sergeant, a real lifer. He said, "I don't have time for jocks, stay out of my way." The captains and lieutenants were amused, stood there listening and not saying a word. I stayed clear of that old guy the rest of my time.

In week ten, we had a graduation ceremony from boot camp, and relatives could come to watch. No one came from my family and I did not expect them to. Our squad was in formation while the drill sergeants were giving out the orders stating where to report after boot camp. When mine was called, all he said was, "Boo-shay, you know where you're going," and then he handed me the orders.

I was never so happy to get out of a place in my life. It was life changing. Everyone went their separate ways. Some ended up together in the same advanced individual training sites. I did not see anyone after that except for one kid a couple of years later in Wisconsin. I often wondered about who actually ended up in Vietnam, who lived and who died.

CHAPTER 38: US NATIONAL HOCKEY TEAM

I was looking forward to going home to Minnesota. I had my orders and my plane ticket, and I was on the bus to the airport. I was happy and I felt as if I was just let out of prison. All the rules and regulations in the Army, going through reception center and boot camp for ten weeks, getting yelled at on a daily basis was a growth experience. Being forced to get up at 4:30 a.m. to do a daily routine day after day would change anyone.

The US hockey team manager Hal Trumble had prepaid a ticket for me to fly back to Minneapolis. The others went to their advanced training units. We would start training camp at the Metropolitan Sports Center soon and some of the players were already skating. They scheduled an exhibition schedule with about 50 games throughout the US and Canada. After returning to the A Pool after the 1970 Tournament the players and staff were excited to start training. We would need to develop a competitive team for the 1971 World Championships in Bern, Switzerland. We would compete with the best in the world. I had not skated since April and it was November. It was a big difference from the year before, when I skated some 100 plus games. I was lean and in good shape from boot camp, so it would not take me long to get back into it. Skating is like learning to ride a bike: Once you learn, you never forget.

FORMER WARROAD HIGH SCHOOL
TEAMMATE LYLE KVARNLOV AND HENRY.
COURTESY OF KENNY KVARNLOV.

HENRY BOUCHA, #10 USA.

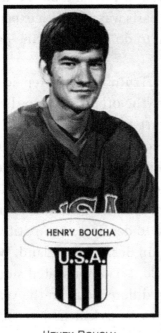

HENRY BOUCHA,
USA HOCKEY.

Figure 56

My brother David picked me up at the airport that day in Minneapolis. I had worn my civies (civilian clothes) and had my duffle bag full of my military clothes. I would stay with brother Dave and family until I could get a place of my own. My car and my hockey gear were in Warroad. I made arrangements to go to Warroad for a few days. Debby was 8 months pregnant, due in December and she was not enjoying the pregnancy. It was best for Debby to stay in Warroad with her mother.

The 1970-71 Hockey season was going to be exciting. It would be the first time that a US Hockey Team played together all year and would compete in a world championship. In the past, the team was put together at the last minute or only played together a short time before competing. This time would be against the A Pool, the best in the world: Russia, Czechoslovakia, Sweden, Finland, West Germany, and the United States were all in the Group A World Hockey Championships that year.

The tryouts for the US team were by invitation only. Players were coming and going on a weekly basis. They were flown in from all parts of the country. The US staff was trying to find the best available players to represent the United States in the World Championships in March. The team carried thirty to thirty-five players through the exhibition season. During our regular season we carried 25 to 27 players with a few players coming to play a few games here and there. All of our games were exhibitions, since we did not play in a league. Our schedule consisted of playing top college teams, foreign national teams and pro teams from the Western and Central Professional Leagues. These pro teams were very good and extremely challenging. The players were a step under the NHL, so the competition was comparable to what it was like playing against the top competing countries. We needed to be able to skate with them, and beat them to be successful in world competition.

Some of the players were told to find apartments because they would be staying on a more permanent basis. I was told that I could find one too. I was sincerely thankful that I made the team and did not have to go back into the active Army. I was able to go to Fort Snelling and pick up my military pay each month. It was base pay. While I was in boot camp, I set up a program with the military to have most of the check sent to Debby in Warroad for her living expenses. We agreed that she would pay her mother for rent and expenses.

This concept, of having a full time team had never been tried by anyone in USA Hockey. At first, the players were having trouble making ends meet. Some of us players requested a meeting with our coach and manager. We were trying to determine a budget to be able to live, and an amount of a monthly per diem that would work for us. Some of players were married and had kids, some were single. After some discussion, we finally agreed on an amount that we all could live with. It was not much—just enough to pay our rent, gas, utilities, and buy food. That was it. Things were tight. We really had to budget to make ends meet. Some of the spouses worked, the players worked part time, or the family helped them out. I worked part-time at Hubbard Broadcasting (TV station) handling mail and running errands. We were on the road so much that it really did not pay off too work. I did not have money to buy new clothes or anything that I needed. I was just surviving. I was still wearing the clothes I had in high school, and clothes I wore in juniors and it showed. I sent most of my money home to Debby. I remember one night when some of the players wanted to go out. I did not have the clothes and was not dressed very well. They wanted me to go with them but asked me if I was going to go out looking like that? I guess they were embarrassed for the way I was dressed. People in those days cared a little more about what they wore and how they were dressed.

I rented an apartment owned by Sid Hartman and his partners. Sid was a sportswriter for the *Minneapolis Tribune* and was an investor in the new apartment building near the Metropolitan

Sports Center. He was nice and gave me a deal. It was a new building and it had two bedrooms. I made arrangements to rent furniture, just the basics, a bed, dining room table, and a couch and chair. I borrowed a TV, and someone loaned me silverware, dishes, pots and pans to use. We played our schedule and had things very organized. I thought we had a good team, and we always added a few more good players at tournament time.

On December 14, 1970, Tara Marie was born in Warroad. I got the call just before practice that morning. I told some of the players and the coach. I was 19 years old and Debby was 18. In a nice gesture, the coach and manager had cake and coffee for me to celebrate my new, little, baby girl. The reception was held in the restaurant above the arena at the Metropolitan Sports Center.

It was not until late January that Debby came to Minneapolis. She was having medical problems and was sick and went back to Warroad after a short time. The team was coming and going all the time playing mostly on the road so with my schedule, I was not much help to her. We spent some time in Colorado Springs at the famous Broadmoor World Arena, and we were able to stay at the resort to train in the high altitude. We played several exhibition games at the Broadmoor World Arena in Colorado Springs and in Denver.

CHAPTER 39: 1971 WORLD CHAMPIONSHIPS

In mid-February the team made the final cuts, and we were in preparation for the 1971 World Championships in Bern and Geneva, Switzerland.

On March 10 we flew to New York and then on to London, then to Prague, Czechoslovakia. We were to play exhibition games against the Czechs. It would be my first time playing a team from the A Pool. I knew they were good.

The games would prove to be a test for us. I was confident and thought we had a strong team with experience and youth. It was a good mix. I thought we could play with anyone in the world.

It was mid afternoon when we arrived in Prague. It was behind the Iron Curtain but the city was nothing like Bucharest. It was clean and bustling with activity. We bused from the airport through the city to the International Hotel. It was an older, world-class hotel, and it was beautiful. We checked in and were allowed to relax and rest before we had our dinner. There was a mix up with our schedule and we did not have ice time. We played the next night with no morning skate or ice time before our game. At our first game with the Czechs, the crowd was huge, 14,000 plus, and the building was big with wood bleachers for fans to sit on. The eastern Europeans were dressed in those dark clothes as usual. The building was buzzing. The people were excited and ready for the game. The Czech team was a world power like the Russians. They had some great players and had on occasion beaten Russia.

It was in 1968 that the Russians invaded and had taken control of Czechoslovakia by force. The Czechs hated the Russians and had won the World Championship the year before.

As the game started, the Czechs came out flying. We were back on our heels, and they were beating us to the puck, swarming us on every shift. It was an Olympic size ice sheet, larger than the rinks in the United States and Canada. Our goalie was shocked early on and we were trying to hold on. In the middle of the first period, we hardly touched the puck and we were already down a couple of goals by the time our coach called a time-out. The fans loved it. It was deafening in the building. I was in shock too. These guys were great. I thought we did not have a chance of beating them. We hardly touched the puck. What an eye opener! This was the best team I ever played against. It did not help that we did not get on the ice to get the kinks out. I could see that because of the way they played, they could beat anyone. As in most cases when you are down, and hanging on, you have to try to slow them down. You start playing a little rougher. Well, this was no different. We went on the attack, there were some big hits and high sticks, and then the penalties started coming. In this game there was a Czech referee and a US referee whom we brought with us from Boston. The Czech referee had us in the box, and Lenny our referee tried to even it up. It was back and forth like that the whole game. It was a rough game, and the Czechs did not like the rough stuff. We lost decisively, but our rough play got their attention.

After the game we went back to the hotel. The hotel in Prague was much better than the hotel in Bucharest. It was much more alive and had all of the modern conveniences. We went to our rooms and freshened up, then to a private room for our meal.

The next day we were to play the Czech National Team, again. I was still amazed at how good the Czech team was and I tried to imagine how good the Russians might be. There was definitely a difference in quality of play in the A and B Pools. Some of our players had a few bumps and bruises, and I could not imagine how the Czech's felt after the beating we gave them with our rough play.

We were up fairly early in the morning and had breakfast. We walked around the city and looked at the shops. With the change in time zones and travel, we were still jet-lagged and trying to get adjusted. In one of the main squares you could still see the bullet holes in the buildings from the Russian invasion a few years before. I think they left the bullet holes there for all to see and remember. They were significant.

Once back at the hotel, we had our pregame meal, and some of us rested for the game. It was another late game, and we wanted to prove we could compete and try to play better. We would play each team twice, once in Bern and once in Geneva, as a double round-robin tournament. A format where we played each team twice and the winners were chosen by their won-and-lost record.

We were all up for the game and knew what to expect. We needed a better showing. We had to show them that we could skate with them. I felt our travel had affected us in that last game and we could do much better tonight. The arena was full to capacity and loud once again. The previous night, the second and third periods were full of penalties, and a couple of their players needed stitches. During that time, the crowd was whistling so loud that I thought my eardrums would burst. Instead of the fans booing, the Europeans would whistle. It was deafening and just about unbearable with fourteen thousand people making noise in the building.

When the puck dropped, the Czechs were a little hesitant at first, but were forceful and domineering once again. They were big and fast. It was not long and they came at us like flies. The puck movement was crisp and clear. They were everywhere, and all we could do was hang on. They were ahead again on the scoreboard and the crowd loved it. Then, like the night before, the penalties started coming as we tried to slow them down. The referees tried again to keep things in order and to keep things even, but the penalty box was full. The Czech crowd was going wild. They were whistling loudly and chanting. They had us by a few goals and were not letting up. The game got ugly when all we could do was run them and try to slow them down.

1971 WORLD ARENA, BERN, SWITZERLAND.

1971 NATIONAL TEAM GENEVA, Switzerland

1971 US NATIONAL TEAM.
FRONT: CARL WETZEL, DICK TOMASONI, DON ROSS, COACH MURRAY WILLIAMSON,
MANAGER HAL TRUMBLE, GARY GAMBUCCI, GEORGE KONIC, MIKE CURRAN.
MIDDLE: DR. NAGABODS, DICK MCGLYNN, TOM MELLOR, JIM MCELMURY, TIM SHEEHY,
HENRY BOUCHA, BRUCE RIUTTA, CRAIG FALKMAN, CRAIG PATRICK, PAUL SCHILLING,
BOB LINDBERG, TRAINER DON NIEDERKORN.
BACK: PETE FICHUK, LEN LILYHOLM, PETE TOOMEY, KEVIN AHERN,
AND KEITH CHRISTIANSON.

Figure 57

We lost the game significantly, and we were reeling in disappointment. We had to keep our heads about us and try to regain our composure and keep our positive attitudes. We tried to relax and enjoy our time in Prague.

While at the hotel, there was a movie being made called *Slaughterhouse Five.* It was set during WWII. We had a chance to meet and visit with the crew and actors. It was good to see other Americans in foreign countries. I saw the movie sometime later and enjoyed it.

The food was wonderful at the hotel. We really enjoyed the meals. The chefs were world class. During one of the evenings at the hotel, there was a college dance. Tom Mellor and I attended. We sat at a table and just watched as the students mingled and danced to a band. They were our age. The band was like the one in Romania, playing the old 1950s music and signing in English. The ballroom was full, and the students were dressed like it was a prom. There was a table of girls sitting next to us. After drinking wine, laughing, and joking, we talked to the girls. We said things and thought they could not understand us. We were shocked when some spoke English. They understood everything we were saying. We were making jokes about some of the people and the music. We were embarrassed, but the girls were nice about everything and wanted us to stay and visit. It was curfew time for us, and we had to go to our rooms. It had been wonderful to be in Prague. It was something that I will always remember. It was a beautiful city, and the people were hospitable.

As we arrived in Geneva, it was overcast and rainy. A bus brought us to the hotel, and we checked in. We had ice time later that afternoon. Some of the players were mending their injuries from the battle in Prague. Some of the injuries were more serious than we thought. We were in Geneva to play an all-star team the next night before going into Bern for the tournament. We sat the injured players so they could rest. The team we played was good, but we managed to beat them in a close and entertaining game. The crowd was enthusiastic and we enjoyed talking to some of the Americans after the game.

We left the hotel on March 17 on a bus to Bern, only a few of hours away. We were to check in and then practice at the tournament venue. As we arrived at our hotel, we pulled up next to a tram that was on rails going up a big hillside. As we departed the bus, we could see our hotel was sitting on top of a small mountain in the city of Bern. Wow, what a great view. We found out that the last tram of the night was at 11:00 p.m. and if you missed it you would either have to climb down the mountain or wait until the next day when the tram started running again.

We took the tram and arrived at the hotel. It was beautiful and had the elegance of an old world hotel. The view was spectacular. The rooms were large and comfortable. It was very quiet. There was no street noise, just the little sounds of the hotel. As we checked into our rooms, and put our stuff away, my thoughts were on the games in Prague and on the tournament. I was still amazed at how good the Czech's were, and I assumed how good the other teams must be. The Czech's sure took it to us and shattered our confidence.

It was exciting being here, and we knew we were in for a battle. What a difference in competition between the pools. The Czechs were so much better than anything that we had experienced so far. I thought this is what the NHL must be like. I was not sure I was ready for anything like that. I was wondering if they could keep up the passion and the high tempo day after day. It was fast and furious. It was so profound that I questioned my abilities to play at that level. I found out in Western Canada that playing day after day was very difficult, and it was hard to stay energized for each game and play with passion.

We went to practice at the tournament venue. The arena was fairly large and sat around 10,000 plus on bench seating. On the side of the rink and behind the seating area was an open air venue. The roof was high and the lights and flags were hung above the rink. The open air made the sounds on the arena muffled. There was an outside practice arena that teams could access for practice. The dressing rooms were large. I was surprised when they brought in a large kettle of tea with honey and lemon after practice and during games. I was getting use to it. I started to drink tea often and drank it during the games.

At the hotel, as we made our way down for dinner, the Russian National Team came walking in. They were dressed in their red sweat suits and they walked in with all of the confidence in the world, and why not; they were world champions and Olympic Champions for many years prior. We made our hello nods and passed by them. We ate in a private dining room, as did the Russians. It would be interesting staying in the same hotel with them. It would be interesting being able to watch them. They were gracious but no one spoke English, so it was hard to communicate with any of them. On occasion there would be an interpreter to interpret a few words back and forth between the players.

As we waited for our dinner, we sat there for some time eating these wonderful hard rolls with real butter and they were delicious. We asked for seconds, and then more. We knew that our meals would be long and we knew what to expect at our meals. They would be served slow, one course at a time, and we would be there for at least an hour and most likely longer.

We enjoyed badgering each other and voted on the "Ugly American Award," which we as a team would give to an individual who embarrassed himself, our team, or our country by doing something odd or wrong in public. Usually though, you got railroaded by your teammates and you got the award for something hilarious you did not actually do. Everyone received the award over the course of the trip. This year the award consisted of a red, white, and blue ribbon necklace and a head of a troll with long ugly hair attached to the end of it. You had to wear this around your neck all day whenever you were in public, no matter when or where you went, even to a governmental reception. It was embarrassing to wear. A person wearing it would have to explain to whoever asked about it. Once they understood the meaning of the award, they thought it was funny. Some people did not ask. They would look at you weird and just thought you were odd.

We would play the Czechs in our first game of the tournament. We knew what they had and how they played. We had some players still nursing injuries from the exhibition games with the Czechs in Prague the week before. We dressed twenty players: two goalies, twelve forwards, and six defensemen. That was all we had. With our injuries mounting, we were starting off the tournament already short and undermanned. Some of the players played with injuries and they were less than 100 percent.

In our first game, we upset the second-ranked team in the world, the Czechs. They had blown us off the ice in Prague the week before. Wow, they were very timid on the ice this time. They were not on their home ice. They did not want to go into the corners and did not want the rough stuff. They did not want to play this game against us and it showed. We skated to a 5–1 win. We shocked the world that night. *ABC's Wide World of Sports* called us and was ready to send a crew over to televise our games. They decided to wait to see how we would do against the Swedes a couple of days later before they made a commitment to cover the games.

After the game, we were stunned too. We celebrated and went back to the hotel. We met in a private meeting room to discuss the recent game and the next game against the Swedes. The coach was giving us his congratulatory speech, when the Russian coach, Tarasov, and the Russian team were passing in the hallway. When Tarasov saw Murray, he came barging into the room with a smile on his face to congratulate us for beating their nemesis, the Czechs. He picked Murray up by his head and gave him a big kiss on the lips, as is the Russians custom. When Coach Tarasov finally let Murray down, Murray stood there in shock with the dumbest look on his beet red face. We were roaring. Murray finally smiled and thanked him, and Tarasov smiled and waved and left the room. As Murray turned around toward us, we were all still roaring, Gary Gambucci said, "It was a good thing he did not know how to French kiss!" Everyone roared again.

We were on cloud nine and had gained some confidence, but our injuries were mounting. One of our goalies came down with a leg injury, and now three forwards were playing hurt and one out. Our next game was against Sweden. We had a day off between games and we practiced while the injured rested. After our practice, we looked around Bern and shopped and were able watched some of the other games. There wasn't much to do at the hotel. We were isolated once we were at the hotel and it was hassle going back and forth on the tram, or to get a cab. One of the games that day matched the Russians against West Germany. It was tied 2–2 at the end of the first period. The Russian coach, Tarasov, was so upset by the way they played the first period, that during intermission, he took the team out to the outdoor practice rink and skated the team the whole time. When the Russians came back on the ice, they scored three quick goals and scored another five in the third to put the game away.

It was interesting to be around the Russians at the hotel. They would not sit around or spend time in the lobby. They were always moving and doing something to keep active. They were kicking the ball and playing soccer outside. We were sitting inside visiting, playing board games, reading, and hanging out. Most of the time while we were watching them, we were eating those delicious hard rolls between meals. It was noticeable to me that the Russians were doing the right thing by moving and keeping active. Personally, I felt too sedentary at that hotel. We should have been more active. I remember how I felt during that time. I attribute our sluggishness to inactivity and sitting around eating those delicious hard rolls. Believe me we ate a ton of them. I know I felt sluggish through the first round of the tournament. It was better the second week when we stayed in Geneva. We got out more and move around, and were able to walk around the city.

LEN LILYHOLM AND HENRY BOUCHA IN SWITZERLAND 1971.

Figure 58

Against Sweden, the game was pretty even. We went back and forth, and both teams had their scoring chances. The game was tied 2–2 when I scored the go-ahead goal, but it was disallowed. One of our players had jumped over the boards onto the ice inside the blue line during a line change while I brought the puck into their zone. I used their defenseman as a screen and shot the puck from inside the blue line, and it went in. It was a weak goal, but it put us ahead in a close game. It would have given us a goal advantage and may have changed the outcome of the game.

Sweden came back right away, scored, and went ahead. It changed the momentum the other way. It stayed that way until they got an empty-net goal. Needless to say, *ABC's Wide World of Sports* did not come. Later they said it must have been a fluke to beat the Czechs. Again no one had any faith in us, and it was disheartening. We needed that win. With our injuries mounting, we played short handed the rest of the tournament. We had five players playing with injuries. The Russians won 10–2, and then it was Finland 7–4 and finally West Germany 7–2. With a full healthy team we would have won most of those games. We ended the first week of the tournament in last place, with 1 win and 4 losses.

It was on to Geneva for the second round of the tournament. We left Bern for Geneva and arrived later in the day. We checked in at the hotel and were summoned to a team meeting. It was our last week of the tournament, and we needed to finish out of the cellar. The pressure was on, and the injuries to some of the players were not healing as expected. Some of our injured players would dress, and the others would sit.

WATLER BROWN MEDAL.

Figure 59

The second week started with the same schedule as the first week, with the United States playing the Czechs. They were a different team this time around. They came out flying and beat us 5–0. It was Sweden the next game, and they squeaked by us 4–3 in a game we should have won. Then it was the game against the Russians, and they won 7–5. It was the closest game we had with them. We had our chances to win it on a couple of occasions. The Fins were tough and had our number that year for some reason. They played well

284

against us, beating us 7–3. Well, we were now sitting 0 and 4 and were going up against the West Germans, who beat us the first week of the tournament. We had to win to stay out of the bottom of the tournament, and we needed to beat them by more than five goals. We won the game 5–1. But we needed one more goal to stay ahead of them and out of the cellar. We did not get the goal and we ended the tournament in last place.

During the week in Geneva, we were invited to the Geneva Country Club for a reception. We were able to meet the actor William Holden, Charles Schultz (Peanuts) and other celebrities. We stayed a couple of days and then returned to the United States. It was hard to go home with a feeling of regret and defeat, and the last place finish in the tournament. We were injured and played short most of the time, and learned some valuable lessons during the tournament. It was time to regroup and set our goals for the 1972 Winter Olympics.

CHAPTER 40: BACK IN THE ARMY

It was a long trip home after our losses in the World Championships. There was not much to tell the family about the games. We saw some great places, beautiful sights and visited some interesting cities, but as for the games and USA Hockey, it was a disaster. It was back to the drawing board.

When we arrived in Minnesota, we all went our separate ways. I went back to my apartment in Minneapolis and rested. Over the next week, I cleaned the apartment and returned everything and brought things back to where they belonged. I made my way home to Warroad to see Debby, Tara, and the rest of the family. I had not seen Tara since early February and only for a couple of weeks while Debby was in Minneapolis. It would be good to visit with the family for a while, and get to know my daughter. I brought gifts and things from Prague and Switzerland for everyone.

I had an open airline ticket to Louisville (Fort Knox, Kentucky) where I was to report back into the Army. No one knew when I was to report. If I had been smart, I would have called my old company, gave them my contact information, and waited for my orders to come in. My company then would have called me to report. I didn't know that at the time. My team manager, Hal Trumble told me to just take a week off and then report. So after a week at home, I made my way to Fort Knox. When I arrived at my old company, they were surprised to see me and asked me what I was doing there. I said I was told to report here. They said okay and put me into a barracks and said my orders must be on their way. I waited and tried to stay out of the way. I thought about going back home again but I did not have any money to travel. After a week, they gave me duty in the office doing daily reports. I was there for a month before my orders arrived. I could have been home those weeks, on Army time. What a waste.

After my orders came, I was sent to Fort Gordon, Georgia. It was a long bus ride to Georgia. It was spring and I knew it would be hot. I had a lot of time to think on that trip. I was alone. I did not know anyone, and looking out the window reminded me of my bus trips in Winnipeg during my junior hockey days. I thought of my family back in Minnesota and of the unknown and uncertainty going to Fort Gordon. I was going into military police training, and the idea of another ten weeks of advanced military training was not pleasant. I had no choice. I would just go with the flow.

When we arrived at Fort Gordon, we were given our barracks and were scheduled into the routine cycle for training. The system was the same. About 250 men separated into platoons, and each platoon separated into squads that resided in barracks. We had daily routines of PT, classroom, and marching. We were up at 5 a.m. and had breakfast at 5:30 a.m. and formation at 6 a.m. We were finished around 5 p.m. and then had dinner. We usually had some free time after that. We stood in line to go to the bathroom, stood in line for breakfast, and stood in line for everything else. It was the way it was. Training was more lax than boot camp.

I found out later that Larry McLaughlin from Warroad was in training in the signal school at Fort Gordon. We got together. Then about week four of my training, my neighbor Dave Rose showed up for military police training also. He was across the field from me, going through a different cycle. We spent time together. Later on, when Larry and I were in our last weeks of training and we were permitted leave for a weekend, we took a bus to see another Warroadite, Steve Stoskopf who was in the Army in Savannah, Georgia. We partied it up for a couple of days. It was a blast. In all, there were four of us from Warroad close by. Nils Nelson, another Warroad boy, was at Fort Benning, but we didn't see him.

While at Fort Gordon, I bought a clipper and cut hair for the boys. I charged only a dollar for a haircut, and I was busy all the time. With no formal training, I did okay, and I made some spending money. I sent most of my monthly paycheck home to Debby and Tara and I lived on less than a $100.00 a month. I often wondered if Debby paid June rent from the money I was sending. Debby had a way of thinking that she was entitled to live there rent free, and that she did not need to pay, so on several occasions I reminder her to give her mother some money. I received a telephone call one day. A clerk came over from the CO's Office and found me. I thought maybe something was wrong. When I answered, to my surprise it was John Gilbert from the *Minneapolis Star Tribune.* He said, "Congratulations," and I said, "Thanks, but what for?" He said,"Haven't you heard?" I said, "No." He told me that the Detroit Red Wings of the NHL had drafted me. I was taken in the second round at number sixteen overall. I said, "Wow, that's my favorite team, and has been since I was a kid." I thought that was unbelievable. So that night after we finished our training, I called home and everyone seemed to know and they were excited. They had heard it on the news. Everyone was talking about it throughout the state of Minnesota. I thought it was a high draft choice since I had another year to go in the US Army and could not play. I had to fulfill my obligation to the Army before playing, but it was a win win situation for me. It allowed me to play for the US Olympic Team in Sapporo, Japan. It was a dream came true, and some long term goals reached. I just needed to stay healthy, get as much experience in International Hockey as possible and be patient.

During our final weeks at Fort Gordon, the excitement of being able to go home for a couple of weeks was building. We did all of our testing for weapons, procedures, jeeps, etc. I ran the PT test and received the five hundred points certificate, the best you could get. I received a certificate of recognition and a trophy for it. I had made some good friends at Fort Gordon. It was unfortunate that most of the 250 troops were going to Vietnam. I knew that I was going to play with the US National Team again, so I was not too worried about where I would end up. You always had that sneaky suspicion that the government might throw a curve at you, at any time. You just needed to wait until they handed you your orders. It was mid-July, and it was too early to be called for training camp. I knew I was going somewhere. There was talk of some of us going to Germany.

When we received our orders: I was going to Germany with about twenty-five other guys from the company, and the rest were to go to Vietnam. I felt fortunate, but I felt sorry for those who would be in Vietnam. I had two weeks at home before reporting to go to Germany. When we picked up our orders and flight tickets, we were all in a frenzy to get home. We took a bus from the post to the airport in Atlanta. There was one other guy from the Minneapolis area who was going my way, and we were on the same flight. We ended up checking our bags and heading to the gate together.

We were finally done with training in that horrible Georgia heat. It would be good to get home to northern Minnesota and cooler temperatures. When we arrived at the gate, the flight attendant said, "We have two seats in first class. We can upgrade you. Would you like them?" We looked at each other and said, "Yes, of course." We boarded first, and the stewardess helped seat us and asked if we would like something to drink. She smiled and said it is free. We were in seventh heaven. We had the biggest smiles on our faces as we got off the plane. Good thing the flight was not any longer. No one was there to pick me up, but his family was there. He was drunk as a skunk and having fun. I looked at them hugging; shaking hands and he had the biggest grin on his face as I passed by and thought what a beautiful sight. I hope he remembers that moment.

I took a cab to my brother David's in Minneapolis, and stayed until I figured how I would get up to Warroad. The two weeks visiting in Warroad, being able to see Debby and Tara and my family was nice. Spending time with everyone was wonderful, and it went fast. I was to report to Fort Dix, New Jersey, and then I was to fly to Frankfurt, Germany. It was always difficult traveling from Warroad to Minneapolis. There was no bus, planes, or trains going in either direction, so you needed a car, or a ride and an extra day of travel. I made my way to Minneapolis once again and stayed with brother Dave and family. I put my uniform on and made my flight to Newark, New Jersey, then took a bus to Fort Dix. Going to Germany would be my third trip to Europe in the past two years. I was excited to see Germany, but I was not excited to go back in the Army. It was only for two months or so until I got my orders to report to Minnesota.

Once I got to Fort Dix, I found out where I was supposed to be. I found some of the other guys who were in Georgia with me. We were all there in anticipation for our deployment to bases in Germany. We were all speculating. A sergeant showed up and made sure everyone was there and said our flight would leave in the morning. He showed us where we could bunk for the night.

When early morning came, we got the wake up call. We ate a quick breakfast and boarded the transport. We were all going to Frankfurt and would be held there until we got further orders. It was a long flight but we made it in one piece. We were at the reception, and processing center for a couple of days. While we awaited orders, we stayed in a barracks. We hung out and watched the local entertainment. The German beer was good but strong and we had a good time. When our orders came in, we were sent in different directions to different posts in Germany. My small group was heading to the Missou Army Depot, just outside of Kaiserslautern and close to the small town of Bruchmuhlbach.

Our group was put into a deuce and a half (a 2 ½ half ton truck), and we trucked down the autobahn (highway) to our destination a few hours away. As we were looking out the back of the truck at the scenery, we could see cars coming up behind us at over one hundred miles an hour. They were buzzing by us as if we were standing still. There was no speed limit on the autobahn.

Once we reached the Missou Army Depot, we were brought to the CO's office at the 189th Military Police Company. Some of us went to the 164th Military Police Company. We were briefed and given our assignments for barracks. I was in an eight-man room, with my own bed and locker. We were assigned to one of three shifts for duty. The shifts consisted of days, evenings, and "graveyards." We would rotate those three shifts and then have three days off. It was nice compared with boot camp and AIT training. It was like a regular job.

I went with the daily routine and tried to stay out of trouble. My hair had not been cut since I was in Georgia, and my hair was a little long and with my cap on it pushed my hair down over my ears. While I was on police call (picking up cigarette butts) with everyone else by our barracks, the CO noticed my long hair from his office window. He came out, chewed me out, and told me to get my hair cut. I said, "Yes, sir."

After he went back into his office, we finished up, and it was too late to get my hair cut as the PX barbershop was closed. So I let it go a couple of more days, and he caught me again outside our barracks. He really let me have it. He talked to my sergeant and gave me extra duty for two weeks. I got my hair cut, but I was doing extra duty by cleaning bathrooms. I did not say anything I just did what they told me. They even had me cleaning the walls and floor tiles and grout with a toothbrush. Then one day, my sergeant came and got me while I was cleaning. He said the CO wanted to see me. I went into his office, and he had a smile on his face. He had my orders and said with a smile, "So, it says here you're going to report to the US Olympic Hockey Team. Is that right?" I said, "Yes, sir." He asked me some questions about the Olympics, and we had a good visit and conversation about the US teams that I played on in the past and the world tournaments. He said, "Well, let me know if I can be of any help while you're here, and don't worry about the extra duty, it has been canceled." I thanked him and went back to my barracks. I never had any problem with anyone after that. I did my job and stayed out of trouble. We had some good times and I made some lifelong friends while I was there.

Tom Kohl was a good friend that I met in Germany. He was from Downers Grove, a suburb of Chicago. We had a great time in Germany and many more good times in Detroit and Chicago. There were others, I can only remember the nicknames of some of the people. One was Pineapple, of course he was from Hawaii. I did visit him in 1972 when Debby and I were in Hawaii. It freaked him out when I knock on his door and he answered. We had a good laugh. Then I saw a guy in Boston and a friend in New York over the years. Time fades away the memories of some of these fine times and wonderful journeys we were on. The names come back to me on occasion and I smile to think of those good times. We had our laughs.

The *Stars and Stripes* military newspaper interviewed me for a story on the players who were serving in the military and playing hockey for the USA. It was good story that was published while I was in Germany. I was able to attend a rock concert in Speyer over a long weekend. We camped out with friends at a local popular lake and had a few beers with the boy's downtown. We did a little sightseeing and ate some good food. I really did not have much time to tour or extra money to spend. I did my job, and it all worked out well. Toward the end, I ran and worked out regularly.

Once I got all of my paperwork for transfer signed and turned in, I caught a ride to Ramstein Air Base to get a hop to the United States on a military transport. I had to wait my turn. There were several flights going to the US daily. You would try to get near your final destination, and the office would help you get as close as you could. I took the first flight I could. I was not sure where I was going to land in the US and did not care as long as I could hop a ride. So I took whatever I could get. The team would pay my flight to Minneapolis from anywhere in the US. It didn't take long once I was on the flight list. I wound up flying into Charleston, South Carolina.

CHAPTER 41: 1972 OLYMPICS

I arrived that night in Charleston. I had about twenty-five dollars in my pocket. I called our team manager, Hal Trumble, and he prepaid a ticket to Minneapolis for me. I picked it up at the ticket counter, and my flight was not until the next day. I was tired, and I did not have enough money for a room. I thought I would wait and sleep in the airport. While talking with some other Army personnel, most were in the same boat as I was. One guy said we could pool our money and get a room. He seemed okay, and I was tired and a good shower would be nice. I had not showered for two days. We got the room; I showered and went to sleep. His plane left before mine. I was not leaving until late morning, so I had plenty of time. I woke up and looked around. He was already gone, and I did not think anything of it. I still had plenty of time to get over to the terminal, it was across the street. I got up and looked out the window, and was happy to be back in the USA. I was excited to start the day and get home. I looked around for my plane ticket and money. *Oh, no,* I thought, and then I re-checked my pants pockets and everywhere else. The guy had taken my plane ticket and all of my money and left me there flat broke. He was long gone. I was stranded with no money and no ticket.

There was nothing I could do except to call Hal Trumble again and tell him what happened. He laughed and said, "You're kidding." I said, "No, I'm not. I am stranded in Charleston, South Carolina."

1972 US OLYMPIC SILVER MEDAL TEAM.
FRONT: PETE SEARS, KEITH CHRISTIANSON, COACH MURRAY WILLIAMSON,
MANAGER HAL TRUMBLE, TIM SHEEHY, MIKE CURRAN.
MIDDLE: TRAINER BUDDY KESSEL, BRUCE MCINTOSH, JIM MCELMURY, LARRY BADER,
FRANK SANDERS, RON NASLAND, WALLY OLDS, CHARLIE BROWN, TIM REGAN,
TEAM DOCTOR- DR. NAGABODS.
BACK: MARK HOWE, CRAIG SARNER, TOM MELLOR, HENRY BOUCHA, DICK MCGLYNN,
KEVIN AHERN, ROBBIE FTOREK, STU IRVING.

Figure 60

He said, "No problem. I'll prepay another ticket for you, and cancel the other one." I left on my regular scheduled flight. I got into Minneapolis and called brother Dave for a ride to his house. I made arrangements to go to Warroad to see Debby, Tara, and the rest of the family for a few days.

I started skating as soon as I returned from Warroad. There were over 40 players at camp. We had players coming from all over the country for tryouts. We skated in Bloomington for a couple of weeks, and then moved the camp to Bemidji. In Bemidji the players were housed in the dorms at the State College. Murray moved me into a cabin so I could bring Debby and Tara in for a week. That was nice of him, we had not been able to see each much since the summer of 1970. I was grateful.

We would eventually end up back in Minneapolis and I was looking for a place to rent for the season. Dave's wife, Donna—we called her Tudy—had a stepbrother by the name of Herb Trimborn. He graduated from Warroad High School in 1963 or '64. He and his wife LaRae, managed an apartment building in Bloomington. He said he would set me up when I moved back to Minneapolis for the 1971-72 hockey seasons. He said to tell the other players who needed a place to come see him. I said "okay." I hadn't seen the apartments yet. I trusted Herb, and I was sure he would take good care of us.

Tudy, bless her soul, died of cancer in 1992. She was a fine woman. She was very shy, caring, and lovable. She never said a bad word about anyone. Her stepbrother, however, was a spitfire, a mouthy, compact but powerful little character. He was the chain-smoking, hustler type, always after the almighty dollar. On the other hand, he was a hardworking and likable guy. He was all that and had a quick wit and he was hilarious.

In Bemidji, in the brisk, early morning weather, we ran around the field house and underneath large pines and other trees, crunching on the leaves that fell the night before. Although I disliked running, it was brisk and refreshing. We skated hard, conditioned, worked on plays, on special teams, and hit the weight room. We went through the routine twice a day. I could tell this year was going to be different. In the past we skated and played our games, and that was it. Conditioning was vital, but we skated our way into shape. We learned a lot from the previous year in Bern. We had a terrible showing and had a lot of injuries. Weight lifting, stretching and preparation would be the key this year. We had something to prove, and that was a great motivator.

Murray had taken into consideration how the Soviets trained in the weight room, did their dry-land training, and practiced on the ice. After being embarrassed in the 1971 World Championships, those of us who were there knew what we had to do to compete. Injuries would kill a team's chance during the tournament. We also worked on injury prevention by doing more stretching and innovative training processes. I liked it. It was different but effective.

We were in Bemidji for a few weeks before breaking camp. We played a few exhibition games in the area and were going to Duluth to play against a couple of teams out of the Central League. The Central League was made up of players who were under contract with the NHL clubs. The players were in development and were in that league to get more experience.

When we returned to Minneapolis, I stayed with my brother Dave and his family. I looked at the apartments Herb and LaRae were managing. The building was only a mile from the Metropolitan Sports Center, so it was very convenient. It was furnished with everything, from towels to silverware to furniture. It was a short-term rental apartment building that stewardesses, pilots, or business people rented. You could rent for a few days, a week, or a month at a time. It was not high quality but would do just fine.

It was close to brother Dave's too. I rented an apartment, and a couple of other players rented there also. Some other players rented apartments nearby, so we were all close. Debby was anxious to come to Minneapolis with Tara. We would be home for a few weeks before going to Colorado Springs for another series of training in the high elevation and to play exhibition games out of the Broadmoor World Arena. It was nice to train out there. It was always warm, bright and sunny. We stayed in a dorm just across the street from the world-famous Broadmoor Hotel. It was part of the Broadmoor complex and we had our own chef. The food was amazing. At that time, Debby's brother, Terry, and his wife were living in Colorado Springs. Terry was in the Air Force and was stationed there. They came to our games and took me out to dinner. It was good to see someone from home.

It was near Thanksgiving when we returned to Minneapolis. We played and toured out east with some great college teams before Christmas. We schedule a holiday series with the Czechs, and the Russians. In Minneapolis we prepared and worked hard for the games. It would be a great test for us, and we were anxious to see how we matched up with these teams. Most of the regular national team players were on these teams, and some new ones.

Sweden canceled us out of their tournament in January. They did not think we could complete with the world powers. It hurt and we were disappointed. It embarrassed us and made us more determined, and we wanted to show them that we were worthy. It stuck in our minds the rest of the year and into the Olympics.

Against the Czech, we finished strong, we split the series with them. The Russians were a different story. They had the Red Army Team with some new players in the lineup, but they were as strong as ever. We lost to them in Colorado Springs and then in Minneapolis. During the game in Minneapolis, we brawled with them. My nose was broken when one of the Russians came out of the penalty box and sucker punched me from the side while I was wrestling with another Russian player. I found out how weak I was compared with the Russians. They were solid, even the smaller players. You could tell they had trained a long time in the weight room.

We played the Russians in Saint Louis, and it was one of our better games. We had them on the ropes, but they prevailed 7–5. They embarrassed us in Philadelphia and in New York. The Russians were good, and it would be a miracle if we could keep it close. They were in their prime, and we were a bunch of college-age kids who had a dream.

Despite losing to the Russians, we were playing well and the team was coming together. We trained hard in the weight room and on the ice. We were winning most of our games against the pro teams, and we felt good about where we were–going into the Olympics. The coaching staff was still looking for a player or two, and we were close to making their final selections for the Olympic roster. The management made a couple of last-minute player additions. We just returned from Dallas/Fort Worth, where we won both games. We were cautious in those games, and aware of the injury possibilities, no one wanted to come up with an injury before the Olympics.

After returning to Minneapolis we were in preparation for the Olympics. We trained hard for a week, both on and off the ice. The day had arrived and we were excited. All of the US Olympic teams were to meet and report to Denver for orientations, get our instructions and depart on one plane. We were in Denver for a few days while we were outfitted with our travel gear, sweat suits, parade outfits, etc. We practiced while we were there for a couple of hours per day. Once the teams we assembled, outfitted, and ready, we boarded a Pan Am flight that took us to Seattle, to Anchorage, and then to Sapporo, Japan. However, we could not land in Sapporo because of heavy snow, so we were re-routed to Tokyo to stay overnight or until we could land in Sapporo.

The hockey team stayed on the same floor at the hotel in Tokyo and we gathered in one room. It was amazing that each room had these nice refrigerated units with candy bars, pop, and other goodies in them. We thought they were free, so we took pop, candy and snacks. When that room ran out, we would move to another room and do the same thing. Finally, we went to bed, and during the night I was awakened. As I looked up out of a deep sleep, I saw the light in our room was swaying back and forth. It was an earthquake! It woke me up but I was so tired that I just looked at it and went back to sleep. When we got our wake-up call, I woke up a bit disorientated and jet lagged because of the time change. We also crossed the International Date Line. We had no idea what day or what time it was. I showered, packed and went downstairs for breakfast. As I got to the front desk, our coach was in a fury, and he was arguing about the bill. All of those things that we had consumed in the rooms during the night were on our bill. He was furious, and after a few choice words, he paid the bill and then had a few comments for the players about eating all of those snacks.

We were excited to see Sapporo. Once we arrived, I was amazed at all of the snow. I had no idea that Japan even had snow. The airport was small but bustling with people. We retrieved our bags, and the bus took us to the Olympic Village. We received our orientation in the reception center, as well as our identification, passes, food vouchers, and apartment assignments. There were four of us to an apartment. They all had two bedrooms, a bath, and a living room. The buildings were four stories and built like regular apartment buildings. The apartments were to be used as housing after the Olympics. The apartments were small, like the Japanese people, so most of us had to duck when entering the rooms.

The complex was well secured with front and back gates and armed guards at each entrance. Guards and police in small cars patrolled the outer fence. In the village was a common area where athletes could gather, get a haircut, a disco, shops, restaurants and other stores to mingle and socialize.

The main restaurant for the athletes had world-class chefs. It actually had four separate parts to it. It had European, Far Eastern, Japanese, and American food served in each section. We had a ticket for every meal, and you could choose to eat in any area you wished and eat as much as you wanted. We had a chance to see the stadium where we would play our games, and we were able to practice. The lighting in the arena was good and it sat around 12,000.

They arranged for us to play two exhibition games in Tokyo before our schedule started at the Olympics. So it was off to Tokyo for a few days. It was a short flight, and we were bused from the airport to the hotel. The hotel was downtown, and the bus ride was amazing. I could not help but remember WWII and seeing many films about the Japanese. The city was old yet modern, with bustling streets. There were thousands of people and thousands of automobiles driving in frenzy. It was alive and things were happening and activities were everywhere.

After we checked in and settled into our rooms, we had a team meal and received a few words of advice, and then they allowed us to walk around the city. We had curfew, but we had a few hours to see some of the sights. As we walked down the sidewalk, we were taller than most of the Japanese. We had our USA jackets on, and they would say hello and maybe say a few words in English to us as they welcomed us to the city and to their country. They were extremely polite, gracious, and happy people.

We stopped in several shops and found some gifts, and as we were walking down the street, we noticed a McDonald's down the way. We just had dinner, but we could not help but want a Big Mac and fries, so we headed over there. When we arrived, we talked to some American soldiers; they were surprised to see us and wished us luck in the games. Some were stationed at Osaka Naval Station near Tokyo, and some at other bases. They said they came into the city all the time by rail and that the Osaka station was just a half hour from there. We ate our meal and walked around some more before heading back to the hotel. I was talking with one of our teammates, Dick McGlynn, from Boston, who was known as our team character. He always had something to say and was always joking or picking on someone. There were five of us that were active Army playing on the Olympic team. His big idea was that if Osaka was that close, maybe we should get up in the morning and take the train to the PX. We could get great deals on some stereo equipment and have it shipped back to the United States. He always seemed to have money. His dad was the Mayor of Medford, MA and he must have been supporting him. Most of us did not have that kind of money to spend. "It would be a great deal", he said. Tim Sheehy and I decided to go along with him. I really did not have the money to spend on stereo equipment, but I went anyway. We had a game that night, and we needed to be back at the hotel by mid-afternoon. We took a cab to the station and boarded the train. They had a big sign that said in English "Osaka Naval Base" at the stop. We got off the train and went to the PX, no problem. Dick and Tim bought some equipment and had it shipped back to Minnesota.

All was well. We got back to the train station okay, and we thought we had plenty of time to get back to the hotel before anyone knew we were gone. There were no signs saying in English which way to go back. We got on the train, but it was going the wrong way. We were heading away from Tokyo, and it was getting late. By the time we realized it and got turned around and were headed back to Tokyo, we were cutting it close.

When we finally got back to the right place, we got a cab at the station, and the driver didn't speak any English. We told him to hurry to the hotel, and he was driving like a maniac through the traffic. We got to the hotel, and the bus was gone. The same cab driver was waiting there and looking at us, so we jumped back into this little cab and tried to ask him where the arena was. He was trying to understand us. He finally realized what we were saying. We did not know the name of the rink where we were playing. Oh, my God, what would we do? The driver thought he knew where the arena was, so we took off. While on the bus coming in from the airport the day before we had driven past it. We all had a good look at it, and we were able to give the cab driver a description of it. Amazingly, he understood. By this time we were in a total panic. We were in trouble, and we did not know if we were going to make the game at all. The cab driver was driving crazy and passing everyone in front of him, and we were wondering if we were going to have an accident. He was a maniac. Dick was sitting in the front seat, saying, "Oh, Oh, Oh, Wow, did you see that?" Then he let out a big laugh as the cabby swerved through traffic. Yeah, we saw it all right. We were frozen in the backseat, praying.

We finally made it to the rink and gave the cabby a big tip. They would not let us in the building. Then we had to talk our way in. They did not think we were players. We sent someone to our locker room and got our trainer, and he came out to get us. Oh, my God, as we entered the arena, our team was on the ice for warm-ups. When we got into the locker room, our coach went berserk. He was screaming and yelling at us, and I thought he was not going to let us play. I was the leading scorer and Tim was the second-leading scorer, and we are playing the Czechs in a sold-out building. So after he calmed down and thought about it, he let all three of us play. He was not about to let his two top scorers not play, McGlynn was the instigator but Murray let him play too. We lost, to make things worse, and the team did not play well. We had another game the next night against Poland, and we needed to get back on track. There were some one-on-one meetings the next day. We won the next exhibition game against Poland. At those meetings, the coaching staff suggested that we focus on our task at hand, and to be ready for some tough competition, and stay away from any distractions, to put it mildly. When things like that happen, it's no joke, we disrupted the teams focus and as a result we lost. I felt bad for my teammates and we apologized for that incident.

We flew back into Sapporo, excited to start the festivities and get settled back into the Olympic Village. The opening ceremonies were in a few days. We were all thrilled and excited to be there. We settle in and practice and got accustom to our surroundings.

On opening day, we got up and had breakfast. It was a beautiful, bright and sunny day. We dressed in our parade uniforms. I don't know what we were supposed to look like, but most of us were glad we only had to wear them once. We had blue leather boots that were up to our knees and that looked like Santa Claus boots with the white fur around the top. We had pants that were stretchy-looking blue jeans with a belt. We had a white wool turtleneck. We had a full-length blue leather coat, with a long red-and-white candy-striped scarf that we wrapped around our neck and threw over our shoulders. A blue broad-brim leather hat, with gloves to match, completed our uniforms.

The women looked charming and elegant. They looked great in red capes and hats like Betsy Ross wore. As we were gathering in front of our building, we took pictures of each other. The bus brought us to the outdoor stadium, which was filled to capacity. The Honorable Emperor of Japan was there with his family, as were all of the Olympic dignitaries and invited guests.

As we assembled outside the stadium, we were all very excited and were able to visit with some athletes from other countries. We had difficulty walking on the snow. Our boots had leather souls and were slippery on snow and ice. When we marched into the stadium, we had to hang on to each other to keep from falling down. Still, it was an amazing experience and a moment that I will always cherish. When I heard the announcer say "And here is the United States of America," I actually choked up. This was the dream, something I would think about as I was playing road hockey or playing on the river, many years before.

We watched the Olympic hockey teams come into Warroad and play our Warroad Lakers. They always were nice and talked with us kids. What an experience for a young person to be able to see that. Then to fast-forward ten years and be able to walk into the Olympic stadium and experience it firsthand made you want to jump for joy.

FROM LEFT: LEFTY CURRAN, ROBBIE FTOREK, HENRY BOUCHA AND KEITH CHRISTIANSEN.
AT THE OLYMPIC VILLAGE IN SAPPORO, JAPAN.

OPENING CEREMONIES.

HENRY AND JACK PLOOF AT THE OLYMPIC
VILLAGE PRIOR TO THE OPENING CEREMONIES.

Henry Boucha (USA)

US OLYMPIC TEAM.

Figure 61

Once we walked in and went around the oval, we settled into our place and watched the people and the ceremonies, including the lighting of the Olympic flame. We listened to all of the speeches and heard the emperor open the games and watched the balloons rise in the winter air on a clear, bright sunny day. It was glorious and monumental. Once the ceremonies were over, we marched back out of the stadium and got on our bus and went back to the Olympic Village to change and prepare for our Olympic schedule.

To get into the Olympic medal round, we had a play-in game against Switzerland that we absolutely had to win. All teams had play-in games, except the Russians, who as defending gold medalists were exempt. It was a close game and we had to work hard, but we prevailed 5–3. Our team was healthy, with no injuries to worry about.

In the next game we played Sweden. We had two close games in the 1971 World Championships. We felt we could have won. Sweden, however, was ranked pretty high coming into the Olympics and was favored to win a medal. Sweden played outstandingly. They had great goaltending and won the game 5–1. The games would not get any easier. We were scheduled to play the Czechs in two days. In between games, we practiced in the mornings and had a chance to go see some other events.

We checked out the disco and meeting areas and visited with some of the other athletes. It was exciting and everyone seemed friendly and wanted to get to know you. The language barrier was difficult, but we managed to have fun anyway. There was always an interpreter around to translate for you and if not we still managed to use hand gestures and have fun. We never lost focus; our games were always in the back of our minds.

Our next game was scheduled for a late-afternoon, the second of three games that day at the venue. We had a light breakfast and a light skate in the morning. It was always nice to calm our nerves and to be able to spend time in the locker room for awhile and get prepared. We watched part of the Russian/Sweden game. It was a fantastic game, fast and furious. The Swedes were playing well and would challenge the Russians for gold that year.

We bussed back to the Olympic Village to have our pregame meal and rested for a while before the game. We heard that the Swedes had tied the Russians in their game, 3–3. Wow, that had not happened in years. There was a tremendous number of NHL scouts at the games. The Detroit Red Wings scouts were there, watching to see if any of the players were ready to make the jump to the NHL. There were five of us players on their protected list or draft choice.

We played a Czech team that had some of the regular national team players on it in the United States around Christmas. Then we played the regular team in Tokyo, losing in that exhibition game. We had split with this team in the World Championships in 1971.

We were ready. We came to play and it showed. We scored first and felt that we were dominant, killing penalties and using our bodies in an all-out attack. They were back on their heels this time, and we won the game 5–1. Although many called it an upset, we won decisively. It was nice to celebrate a win at the Olympics in the medal round. We were 1–1 going into a game with Russia. We had a day off the next day, so we practiced and went out to see some of the other events.

During that time, Jack Ploof, my boyhood friend from Warroad. He was living and working in Okinawa. Jack worked for a communications company and was stationed there. He was close and wanted to come over to the Olympics and see me. He called me in the US and told me he would try to get in touch with me once I reached the Olympic Village. One day I got a call from the main gate, stating that I had a call and ask if they could put the call through. It was Jack. He said he was at the Sapporo airport, and he asked what he should do. I told him to come to the Olympic Village and call me from the main gate. Sure enough, the phone rang and it was Jack. He said he was at the front gate. So I picked up an extra USA jacket and went to see him. At the main gate, we greeted each other and laughed. I suggested we go for a walk, and we walked away from the front gate. I told him to put the USA jacket on, that I was going to try sneak him into the Village and he could stay on the couch. We walked around to the back gate, as we walked up to the gate, we just said, "Hello, how are you?" The Japanese guard just smiled and let us through. The guard did not even check Jack's ID or look for any identification. Jack looked like an American—blond hair, blue eyes—and had a great smile. We were in. I could not believe it. We went to our apartment in the village. He was able to see everything we saw and go to places inside the village that no one else could experience. He was overwhelmed. I gave him meal tickets, and he came along with us to the venues and to the games and participated in everything we did. I introduced him to the coaches and the other players and he was right at home. He became part of our entourage. This could never happen again. Especially after the 1972 summer games in Munich, with the kidnappings and killings, the security became stricter.

Sapporo was magnificent and extremely friendly. They had ice sculptures the size of buildings downtown on the main street. They were lit up with colored lights, and the artistry was in great detail. They were beautiful. The whole community was festive. You were greeted with a smile wherever you went and treated like a celebrity.

Against the Russians, we would need to play a near-perfect game if we were to have any chance of winning. They were the defending Olympic and world champions and the team that would go down in history at some point for winning the world championships and Olympics so many times over the years. They beat us at every part of the game, winning 7–2. We were bewildered. We were not in the same league as they were, but we had to move on, get over it, and hope the best was to come. We would need to play a sound game in two days against Finland. We thought we could beat Finland, although they beat us in both games in the 1971 World

Championships in Switzerland. In preparation, we had to forget about the Russian defeat and concentrate on this game. We could not afford to lose again. Finland was coming off a 7–1 trouncing by the Czechs, so we felt that the team may be down and we could take advantage of the situation. We had a day's rest, and we were healthy going into that game. Meanwhile, Sweden beat Poland by the score of 5–3. It was not a good showing for the Swedes, but they won and that was the name of the game.

We were playing a late-afternoon game, and as before we went to the rink, had a light skate, and observed for a while at the arena. We caught part of the Czech/Sweden game before heading for our pregame meal and a rest. We found out that the Czechs had beaten the Swedes 2–1. We needed this game against the Fins if we were to have any shot at a medal.

When the game started, we were all over the Fins. We hit them, fore checked the heck out of them, and took control right off the bat. We ended up winning 4–1, and we had an outside chance of getting maybe a bronze. We heard rumors the Swedes were having some internal problems but really didn't know what that was all about but it seemed they were faltering. We had to play hard and control our own destiny.

With the next day off and our final game coming up with Poland, we tried to relax, take in some of the Olympics, and enjoy our time away from the rink. We ventured out to the other events and socialized with some of our new friends. We had a tremendous time.

The next day was game day. We knew we were favored to win the game, but we still needed to come to play. We knew we might have a shot at a bronze medal. There were still games to be played that would determine the outcomes. Our record stood at two wins and two losses. We needed this win. There was nothing anyone could say that had not already been said. We were in great shape and we stayed focused. We did our own thing everyone has their rituals and schedule before playing in a game, some more extreme than others but it is still a routine that we all go through to prepare ourselves for action, and get motivated in our own way to play our best.

As soon as the puck dropped, we took advantage of the Poles' mistakes and scored. We played great and our goalie, Lefty Curran, stood tall in the nets once again. Lefty was having the tournament of his life, and we could not have done it without him. He was absolutely terrific. We won the game 6–1. We now had three wins and two losses.

We had to wait until the next day to find out where we stood. It was Sweden vs. Finland; we figured the Swedes would win that one hands down. The Swedish team was in turmoil for some reason. We heard some of the players were having problems. This would take away from their focus and it would be hard to play. If they lost to Finland, it would elevate us into second. We planned to go to the game and cheer for Finland. Why not, look at what was at stake?

Then it was the Russians vs. the Czechs. If both the Czechs and the Swedes lost, we would win a silver medal. It was hard to sleep that night. We celebrated our 3–2 record and a possible bronze medal. If Sweden beat Finland, and if the Russians beat the Czech's, we would have identical records with the Czechs. We beat the Czechs, so we would have the Bronze. However if Sweden lost to Finland, Sweden would go from Silver to forth and no medal. It was out of our control. We had nothing left to do but wait, hope, pray, and watch.

Well, as it turned out, both games were in our favor. The Fins beat the Swedes in an upset 4–3, and the Russians beat the Czechs 5–2. Here's how it played out: The Russians took the gold, the United States took the silver, and the bronze went to the Czechs. Although the Czechs and the United States had identical records, we had beaten the Czechs, giving us the silver medal. The Swedes had a total collapse in the last two games and finished out of the medals. We couldn't believe it. We celebrated.

1972 OPENING CEREMONIES.

Associated Press

Keith Christiansen of International Falls represented the United States hockey team and stood on the podium as team members received silver medals Sunday at Sapporo, Japan, after placing second in the Winter Games.

MEDAL CEREMONIES.

Figure 62

OLYMPIC SILVER AND PARTICIPATION MEDALS.

Figure 63

The medal ceremony was exciting. We all stood there and received our medal, one by one. There was a huge crowd, and we stood and listened to the Soviet national anthem, with our silver medals. It was an amazing moment, but where were the US cameras and the reporters? There was nothing—no interviews or cheers for us. We felt abandoned and walked away feeling underappreciated. We knew what we accomplished, and we knew how important it was to USA Hockey and the US Olympic Committee. The US TV media left the country and we had no fanfare or recognition.

We celebrated most of the night and were scheduled to leave the next day. We had trouble getting up, organized and going. On the flight to Anchorage, we received a message from President Richard M. Nixon congratulating us on our silver medal. It was a long flight to Anchorage. We slept most of the way. It was truly amazing; every time we woke up we had a smile on our face. When someone came by with a message, it seemed to be good news. We heard that the Army was giving troops a six-month early out because they were pulling troops out of Vietnam. I qualified for that. That was wonderful. That means I could muster out when I got back. Then, in another message, I was the number one draft choice by the Minnesota Fighting Saints of the World Hockey Association.

When we landed in Anchorage to fuel we did not get off the plane. We fueled and took off again for Chicago, another 6 plus hour flight. It was a long fourteen-hour flight from Sapporo to Chicago. Then we still had a flight to Minneapolis. We were excited to get home. When we finally arrived in Chicago, we all wore our silver medals when we departed the plane. We did not know what to expect. We thought maybe there would be welcome home celebration and media interviews. We walked off the plane and there was nothing. We walked off the ramp to the terminal just like any other passengers. This was the United States Olympic plane coming directly from the 1972 Olympics in Sapporo, Japan. There was nothing there and no one to greet us—no signs, cameras, or reporters. Disappointed, we walked down to our gate and sat around and waited for our flight to Minneapolis.

CHAPTER 42: HOMECOMING

When we arrived in Minneapolis, we knew someone would be there to greet us, even if it was just our families. Again, we wore our medals. As we got off the plane, there was a TV camera, a reporter, and most of our families as they cheered us down the ramp and into the terminal—an event that lasted about ten minutes. Debby was in town but did not come to the airport. She waited for me at the apartment. We got our baggage and made our way home. Coming home was anticlimactic but it was good to be home.

Once I got to the apartment, I was greeted by Debby. It was nice to come home to someone. I took a much needed shower and we spent some time together. I called family in Warroad and they were glad to hear from me. Everyone was excited that we won a silver medal and we had success in the Olympics. It was nice to be home and just relax. It had been another long season, with the stress of competition and winning a medal at the Olympics. We answered our critics with a silver medal and thought that would shut them up once and for all. It was for all of those people who loved you when we were winning and disowned you when you lost. Now they all wanted to be a part of it. We had our critics all year, from the bene-factors, supporters, fans, some USA Hockey people and many oth-ers who quit on us or didn't believe we would accomplish anything, especially win a medal. Well, we proved them wrong. It was a nice feeling.

We got a call the next day from our manager telling us that the team was invited to Las Vegas. The team would be hosted by Ralph Engelstad, a casino owner in Las Vegas. The whole team, wives, and girlfriends would be able to go. We would play his Las Vegas Outlaws Team in two games over the weekend. We could handle that. We called June, Debby's mother right away, and she agreed to watch Tara while we were gone.

Meanwhile, the Minnesota Fighting Saints called and wanted to talk. I had not really thought about that very much. I was still in the US Army, and getting an early out would dictate what I could do next. I had not even talked to an agent or an attorney about representation.

I got a call from our coach, Murray Williamson. He said Ned Harkness, GM of the Red Wings would be in Las Vegas to talk with me. He suggested that I play it cool and that he would help me. He told me that I did not need to do anything but wait and see what they had in mind. I could wait and discuss my options with someone later.

Ironically, the Red wings were in town to play the North Stars, and Hal Trumble, our manager offered tickets to go. So most of the team went and watched the game. Tim Sheehy came up to me and said, "Hey, they got your name on the Detroit roster for the game." I said, "What?" Then he showed me the program. Sure enough, it was there. I did not know what to think as I watched the game. I was wondering if I could even play with these guys. They looked pretty good from where I was sitting.

The next day I checked with the military. I qualified and could obtain an early out. I was still assigned to the team, so I had time. I would need to pick a time and a place. I would wait to figure that out later. Things seemed to be happening fast.

After a nice flight to Las Vegas, the weather there was like summer. We were celebrating as we checked in at the hotel. We did not play until the next day, so we had dinner plans and saw some of the sights of the city. Debby and I never vacationed before, so it was all new to us. We enjoyed ourselves. We saw Paul Anka at a dinner show at Caesars Palace, gambled a little and strolled around. Things were good.

Our game was the next night, and we had no idea who the Las Vegas Outlaws were. We had not skated since our last game in the Olympics against Poland, so we were all a little rusty. We partied and celebrated late. We slept in late, and the team ate lunch together. After lunch some of us rested, and others went out to the casinos to try our luck again. We all met in the lobby before the game, and we took a bus to the arena. The wives would follow later.

It was game time, and Ralph Engelstad was quite the promoter. The building was full as we stepped on the ice for warm-ups. Although we were rusty and had not played or skated in a week, it all came back very quickly. We looked over the Las Vegas team as we skated around, and they seemed enthusiastic. I am sure they wanted to make a good showing and maybe even beat us. We were proud bunch of guys and were not about to let something like that happen.

When the game started, we realized that compared with the likes of the Russians and Czechs, these guys were slow. We skated circles around them, and they seemed very amateurish. They were getting chippy because they could not skate with us. Our skating and passing was superior, and we were up by several goals after the first period. Ralph Engelstad came into our locker room and gave us each one hundred dollars to keep the score close so the people would come back the next night. Their team was frustrated, and could not do anything against our defense, and our offense was too much for them. No matter what they did we beat them. There were a few fights and we won all of those too.

CHAPTER 43: THE DETROIT RED WINGS

While sitting in the hotel lounge after the game, our coach came in with Ned Harkness, the general manager of the Detroit Red Wings. He introduced me to Mr. Harkness who said he would like to visit with me in private. We went to his room and we visited. He told me about the organization, the team and their future plans. He said we would like me to play for Detroit. He offered me a contract. "Go talked it over with your wife and come back here and let me know." I looked for Debby who had gone out to a casino but had no luck finding her.

I went to talk with Murray Williamson. I showed him the offer and got some advice. He told me they really would like to sign me and take me back to Detroit tomorrow. He said, there are sixteen games left in the season, and he thinks you can help them win a playoff spot. It would be a feather in their hat to sign you and take you back. Murray and I talked over the contract offer. He said, "Go back with a counteroffer for more money and see what they say." I said, "Okay, I would think about it and I would do that."

I kept thinking about the Minnesota Fighting Saints and how they were interested in signing me too. I was their number one draft choice. So it was a big decision.

A thousand thoughts went through my head. I was thinking how I would watch the Red Wings play on *Hockey Night in Canada*. I always wanted to play for them, and as a kid I would have played for nothing. I reflected back to when I was about ten years old, and I sold candy just to go see them in Winnipeg. I recalled how much effort I put into winning that sales contest. Now, here I was sitting with a contract to play for my favorite club, the Detroit Red Wings.

My choice was that I wanted to play with Detroit. I wanted to get established in the NHL. I thought I could go to the WHA in the future. The World Hockey League was just starting out. I was young, so I thought I had plenty of time to jump league down the road. So with those thoughts my mind, I wrote in more money and if they took it, my mind was made up.

I took the contract with my changes back to Ned Harkness. After some discussion things appeared to be in order. As I signed the standard player's contract, it seemed as if I was in a dream. It seemed that everything I did as a kid was flashing before my eyes: the road hockey games, skating on the river, selling candy, seeing the Red Wings play in Winnipeg, and watching them on Hockey Night in Canada. It was overwhelming, and I really did not care about the money. It was the prestige of playing in the NHL—my dream. I took the money anyway.

Ned welcomed me to the organization. He said "I will make reservations for you and your wife to fly to Detroit with me in the morning. We will leave at 8 a.m." I was a Red Wing!

I walked out of that room on cloud nine. I walked over to Murray Williamson's room and told him. He jumped up and shook my hand. He had a big smile on his face and said, "Come on, let's celebrate." We went to the lounge, and we met up with some other players and celebrated.

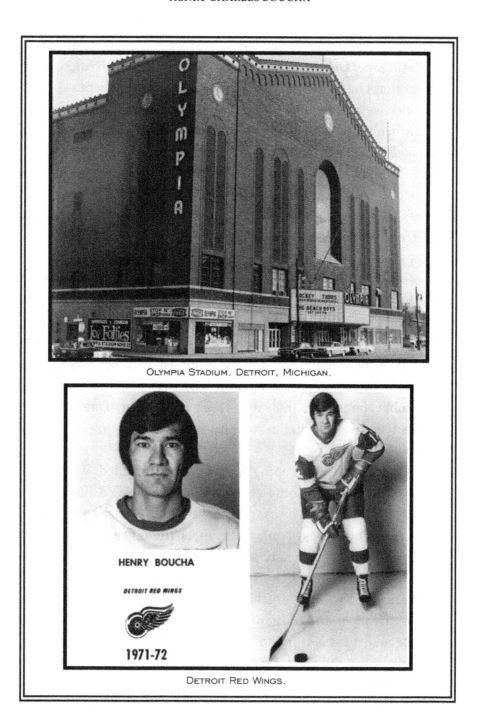

OLYMPIA STADIUM. DETROIT, MICHIGAN.

HENRY BOUCHA

DETROIT RED WINGS

1971-72

DETROIT RED WINGS.

Figure 64

I stayed quite late. Players and wives were coming in and congratulating me. Debby arrived from one of the other casinos, and I told her that I had signed with Detroit. She just stood there stunned. I told her we were flying to Detroit in the morning, and we better call her mother about Tara. We finished our drinks and said our goodbyes and left. We went to our room. It was late and we talked. We had to get up early. We called her mother and told her the good news, and then I called my mother and dad to tell them. Debby's mother said, "Don't worry about Tara. Call us when you get to Detroit, and we can work something out."

We did not get much sleep that night. It was already late, and we kept talking about the trip to Detroit. I was thinking about playing with the Red Wings, and I tossed and turned most of the night. We got up early, packed our bags, and took a cab to the airport. We flew nonstop to Detroit. When we arrived, Mr. Harkness put us up at the Marriott at the airport. He said, "Rest and we will pick you up at 8 a.m. in the morning, and bring your bags." As he was walking out of the lobby, he turned and said, "Don't forget your skates." and he said the team was playing in New York tonight and you can watch them on TV.

It was already early evening, and we were exhausted. We relaxed in our room, ordered some room service, and called home. Our schedule for the next day was to be picked up early, driven to Olympia Stadium for a press conference, meet the office staff, go for a morning skate with the team, and then go back to the hotel. We had a game that night against the Toronto Maple Leafs in Detroit.

The team was playing the New York Rangers at Madison Square Garden that night and the game was on TV, so I watched it. I could not believe that I was going to be playing with these guys tomorrow in Detroit. It just did not seem possible. I would have to pinch myself to see if this was a dream. I was more than excited. I do not think I slept that night either. When the morning came, I felt as if I had not slept in a week. I was going on pure adrenaline, and I thought if I sat too long I would fall asleep.

They lost the game that night in New York and chartered home to Detroit. So the pressure was on to win at home tomorrow night. With Detroit tied for the last and final playoff spot with Buffalo, we had to win and keep winning.

We were ready with our bags packed when the call came. One of the staff from the Red Wings office was at the front desk. We went down and Jimmy Skinner, Western Scout introduced himself. We got into the car and headed toward Olympia Stadium. I remember going down I-94 and seeing the big tire on the way into Detroit. I was so nervous, with a thousand things going through my head. The scout was making small talk, and Debby just sat there and did not say much. She smiled once in a while and just nodded while looking out the window. This was all new to her too. I do not think she liked the looks of the city. It was a cloudy and dreary day, and it was spring, so the city looked trashy and dirty. When we arrived at Olympia Stadium, it was broad daylight and the neighborhood looked pretty scary. The parking lot was all fenced in, and it had guards at the entrances. They checked us as we entered. We parked and walked in. They said to leave the bags but bring my skates. The building was huge. It was old, classic and built with old-world charm. It was the building where the Red Wings won several Stanley Cups over the years. It was home of the famous Production Line, with Gordie Howe, Sid Abel, and Ted Lindsay. Wow, I was here. We entered the building and went into the Red Wing office first. We were introduced to the staff. They were friendly and welcomed us to the Red Wing organization.

We were then taken to the media room, where the TV cameras and the reporters were. The general manager, the president of the organization, Vice President Gordie Howe, and several others from the organization were there. Ned Harkness announced that I had signed a contract to play with the Red Wings and that I would play in tonight's game against Toronto. I was asked to say a few words. I was nervous but I introduced Debby and told them that I was happy to be there and to have signed a contract to play. I told them that Detroit was my favorite team and had been since I was ten years old. I talked a little about winning the Silver Medal at the Olympics, and about my current Army situation. I also said that I hope I could make a difference. When I stopped talking, the floor was opened to questions. There were a lot of questions about Debby and me, Warroad, Junior hockey, the US Teams and the Olympics. There were a lot of pictures taken, and everyone wished me good luck as the press conference ended. We went back down to the front offices.

It was time to go to the locker room and meet the coach and players. I was really nervous again at that point. Debby waited in the office as Gordie Howe and Mr. Harkness walked me over to the locker room. The locker room was like any other I had been in, except it was bigger and nicer. The players looked the same, although they were not as big as I thought they would be, compared to how they appeared on TV. They were friendly and were joking around. I was given a seat/stall and asked what size I wore, and I was fitted with my uniform. They also gave me sweats to wear in the morning skate. The coach came over and asked what position I played, and I said left wing, even though I was a right-handed shot. Ned Harkness was an American who coached at Cornell and won an NCAA championship. He came to the Red Wings as coach but was later booted to the front office. Most clubs had all Canadian players, coaches, and staff, and they didn't like Americans much. Mr. Harkness told me to tell the coach that I played left wing because they needed one, and he thought I would do a good job. So I told the coach that I played left wing. I actually never played it before that day. The coach said. "Good, we'll see how it goes."

We skated light drills, worked on breakouts, passing drills, and that was it. We showered and were told to be at the rink by 5:30 p.m. They brought Debby out to watch the practice for a while. After practice and our team meeting, I walked back to the office to get Debby. They gave me a car to drive and said that I would be staying in an apartment in Dearborn. They said to stay there until I could find an apartment to rent and get myself settled.

After getting our bags into our car, Jimmy Skinner led us over to the apartment. He let us in, gave us the keys, and a map of the city. He said, "You're all set, see you tonight and try getting some rest." I was tired, and it had been quite a few days of traveling and excitement. I slept some, but I did not want to oversleep. I started thinking too much and was not sure if I knew my way to the arena, so I wanted to leave early. I got dressed and took off. Debby was tired and did not want to go, so she stayed at the apartment and rested.

I left for the arena and took the wrong exit. After some driving around, I figured it out and arrived at Olympia Stadium a little later than I wanted. As I pulled into the parking lot, the guy said, "You cannot park here." I said, "I'm the new player." He said, "I don't have you on my list?" After some explanations and begging, he let me through but told me to park across the lot by the north fence. Come to find out, the players parked right by the side entrance. I parked my car all the way across the parking lot and I ran to the players' entrance—and they would not let me in either. Both the players and fans used the same building entrance. The man guarding the entrance said, "Where's your ticket? "I said, "I am a new player and I should be on the list." He said, "What is your name and no, I don't have you on my list.

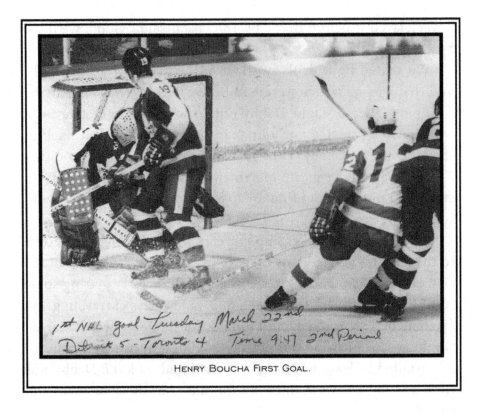

1st NHL goal Tuesday March 22nd
Detroit 5 - Toronto 4   Time 9:47 2nd Period

HENRY BOUCHA FIRST GOAL.

Figure 65

Where is your pass and ticket?" I said, "I am the new player."
"Well, I don't have you on my list." So he got a guard who was
standing there to go to the locker room to get someone. One of
our trainers came out and saw me, so they let me in. After all of
that, I was a little late. I was embarrassed but everyone laughed it
off. Once I settled down and was getting dressed, Gordie Howe
walked through the locker room. There was Alex Delvecchio sitting across from me. Mickey Redmond, Marcel Dionne, and Red
Berenson—all players I had watched on TV. Billy Collins was
laughing and joking with me about the Minnesota State Hockey
Tournament. He was with the North Stars and saw me get hurt
in that final game.

When I arrived, the game jersey and everything else I needed were laid out for me. We were catered and pampered by these trainers and equipment men. I was quiet and did not say much to the others. I just minded my own business. The coach came in and talked about matching lines and who was going to play against whom. Then we went out for warm-ups. My legs were shaking as we got out there. I just needed to skate around and get loosened up. I was way too nervous to stand on the blue line and shoot pucks. As I skated around, the Toronto Maple Leafs came out on the other end. I saw Dave Keon, Ron Ellis, and a few other guys I knew from TV. I saw Jacques Plante in the net warming up. Oh, my God, this is fantastic. I could not believe I was there. I looked up into the crowd of sixteen thousand people and could not believe I was skating on this rink in Detroit. What I noticed most was the uniforms of the teams, the colors seemed to pop out more—the Red Wings' white home uniforms and the Maple Leafs' blue road uniforms. There I was playing my first NHL game. I was emotional.

In the locker room after our warm-ups, our coach came in and gave the final game strategy, and then we went onto the ice. I still could not believe I was sitting on the bench with a Red Wings uniform. I didn't know when I would get into the lineup, if at all. There were a few shift changes and then Toronto got a penalty. Johnny Wilson, the coach, tapped me on the back and said, "You, you—get out there on left wing." It was a power play for my first shift on the ice. Mickey Redmond set me up in the high slot, and I let a one-timer go and hit the pipe. If I would have stopped the puck, and then shot it, it would have been a sure goal, but I did not. I was too nervous. We did not score on that shift, but I made it though without making any major mistakes. Toronto scored and then scored again, and by the third period it was 4–0 for Toronto. I was playing on a regular shift by then and was fore checking hard. I knocked the puck loose and chipped it in over Jacques Plante. Wow, my first

NHL goal in my first game. Mickey Redman got the puck and gave it to me. I gave it to the trainer, and he kept it for me. That goal started a rally and we ended up coming back and winning 5–4. It put us into fourth place. It was a great first game, and I had a good feeling of accomplishment. My stress was gone, and I was tired. I could not wait to get to bed for much-needed rest. I found the apartment and had something to eat. Debby and I talked about the game. I called home and some friends. Then it was an early night with no celebrations. I slept like a baby. We had a few days off with only practice in the mornings.

CHAPTER 44: DETROIT, MY NEW HOME

There was so much to do yet. We needed to find an apartment, buy or rent furniture, get our car from Minneapolis or buy a new one. We made arrangements for Leo, June, and Tara to fly to Detroit. I had not even moved out of the apartment in Minneapolis yet. I called Herb Trimborn in Minneapolis, and he said, "Don't worry about it, come when you can."

Hockey had been my life, and now I was living the dream. In reality, I still had to muster out of the Army. I was still active, and was tied to the US Olympic Team. It was a real blessing to have made the Army's Phasedown Release Program.

Meanwhile, Leo, June, and Tara arrived in Detroit. We stayed together in the apartment provided by the Red Wings. We found a nice apartment in Taylor, Michigan, a suburb of Detroit. The apartment was comfortable and on one level. It had two large bedrooms and a nice kitchen and living room. It was close to everything, and we would enjoy living there.

Alex Delvecchio set me up with his friend who owned a furniture store in Dearborn. He said they would treat me right. We went to meet the owner and looked at furniture. It was amazing to me, that we finally had money to spend. We were so broke for such a long time, and it was unusual to have money in our pockets and in the bank. We could buy almost anything we wanted, within reason. We took a look around the store, and we really did not know what we were looking for. The owner finally said, "Let's go out to your apartment, and see what you need." We drove to the apartment and he and his associate looked it over. He said, "Why don't you let me decorate the apartment for you? You'll love it." Debby and I looked at each other and said, "Why not?" He said if we did not like it we could change things and get something else.

We gave him the keys, and he said he would call us when they were finished. A few days later, he called and said the new place was ready. We hurried over there to take a look. It was beautiful. Debby just sat down in a chair and giggled like a kid. The furniture was beautiful, a couch, love seat, chairs, pictures on the walls, end tables, coffee tables, lamps, dining room set for six, bedroom furniture, and a new washer and dryer set. It was impressive, and we were amazed. We were never so happy, and we felt blessed. June and Leo were really happy for us. They stayed with us through the move and then flew home.

It was spring and the weather was getting nice. We were happy in our new apartment, and we had everything we needed and then some. We found a babysitter, and Debby attended a few games. I bought a new car that spring. Debby got calls from the wives to get together. Life was good and things had worked out for us.

During one of our home stands, I flew to Chicago for the day. I arranged to muster out at Fort Sheridan, Illinois. I called my friend Tom Kohl, my Army buddy from Germany, who was out then too. He picked me up at the airport and was able to drive me to the post. It took most of the day to get all my papers signed, and muster out. We had lunch and he brought me back to the airport, and I flew back to Detroit that night. I was at practice the next day. It was good to finally finish up my obligation to the Army and to be done with that phase of my life.

During my time in Detroit, Tom and I got together several times, and it was always good. I got to know his family, and we got along well. He had been a sergeant in the Army. We served in Germany together, and we had good times and many memories of that tour.

Meanwhile, we had a long road trip coming up out west. We would be gone for a week. Debby wanted to fly home and wait there until I finished up the season. I would drive home later.

It was during that time when word was out about Team Canada playing the Russians in the Summit Series the next fall. A few of the Red Wing players were invited to that camp. They asked me about the Russians. I said, "They were great. They have strong skills, and they were tough." Arrogantly, my teammates said, "Bullshit, we'll kick their ass. Wait until we (Canadians) play them." I said, "Wait and see. The Russians will surprise you." The guys were over confident, and I laughed to myself, and I could not wait for them to play the Russians. The Russians would teach them a lesson or two. No one would listen to me. I played against the Russians nine times and never got within a couple of goals of them. If they wanted to, they could demolish you.

Detroit could not get over the hump when it came to getting a few points ahead of Buffalo. They lost, we lost, they won, and we won. It came down to the last day, but they finished ahead of us by one point and made the playoffs. We were done for the season. We finished fifth in our division and did not make the playoffs, although we had enough points to finish second in the other division. The league was set up wrong with only two divisions. How could you allow teams that had mediocre seasons into the playoffs when other teams like Detroit had superior numbers, points and were left out? I never understood that. In Detroit we had our after-season party and everyone parted ways for the summer. Some would be back while others were traded, or signed with the WHA.

It was different playing professional hockey with the Red Wings. I was used to being part of a team that cared about one another, and were proud to do battle together. The Olympic team, the Jets, and other teams had camaraderie and team spirit. I was bothered by some of the Detroit players and the attitudes. I thought they did not understand what it meant to be on a team. They did not understand that there was no "*I*" in the word "*team.*" Individual achievements—

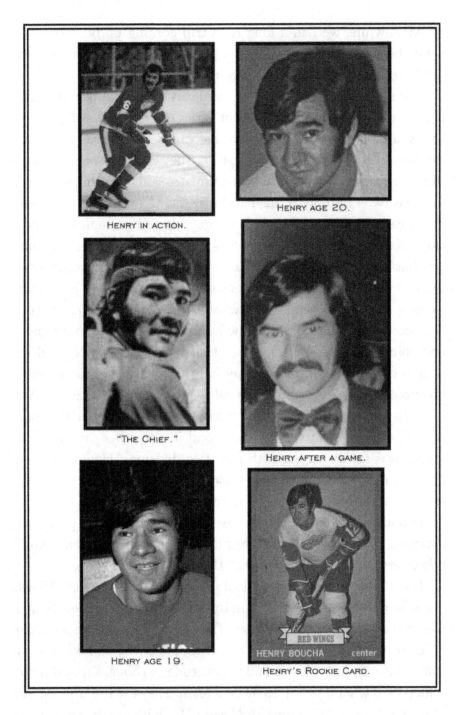

HENRY IN ACTION.

HENRY AGE 20.

"THE CHIEF."

HENRY AFTER A GAME.

HENRY AGE 19.

HENRY'S ROOKIE CARD.

Figure 66

goals and assists—were more important to those players, than a team win. Maybe things would change next year. When we lost a game, if these players got points, they were happy. When we won, if these players did not get a point, they would sulk and pout. It pissed me off. I was appalled by their attitudes. I kept my thoughts to myself. I was a rookie, and I did not have the authority to say a word. I said something one time and Alex Delvecchio put me down for it. I respected him but I thought he was wrong.

After the season Debby and I decided to keep the apartment and leave things as they were. We would be back in late summer, and next season. On the way home, I wanted to stop and see my friend in Chicago. Then I wanted to stop in Minneapolis and visit Hal Trumble, our Olympic team manager, and Coach Murray Williamson. I thought it would be good to keep in touch with everyone. When I called Hal Trumble, he invited me to lunch at the Downtown Blue Line Club. It was good to make those connections and network with people.

When I got to Warroad, we stayed with Debby's parents. We looked for a place to rent for the summer. We talked about buying land and maybe building a house or a duplex. Debby wanted to buy a horse, so we bought one and had it boarded at the Don Ellerbush stable. Don was a minister in town and was a man of strong character. I liked him because he told things like they were, and we got along well.

Other than our trip to Las Vegas, Debby and I had never been on a real vacation or on a honeymoon. June agreed to watch Tara. Debby always wanted to go to Hawaii, so we booked a flight to Hawaii. We stayed on Waikiki Beach for a week, and went to Maui for a week. The trip was good at times, but then there were those times when I thought our relationship took another step backwards.

We tried to find a place to rent in Warroad. Everything we looked at was old and run-down. There was not much to rent. In early June, I took a job with the city for the summer. I ran the summer recreation program and coached youth baseball. I really enjoyed the job. I enjoyed getting up in the morning, teaching and being with the kids. We were still looking for a place.

The Red Wings called and asked the players to come back to Detroit. They hired a physical management group and they wanted us to get checked out to see how we were doing over the summer, so I made arrangements to go back for a few days. Once I got to Detroit, I stayed at our apartment. I was there a few days and finished my obligations and then flew to Minneapolis. I talked to Herb Brooks in the airport and he asked me to stay over and play golf and I said that I would. While there I visited with some others friend and family. When I called Debby she was furious and in one of her moods. She told me that if I did not come home right now, she would have my bags packed and on the steps.

It was difficult, Debby was having serious problems. She was agitated with me and everybody around her. She grew intolerable and she wanted me to leave. It was not working out, June and every-one around her were suffering and stressed out. I could not handle the constant badgering and bickering. I was tired of the stress of fighting with her and the extreme moods swings. I needed to get away. She was bringing me down and I was about to crack. There was nothing I could do. We needed a separation, so I went to my parents' house.

I was thinking of leaving Warroad but I had the summer recreation job and I needed to do something about that. I found someone to take the baseball team for the rest of the summer. Then I went to see the City Administrator, he said he was disappointed but understood.

It was good to have brother Eddy there at our parents' home and to have someone to spend time with. Eddy and I went to visit my brother Dave in Minneapolis. Then we decided to visit my sister Darlene and her family in Idaho. My nephew Roger Dorion was getting married, and I thought that it would be a good time to go visit, and it would give me a chance to think things through.

We were in Idaho for a few weeks. We fished, played golf, and visited with Jim and Darlene's family. Then we flew back into Minneapolis, and I picked up my car. I went to Detroit, and Eddy went back to Warroad. Eddy was to report to play junior hockey in Canada.

When I got back to Detroit, I opened the apartment door, expecting to see the furniture but the place was empty. Without any notice, notes or messages Debby and her parents had come to Detroit, rented a U-Haul and moved everything to Warroad. Every piece of furniture was gone and my clothes were thrown on the bedroom floor. I was stunned. I packed my things and went to talk with the apartment management. They told me they came in and got the key a few weeks before. He let me out of the lease. I thought I better go check the bank. I found both my accounts empty. Debby had been there too, along with her lawyer. They were able to withdraw over twelve thousand dollars. I wrote checks in Idaho and I had overdrafts pending. I had to get a loan from the bank to cover things until the season started.

A friend owned a hotel in Dearborn called the Continental Congress Inn. I checked in there. He was a good friend of the players and took good care of us. I was scheduled to work in Gordie Howe's Hockey School the following week. I got to know Gordie, along with his sons, Mark and Marty, and the rest of the family. I also worked with Bugsy Watson, who played for Pittsburgh. We had a great camp and had a lot of fun. I brought in Tom Kohl and his brother Richie to attend camp as well. They came to Detroit and stayed. They were like family to me. Hockey schools gave players a chance to skate and get into a little better condition before training camp.

That fall I was introduced to Brian Smith, a corporation labor lawyer. Vince Doyle, a sports radio show host, and Norm Cash, a Detroit Tigers baseball player, and Brian put together Triple Crown

Sports. They represented players. Brian was the only lawyer, and he handled the negotiations. Vince and Norm were silent partners and recruiters. While doing a radio show with Vince, he asked if I would like to talk with Brian. He went on to say that Brian was a nice guy and that he represented players. I said, "Yes, I needed to talk to someone about my financial situation." So we set up a meeting to meet Brian Smith. I did not tell Vince about the call I just received from the front office of the Red Wings. The office informed me that they had taken several calls from bill collectors. I did not know what they were talking about. I was stunned and embarrassed. When I went to the office, they asked me what was going on. I said, "I don't know, but I will find out." I did not have any bills that I was aware of. I called and talked to Brian Smith. He said he could help and he would find out what was going on. We signed an agreement for him to represent me in this situation.

When I met with Brian, I told him everything that had happened with Debby; the summer we separated, when she took all the new furniture, (worth over twenty-five thousand dollars), and about (fifteen thousand dollars) from the bank accounts. I told him about an attorney in Minneapolis that was temporarily representing me in the divorce, although the divorce was not final yet. He advised me to give Debby a specific amount of monthly child support and alimony to get it over with.

After investigating the situation, Brian got back to me. He said, "Debby apparently has been charging everything to you and not paying for anything." He said. "This is a real mess. We need to stop the bleeding now, and get it straighten out. It would take a little time." Brian assured me and said, "Do not worry about it, just play hockey and we'll take care of this." They would contact all of the creditors, and I would need to post a note in the *Warroad Pioneer* stating that "I will not be responsible for any bills other than my own", signed by me. So I did that, and we stopped Debby from charging, but the damage was done. By the time we totaled all of the debts; it was nearly thirty thousand dollars in charges and fees.

At that time, and in order get some upfront money to help pay off some of the creditors, Brian suggested we re-negotiate my contract with the Red Wings. We wouldn't have much bargaining power, but it would help me out of my situation. So we did that for a modest raise and extension for another year, plus an option year. I was relieved to have someone on my side.

CHAPTER 45: FIRST FULL NHL SEASON

Detroit had five teams in the Red Wings organization and all in camp at the same time: the Detroit Red Wings of the NHL, the Tidewater Wings of the AHL, the Fort Worth Wings of the CHL, the London Lions of the European League, and the Port Huron Wings of the IHL. There were a lot of players in camp trying out for these teams. Port Huron, Michigan camp headquarters was full. The camp was very good, and I saw several players whom I had either played against or had played with at some point in my career. That year, I also met Tommie Bergman from the Swedish Olympic team. He was a big defenseman and was trying out for the Detroit team. We started spending time together. I found out that Sweden during the Olympics was having internal problems with some players. Two of the players wanted to marry Japanese woman they met while at the Olympics, and it impacted the whole team—the reason Sweden ended up in fourth. I introduced Tommie to the Big Mac, and he was hooked. He would go down to McDonald's two and sometimes three times a day. Tommie made the team and we became good friends over the years in Detroit.

HENRY BOUCHA, DETROIT RED WING.

Figure 67

After we moved back to Detroit during the exhibition season, I found a house to rent in Allen Park. It was just off the freeway between the airport and Olympia Stadium, so it was convenient for me. I was alone, lonely and had no contact with Debby, although we were still married. I really did not meet anyone in Detroit the year before, so life there was all new to me. I was always shy but when I drank I came out of my shell and I was able to talk and visit with people. I used to say, "I needed a drink to get my personality going." A phrase that would haunt me later on. So with that said, that is the way I carried on. I loved Debby but wanted her to be well, normal and to be there with me. Her mental illness devastated and scarred me. I had to leave to save my sanity. While in Detroit, I was lonely, homesick and miserable. Drinking gave me a temporary escape from loneliness during that time of my life. So I frequented the bar scene but my fears never allowed me to be close with anyone. It was a lonely and miserable way to live my young life.

Some of the players were back that year but not all. I was able to get my number 16 jersey (the number I had at Warroad High school) that year, after wearing number 12. I was slowly getting to know my way around. It seemed that the players who were in transition always ended up at my house and stayed with me. That was okay. It gave me company, and we always found things to do. It helped me with the loneliness. Living in the big city was something that I was not accustomed to. The other players had either their girlfriends or wives, and we really never saw each other, except at the arena, on the road, or when someone had a team party. During our days at home, we practiced a couple of hours, and that was it for the day. We had a lot of time on our hands.

The Red Wings public relations department asked me to appear at different venues for charities. None of the other players would go to anything unless they were paid to do it. I felt that the hockey community was paying me, so why not give something back.

One of the first things Gordie Howe did my first year was to ask me to come to his office. I did not know what he had in mind. When I got to the office, he said, "I hope you have a little time." I said I did and he took me to Children's Hospital, and we visited some of the kids with cancer. I felt compassion but I did not know what to say or how to act, until I saw the way he treated the children. He was upbeat, talking and laughing with them. He brought them gifts from the Red Wings, and they enjoyed every minute of his time. From that time on, I always went back when asked and I never said no to the public relations department about doing my share of giving back to the community.

I was also involved with the Big Brother Big Sister Program. I was assigned a boy by the name of Danny that I spent time with. He was from Lincoln Park, a community next to where I lived. Later on I spent time with another kid by the name of Jerry and he was from inner city Detroit.

I started meeting people and getting to know the neighborhood. It was nice. I was treated well, and I started spending time with some of the locals. I met Bob Cassell, Bob Rodwell, Doug Sherpard who I socialized with most of the time when I was away from the team. There were young woman who I dated from time to time. I never let myself get involved emotionally. I kept everything inside and I was very private and extremely sad. It was a hard and difficult time for me. I never talked about my feelings with anyone. I had some break downs in energy and it affected my playing at times. At that time, I was not well balanced.

During the first half of the season, I played regularly, then I slumped and I was used sparingly. I started sitting on the bench more than I was playing. I was getting out of shape. I was depressed and I lacked confidence. I was not producing and getting the ice time I needed, and it showed.

While on a road trip out west in Los Angeles, they decided to send me to the Tidewater Red Wings in Norfolk, Virginia. My pride was affected. I was embarrassed and I resented it. I recognized that I was out of shape. I said, "Ok, let's do it." They said they would bring me back up when I was ready. "You'll be back in two weeks," they assured me. "We need you to get back in shape in order for you to help us." I agreed and packed my bags.

While making our approach to Detroit Metro Airport, from L.A., the landing gear would not go down. The plane circled and circled. They announced that we would need to make an emergency belly landing. We were making our final approach when the gear finally went down and we were able to land safely. I stayed in Detroit overnight. I packed and the next day we flew to Hershey, Pennsylvania. I hooked up with the Tidewater team there. I was out of shape. I struggled playing the whole game. I was tired. Still, it was good to play and see some of the guys I knew.

We had a good time in Norfolk. We stayed out on Virginia Beach at the Ramada Inn. So it was like a vacation. When I woke up in the morning, I would look out at the sun coming up over the ocean; it seemed like I was on a ship.

After that first game, I knew my coach was right. I was out of shape and had no confidence. As time went on, I gained my confidence, skated every day, and played a regular shift. I played on the power plays and killed penalties. I felt, I was getting back into shape and enjoying the game again. I led the team in scoring, and we did not lose a game while I was there. After two weeks, I was called back up.

With my confidence restored, my sadness gone, and strength added, I felt like a new man. While playing at Tidewater, I had taken my helmet off and was playing without it. I never played without a helmet before. I was wearing my hair longer, and it was getting into my eyes. I wore contact lenses, and it was a problem when sweat would get into my eyes and contacts.

After practice one day in Detroit, I was visiting my friend Tom Jaffire, Manager of the Dearborn Ice Rink. In the building, they had tennis courts and a sports shop. I was telling Tom about my time in Tidewater. I told him I was playing without a helmet. He asked me how I liked it, and I said I did. It was a different feeling, less constricted. I told him about the hair getting in my eyes, and the problem I had with the sweat in my contacts. While listening to my story, he said to wait a minute. He went into his sport shop and came back to his office with a headband that tennis players wore. He said, "Try this." I said, "Yeah, right. They won't let me wear this." Ned Harkness just started letting us grow mustaches. Ned Harkness came in from the Ivy League a few years back. He preferred the clean-cut image. Then, I thought about Johnny Wilson, our coach, and what he would say—not to mention the players. I thought, no way. I bought two red and two white headbands and took them home with me. I thought about it and tried them on. They didn't look that bad. I bounced it off a few friends. Some laughed and some said I was crazy. At that time, I never thought that I would actually wear them.

The next day, we were to play Pittsburgh at home. I went in for our usual morning skate, and wearing the headband was on my mind. As I sat in the locker room, I looked around at the players and wondered what they might think or say if I wore the headband. I still wasn't sure I would do it. Even if the coach and players accepted it, would management? My confidence was high right now, I was playing regular, and things were going well. I didn't want anything to be a distraction.

I went to the Mustache Lounge and had a prime rib lunch as usual. The lounge was my favorite place during those days in Detroit. I knew the owner and the house band, and they had great lunches. Then, I went back to my house for an afternoon nap before our game. As I lay there, my thoughts were on the headband. Do I wear it or don't I? I fell asleep. I got up around 4 p.m. I got dressed and grabbed the headbands and got in my car. I turned on the radio, and headed to the Olympia. I was upbeat and grooving to the music as I headed down the freeway. I arrived at Olympia, parked in my usual place, grabbed my headbands, and walked into the building and into the locker room. All the while I was thinking, should I or shouldn't I? I thought, I would wait and see what the mood was like in the locker room. Everybody was getting ready, and they seemed to be in good spirits. I still was not sure I would try to wear the headband. We had hair spray in the locker room, although I had never used it before. The players who did not wear helmets used it all the time. There was a room off the main locker room near the showers, and it had shelves of shaving cream, razors, aftershave, combs, brushes, hair dryers, hair spray, etc. A rubber pad was on the floor so we could go in there with our skates and do our hair in the big mirrors before we went on the ice.

Just before we were to go on the ice for warm-ups, I was fully dressed with my jersey on, and I grabbed the white headband and went into that area to look in the mirror. I still wasn't sure but I put a headband on. I combed my hair with a part in it, and I thought it looked good. Then I applied hair spray and put the headband on. I thought, I have a good reason to wear it—to keep hair and sweat out of my eyes. That justified my purpose and was a good excuse. When I came out into the room, everybody looked at me and roared. They all laughed and said, "You're not going to wear that thing, are you?" The players were razzing and teasing me for a while. When the coach walked in, everything went silent. They were all waiting to hear what he was going to say. He walked up the center of the locker room, as usual, telling us who was going to play against what line, when all of a sudden, he looked at me and stopped. He did a double take and said, "What is that?" Everyone roared again, and he laughed and said, "What are you, some kind of chief?" Everyone roared again. Then he took a long look at me again, shrugged his shoulders, and continued with his game plan and pregame speech. All this time, I just sat there with a smile, waiting for someone with authority to tell me to take it off, but they did not, so I wore it out on the ice for warm-ups. People were yelling at me from the stands, calling me "hippie" and other names, but I stood my ground. While standing in the lineup waiting to shoot at the goalie, Bugsy Watson from Pittsburgh came over and said, "What is that? Take that off." He was old school and was laughing. I worked with Bugsy in Gordie Howe's Hockey School the summer before, so we knew each other.

I thought Ned Harkness was going to be waiting for me when I got off the ice after warm-ups, but no one said a word. I thought, now I would have to play well, if I wanted to keep wearing this. It was a good motivator for me to wear it, because I felt I had to prove something every day.

As the season went on, I gained more confidence, scored some goals, and gained notoriety in the league and media. We actually started selling headbands in the concessions in Detroit. The public relations department loved it and I was in demand.

While playing in the National Hockey League the racial name calling and derogatory comments about race (being Indian) by some of the players were there too, but not as bad as when I was in juniors. There were comments and a few statements that hurt and were totally out of line. I dealt with them but it certainly bothered me. I attributed it to ignorance, and had to take a look at that person individually, and assume he was a person without any education or morals. I fought when I had to but never looked for a fight. I was older, and had gone through that stuff before. So I seemed to handle it better but it still was painful and hurtful. Some fans were the same way. The NHL had no guidelines for that conduct and only after African/Americans came into the league was a Code of Conduct established.

In February of that year, I broke a forty-one-year-old record in Montreal. I started the game with Red Berenson and Billy Collins. On the opening face-off, Red poked the puck between Lemare's legs and stepped around him. My winger Cornyeur left me alone, and Billy Collins's winger did the same thing. We had a three-on-two right off the bat. As we skated up the ice, one of the Canadian

Henry's Fastest Goal Plaque.

Figure 68

defensemen fell down, so we had a three-on-one. When Red passed the puck to Billy, I was already down by the net. When Bill passed the puck over to me, I shot a backhand shot toward the net. Wayne Thomas was in the Montreal goal and overreacted and the puck fluttered over the top of him into the net. I scored a six-second goal, breaking Charley Conacher's record by one second. I didn't know that until after the game when the reporters came in. I held the record for eight years, until Doug Smail of the Winnipeg Jets broke it. I received a nice plaque from the league for breaking the record.

The season wound down. We were in the same position as we were the year before, vying for fourth place and a playoff position, this time with Buffalo and Toronto. Even with a few additions to that year's lineup, we still came up short. It was stressful coming down the stretch trying to be the last team in. We just did not get the job done. As was the case the year before, I thought some of our better players lacked character. They did not care about the playoffs if their point's totals were there. Some had no pride in winning, and it showed. It was all over, and we had our team party. Some of the players never showed up, just as they never showed up when things were tough.

I was awarded the Rookie of the Year from the Red Wings organization. I had proven myself in the league and finished strong in the second half of the season. I was looking forward to the next season and what it would bring.

CHAPTER 46: SUMMER OF 1973

I always loved that feeling when you stopped skating after the season. You had a tremendous amount of energy while your body adjusted to being idle and not burning up the daily calories. It made you feel light on your feet, and rested with a ton of energy.

I was talking with my lawyer, Brian Smith about going to Florida after the season. During our conversations, he mentioned that he could get a motor home to use from the TV station. Brian worked for a local TV station in Windsor for different projects. He asked and they said, "No problem." It was April and college spring break was going on. I called my brother Eddy, and he came to Detroit. I asked a couple of buddies from the Detroit area if they wanted to go. The motor home was housed in Detroit at a dealership where it had been stored for the winter. I was excited when I picked it up and drove it to my house. We packed the motor home with food, snacks and beer, filled it with gas, packed our things, got our maps, and took off for Florida.

The trip down was amazing. We took turns driving while the others carried on drinking and playing cards and horsing around. We made sure someone was sober to drive at all times. It could have easily got out of hand with the many towns and bars we passed. It was a unique way to travel and we made to most of it.

We pulled into Fort Lauderdale at midnight a few days later. We were winging it as far as where to park it. We didn't make any reservations or plans about where to stay. We found an RV park not too far away. We drove the RV and parked near the beach and stayed at the RV park at night. We played volleyball and spent time on the beach and bar hopped. We had a good time golfing, partied and met a lot of people. We stayed for about ten days and then started north. We stopped at several places along the way, including Disney World. We took turns driving to get back home. The trip was great, filled with fun and a lot of laughs. We cleaned up the motor home and amazingly, returned it to the dealership in one piece.

I was still in the rented house in Allen Park. The people I rented from moved to California. They put the house on the market that spring. I could stay there until it sold. I moved so many times over the years that it was nice to stay in one place for a change. Even though it was a rental, it was mine just for a few more months. It felt like home. I would be twenty-two years old in June. I had thoughts about taking a few college courses and maybe buying a house.

I received a call from Bemidji High School about coming to Minnesota to speak at an athletic banquet that spring. They apologized for the short notice and they offered to pay expenses and give me an honorarium. I said, "Yes". It was a free trip home and it would be good for the students. I had not been to Warroad since Debby and I separated, the year before. It seemed like a very long time. We were not formally divorced, although I talked with a lawyer. I was upset with Debby about the bills and the way things happened. She was still living with her parents in Warroad. Although I had not talked to her since I left the previous year, I missed her and Tara.

I called my parents and told them that I was going to be in Bemidji and that I had planned to go home to Warroad. They were happy to hear that. Bemidji was 2½ hours from Warroad. It was close enough to go see my parents and get a chance to see Tara. I planned to fly back to Detroit after a few days. After the banquet at Bemidji High School, we visited with family and friends. I stayed in Bemidji

GEORGE, ALICE & HENRY, JANET FLICK AND TARA.

Figure 69

that night. I was up fairly early and traveled to Warroad the next day. I visited my parents and some other people around town.

I called Debby, and I saw Tara. She was 2½ and she was walking and talking. Debby and I talked things over and decided to give it another try. We rented a big U-Haul and packed up the furniture. Our families were extremely happy for the two of us and hoped that we could work things out. It seemed like such a long time apart. I had grown and matured some and I hoped she had also. We enjoyed getting to know each other again. We took our time traveling and stayed at motels along the way. Once we arrived in Detroit, we stayed at the Continental Congress Inn in Dearborn. The owners were friends of mine and helped out a lot during the season.

We looked at several apartment buildings and complexes. We stayed in my friend's apartment while he was out of town to see if we liked that part of town. We looked at dozens of places. Nothing seemed to suit her, and I could tell something was not right. As time went on, we started to argue and disagree about everything. I could see the trend starting all over again. She did not want to be there. Although she didn't come right out and say it, I could tell she wanted to go home. She did not want to admit it. We stopped looking at apartments. Finally, she admitted that this not going to work. She did not like being away from Warroad and the comfort and security of her parent's home. I bought a plane ticket home for Debby and Tara. It was over. I had my family drive the U-Haul back to Warroad.

It was already late spring. I signed to take summer school classes at the University of Detroit. They would start soon. I chose Business Law, and Micro Economics. The classes were in the evenings twice a week. I attended most of the classes, and the ones that I could not make I had a friend take notes for me. We had a lot of homework and things to do for the classes. It was a commitment, and it was difficult to stay focused. I passed both classes but vowed never to do it again.

That summer, I attended the wedding of my cousin Marie Boucha who married Mark Andrews in Kenora, Ontario. I flew to Winnipeg, Manitoba. My brother Dave and family along with brother Eddy picked me up, and we traveled to Kenora. It was a special time with all of the relatives. I stayed a few days and then flew back to Detroit. While in Kenora, I asked my cousin Doug Boucha to help me with my hockey school later that summer, back in Detroit.

MAGAZINE COVER.

RIGHT: HENRY WEARING USA JERSEY AND SILVER MEDAL.

Figure 70

This was my first Henry Boucha Hockey School. We partnered with the city of Royal Oak, a northern Detroit suburb. The hockey school was full, and we ran a good camp for two weeks. We had a skilled staff, with my brother Eddy, Ritchie Kohl, my cousin Doug, and me as instructors. I flew my old trainer, Buddy Kessel from the Olympic team in from Minneapolis. The school was successful and well run. The city of Royal Oak was extremely happy. We had a good time and made a little money. It was always nice to get back on the ice in late August. It gave us a chance to skate and get the kinks out before training camp. I loved to work with the kids, and this was a way to give back to the community as well.

Just after the hockey school, they sold the house I was living in and I had to move out. I wish I could have stayed. I liked it there

353

and it was a nice neighborhood. I moved out and stored some of my belongings at a friend's house. I looked for and place to rent and went through the process once again. The Red Wings office would sometimes receive calls of people wanting to rent their home for the season.

CHAPTER 47: THE 1973—74 SEASON

The Detroit Red Wings fired Johnny Wilson over the summer, and I was extremely sad to hear that. I thought he was the glue that held everything together. He was a good coach. He was the type of coach that was a player, had great knowledge of the game, could blend everyone together, motivate you and would give you a fair shot.

Training camp was coming up, and it was announced that Ted Gavin was the new coach. He did not have NHL experience but had been with the Red Wings organization for years. He was a minor league coach with Port Huron Wings and had been successful. Some players did not like the fact that Ted Gavin did not have the NHL experience. They would not give Coach Gavin a chance and had no respect for him. They would make fun of him and backstab him at every opportunity. I could not understand it. We were a team, all together and why not try find solutions and pull together. It was horrible to see the immaturity, and hear the negative comments and jokes. It was pathetic the way some of the players acted. It was the social disease—and the same players that I talked about earlier. If they did not get a point in a game, they would pout and carry on. I stayed out of it. They would not listen to me or anyone else on the team. I knew it was going to be a long year.

1974 RED WINGS.

Figure 71

During that time, Denny McLain and I were to have a TV show together on a station in Windsor. Denny was a 31 game winning pitcher with the Detroit Tigers during their World Series run a few years before. Denny was having some personal problems and got into some trouble before the show got off the ground. So the show never happened. I was asked by the network to do a screen test but I never did.

After we broke camp in Port Huron and returned to Detroit, I moved back into the Continental Congress Motel. I looked around and managed to rent a house in Westland, Michigan. It was forty-five minutes from Olympia and about fifteen minutes from the airport. It was a nice 4 bedroom house, furnished and comfortable. I had the transition players stay with me again that year. My mother and dad came from Warroad to spend some time too. Mom would have stayed

RED WINGS POSTER.

HB RED WINGS.

HB RED WINGS.

BOB CASSELL CARICATURE.

Figure 72

all winter but dad felt cooped up in the city and wanted to go home. They had been there enough to make a few friends in the area.

I had friends and family from out of town come to visit while I was there, including Tom Kohl and his wife from Chicago, Herb and LaRae Trimborn, Jack Ploof and his wife from Elizabethtown, Kentucky and others.

That fall, I bruised my hip when I fell on the ice; my pad in my pants slid over and exposed my hip to the ice. Our equipment did not have the protection they have today. Our pants had no padding in the back at all and little protection on the sides. My hip was swollen, and was black-and-blue from my waist down to just above my knee. It was a massive contusion that hemorrhaged and had to be drained. I was up most of the night in extreme pain and had not slept much. I went into practice and saw the trainer. He immediately called the team doctor. I went to his office. He opened me up and put tubes in my hip to drain the hemorrhaged area and sent me home to rest. I rested overnight and felt somewhat better. It was game day the next day and I did not skate in the morning. They checked my hip. Some of the swelling went down and I was expected to play that night. The doctor said, "I guess we could put cotton on it and give him a shot for pain." That was enough for management, so I played.

Another time, I had a collision near our goal. Neither one of us had seen each other. We both lay there for a minute. I got up and followed the play down the ice. He went to his bench. While I was following the play down the ice, I did not know what team I was on or where the bench was. I didn't know what was going on. As I got to the other blue line, the play turned around and started back up ice. I was looking for the bench but I did not know what team I was on. Finally, I looked down at my jersey to see and then found the bench and got off the ice. The trainer gave me smelling salts, and I was back out there for my regular shift. Early on we did not know or understand how serious concussions were. We played through them.

I was killing a penalty and was covering the point; the defenseman took a slap shot and hit me on my right foot instep. The shot hit me so hard that it took the strength from my leg and I fell down. The puck bounced toward the other team's goal, and I was home free. I jumped up to take off on a breakaway, but as soon as I stepped on that foot, I fell down. I had no feeling in my foot. I was helped off the ice. It did not break anything. It was a deep bruise. I never had a bruise like it before. The team doctor had me take my skate off. He examined it and had me step on it. He did not think anything was broken so; he gave me a shot of Novocain, and sent me out to play.

It was sore and I was limping badly the next day. It hurt badly to walk around on it. I thought I had a cracked instep. I got the day off from skating and went in for x-rays. Nothing was broken. I reported back to the locker room. The trainer filled a bucket with ice and water and then filled another bucket with hot water and set each beside me. He told me to stick my foot in the ice water as long as I could stand it and then stick it in the hot water as long as I could stand it. I was to do that back and forth until he said to stop. That was painful. That injury lasted a long time. It was tender and just would not heal. They used Novocain on my foot for the games.

Coach Gavin did not last long with the negative pressure from the players. There was no attempt by some of the players to follow his directions or support his coaching style. Some of us worked with him, supported him and played hard. We tried getting the others to respond positively to a team concept and to Gavin himself, but some players were just too shallow to respond to that. He was fired after a morning skate on a game day. We came to a game that night and Alex Delvecchio was not in his usual place in the locker room. He had never missed a game or been late before. We knew something was up. Then Ned Harkness walked in with Alex, and we knew then what was going on. Alex Delvecchio, our teammate and captain, was replacing Ted Gavin as coach.

Alex was not much of a coach, and it proved to be the same old, same old... He was too nice to the players, having played with us. He knew the game but could not strategize or motivate us as a normal coach would. He was too laid back, and now we were no threat in the league standings. The team and organization seemed to be falling apart and going downhill. We finished the season out of the playoffs again, even further than we had in the previous years. We knew there would be a shakeup of personnel in the front office during the off-season. The team would further deteriorate down before Alex was replaced too. We went from a playoff team to a poor team in a matter of one year. We did not have the leadership without Johnny Wilson. He was a great coach and would have made a great GM too. He knew talent, could motivate players, and could pull personalities together. Ned Harkness fired Wilson to save his job. It was evident that the team had not drafted well. The team had not been organized nor managed its talent pool very well and for some time.

CHAPTER 48: SUMMER OF 1974

After a frustrating season with the Red Wings, it was nice to get away from all the drama. We struggled all season and our season was a total loss. Everyone knew the winds of change were coming. Nobody knew exactly what the outcome would be for the team. It was April and again we were watching the playoffs instead of participating in them. No one wanted to stay around. Personally, I got my plane tickets to Florida. I planned to go down for a couple of weeks. I rented a room at a beachfront hotel for a few days and then stayed with a friend from Detroit who had an apartment in Fort Lauderdale. He managed the Playpen South nightclub in Fort Lauderdale. I spent my days playing golf and lying on the beach and at night went to the dinner clubs around town.

My friend Bob Cassell and his wife, Sally, came down from Detroit, and I met up with them. They were staying with Bob's friend Dare Darnell, his wife Anita and family. They had a 13 year old daughter Sherri, who thought she was in love with me, so we teased her about it and had fun. I spent time at their home too. We socialized, cooked out, went to dinner, and rested in the sun. We had wonderful time. Bob, Sally and I rented a car and traveled down to Key West. It was a fantastic drive. One of the highlights was to sit on the pier and watch the sun go into the ocean. We went to the bar Hemmingway made famous, and took in the sites and haunts around Key West.

Bob Cassell was a creative artist and painted a picture of me in a Detroit Red Wings uniform. I gave it to my parents for Christmas one year. Bob and I were good friends while I was in Detroit. Bob came to my hometown of Warroad one summer. One thing Bob could not get over was the clear skies at night when you could see a million stars. Bob grew up in the city and had not seen stars like that before. He saw the northern lights too. Bob stayed around Warroad for awhile. My dad dropped him off at Buffalo Point, before the road, and there was no one living or staying out there on a regular basis. Bob was thinking about doing a vision quest of some kind, and wanted to stay out there in a cabin by himself for a few days. Bob took some kind of drugs, and was lying on the beach. He was stark naked and fell asleep. When he woke up, he looked up and there was old Wabby Handorgan standing there looking at him. I suppose Wabby was not sure Bob was alive, or maybe he thought Bob was some kind of nut. Anyway, Bob jumped up and they talked and got to know each other.

After returning from Florida to Detroit, I moved out of the house in Westland. The house had served its purpose and the location was not the best after all. I put some of my belongings into a storage unit. I planned to go home to Warroad, and spend time with the family. After I got things in order, I went to Chicago to see my friend Tom Kohl and his family. It was always nice to stop and visit, play golf and tennis, and socialize on my way home. The next stop was in Minneapolis, to see Herb and LaRae Trimborn and stay with my brother Dave and his wife, Tudy. We played golf and went out to dinner and had a few barbecues. I also saw a few other old friends and family while stopping along the way for the week or so. It was becoming tradition that I make these stops each year and visit and have some fun. My friends and I enjoyed the time together.

HENRY BOUCHA, EDDY BOUCHA, DOUG PALAZARRI, HERB BROOKS.
US HOCKEY HALL OF FAME GOLF TOURNAMENT.
COURTESY OF THE WARROAD HISTORICAL SOCIETY.

Figure 73

The summer softball season had begun and the weekend tournaments were about to start in Canada. We played for Stu's bar, the Northland Tap. It was a local hangout for us. It seemed every weekend we played softball in some Canadian town. Canada was only six miles from Warroad. We had a great team and won most of the tournaments that summer. Besides that we fished, boated, played golf, and spent time with the family. It was one of the best summers I can recall.

My brother Eddy and I traveled to Kenora, Ontario, for a couple of weeks that summer. It seemed most residents of Kenora were our relatives. My dad, George, was the only one of his family who moved to the United States, and that was 90 miles across the lake. All his brothers and sisters were in Kenora, along with a lot of other relatives.

All good things had to come to an end. Eddy and I came back into Warroad for a little while and said our good-byes, and then we headed for Detroit. In reverse order now, we went to Minneapolis, and then to Chicago, and then to Detroit. We did not stay as long on the way back as on the way out, but we had a great time. I did not have a place to live in Detroit at that time, so Eddy and I checked into the Continental Congress Inn, again. It was my home away from home until I found an apartment. I thought I would try an apartment that year instead of a house. I heard about a place called the Independence Green Apartments. It had a golf course around it. It was big and had a pool and training area. I rented furniture and organized a living space.

In the Henry Boucha Hockey School that year, I partnered with the City of Birmingham, another Detroit suburb, as well as with the City of Royal Oak. I did one week at each place. Our staff was the same, except my cousin Doug could not make it from Kenora that year. Our staff flew in, and we put them up at our friend Mike Giordano's house in Detroit. We played a lot of beer pong in the evenings. The hockey schools were terrific once again. Our staff was great, and the kids and parents loved us. During the hockey school in Birmingham, I thought I broke my arm when a kid I was horsing around with accidently tripped me while I was going behind the net. The door was open behind the net, and when I fell into the door, I hit the edge. My arm was protecting my ribs when I hit the corner of the door with such force. It was excruciating pain; I immediately went into the locker room and lay on the floor moaning and groaning. I went to the hospital to have it x-rayed and it was not broken. I had a dent in my arm from the door, and my side was black and blue.

Late one afternoon, I got a call from Alex Delvecchio, the new Red Wings General Manager. He said, "Hank, I got some good news and some bad news for you." I said, "Okay, what is it?" He said, "The bad news is that we traded you, and the good news is that we traded you to your home state of Minnesota." I was stunned and just said "Okay." He said that I was traded for a fifty-goal scorer, Danny Grant. He wished me luck and told me to call my attorney and Jack Gordon, the General Manager of the Minnesota North Stars in Minneapolis. I thanked him and hung up.

I did not know how to react. I really had mixed emotions. I was stunned, felt betrayed, and yet I was happy. I felt sorry for myself, and I felt excited. It would have been nice to be traded to a contender. I started getting calls immediately from the press and everyone I knew. They had heard the news.

I called and talked with my lawyer, Brian Smith, who said it was a good deal for me to go back to Minnesota. He talked to Jack Gordon in Minnesota. They wanted to build a team around me. They were excited to have me. Brian was looking forward to arranging and negotiating a new contract. I was on my option year and would be a free agent after that.

CHAPTER 49: MICHIGAN DEPARTURE

By the end of the day, the world knew that I had been traded. Even though we did not have cell phones or computers then. The announcement was on the TV and radio. I notified my relatives and friends. It seemed too happen so fast. Training camp started in September, less than three weeks away, and I had a lot to do. It was time to make plans for my departure to Minnesota. Realistically, I did not have much other than my personal belongings. What I had, I could ship. Once again, I would have to count on and stay with my brother Dave in Minneapolis, while I looked for an apartment. Good thing he lived there. He helped me out many times over the years.

My Detroit friends wanted to have a going-away party for me, so we scheduled that. They called it the Boucha Bash. I talked to the apartment manager, and I returned the furniture to the rental place. I packed up my belongings and got them ready to ship. I had mixed emotions and thoughts about leaving. All of those feelings came to me at one time or another. Maybe it was the way the mind and the body work to comfort one's self. Maybe it was a blessing. The Red Wings, once they let Johnny Wilson go, were on their way down. They had no one in the front office that could make good decisions or run a team. So maybe it was a blessing to move on, especially to Minnesota, my home state. They wanted a young player to build a team around. It was an opportunity and a chance for me to play in my home state.

The plan was for me to negotiate a new long-term contract. I was in the option year of my contract, and it was time to cash in. After all, I was the number one draft choice of the Minnesota Fighting Saints of the WHA, and I had bargaining power. It was perfect timing to negotiate the deal.

Back in Detroit, I started to accept the trade, and I was okay with moving. I met several times with my lawyer Brian to outline a plan. He was to start negotiations with the Fighting Saints and the North Stars to secure a long-term deal for me in Minnesota. The two teams were across town from each other and both wanted me. What lawyer would not want this situation? I loved Brian, and his family, and they were like family to me. His wife, Ann was very controlling, and for some reason did not like Brian traveling. That limited his ability to be away from home and affected his performance with the sports side of his business.

He started the negotiations with the North Stars but never pushed to complete the deal before camp. I was concerned about it and talked to him. He said he talked with Watler Bush, President of the North Stars and they were working on a new deal, and it was looking good. I went ahead and (I should not have) started the season without a new contract.

In Detroit, we had our Boucha Bash with our friends. There were a lot of people there and it was a blast. It went on until the wee hours of the morning. We had a great time and I was sad for it to end. We talked a lot about keeping in touch, and keeping the hockey schools in Michigan in the future. We talked about coming back in the summers. It was sad to leave, and to say goodbye.

The day I left, Doug Shepard and Bob Rodwell took me out to lunch, and we had several laughs before they dropped me off at the airport. While flying to Minneapolis, I sat with the placekicker Errol Mann from the Detroit Lions, a former North Dakota Sioux player. He was headed to Grand Forks for a function. We had a nice visit. I wished him luck, and he did the same to me. My brother Dave picked me up at the airport and I went to stay with them until I could find a place on my own. It was just like old times.

CHAPTER 50: MINNESOTA NORTH STARS

My first meeting with Jack Gordon, General Manager of the North Stars, was a couple of days after I arrived in Minneapolis. I had my haircut but kept a mustache. He welcomed me to Minnesota, and we talked about the team goals and philosophy of the organization. He told me that camp would be starting the following week, and asked me if I had skated much that summer. I said that I had hockey schools in Detroit and had been on the ice for the past month.

We also talked about team appearance, and he said, "I see you have a mustache. We do not mind if players have mustaches, but no one else on the team has one" (enough said). He then introduced me to the office staff. After that we went down into the locker rooms to meet the training staff and equipment managers. A few players were hanging out down there, and we visited. After awhile I returned to my brother's place. I stayed with them a few more nights and then moved to the Marriott next to the Metropolitan Sports Center, where we were going to hold training camp. All players were required to stay at the hotel through camp. I roomed with Bill Goldsworthy, the team's captain.

We trained two times a day. We had one session in the mornings and then lunch and rest, and then we were back on the ice for the afternoon session. The North Stars had other teams and players under contract, but they invited only players whom they thought might have a chance in helping the main team here in Minneapolis. All other players were training at different levels in camps at other locations.

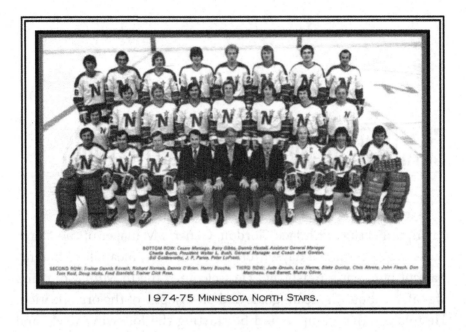

1974-75 MINNESOTA NORTH STARS.

Figure 74

We may have had thirty-five to forty players in camp, and we were given various chances to see what they could do with the many different player combinations. It was a work in progress. The practices were high tempo and fun. We were scheduled to play about ten exhibition games before the season started. I was getting to know some of the players, and the transition to my new team was getting better.

I talked to Brian Smith, he said he was working to get my new contract together with Walter Bush, the owner and president of the North Stars organization. I said, "Great, the sooner the better." Some players were getting speaking engagements, commercials, and endorsement deals. It seemed that those players were attached to Alan Eagleson, who was a player agent and the head of the NHL Players Association. He used his position of power to get most of the major offers from companies that would pay endorsements to players.

MINNESOTA NORTH STARS.

Figure 75

I visited with him briefly in Detroit, and I was planning to talk to him about representing me. Once a year, the players association had training and informational meetings regarding the association. In one meeting in Detroit, he was arrogant and made a derogatory remark about me in front of some players, and although it may have been a joke, it struck me wrong. I never liked him after that. So as a result, I never asked him for his services. He later was convicted of fraud and malpractice and served time for his actions. Enough said.

371

As the exhibition season started, we played okay. We weren't going to be a great team, but we had some pretty good guys. We needed to build on what we had to become a better all-around team. The North Stars had not drafted well either, and some of the draft choices were questionable, and not panning out. The trades were about even or worse than even, and we were not gaining any ground in building our depth and talent base.

During camp Blake Dunlop and I both got apartments in Burnsville and rented furniture. The apartments were about twenty minutes from the arena. They were nice with sunken living rooms, fireplaces, and decks. I was given a car by a dealership to use throughout the season. It was nice. I had similar benefits in Detroit in the previous years.

I was introduced to Randi Peterson during training camp. She was a friend of Dennis Hextall's wife. We got along well and started dating. Randi was an RN and was working at a local hospital. She was beautiful and had done some local modeling. I met her family and they were wonderful people. They were from the Minneapolis area, Phil (her father) worked in public relations and Joan (her mother) work at the market in downtown Minneapolis. They had a home in St. Louis Park. Phil was a WWII veteran and we got along well.

It was different playing in Minnesota. I was used to the old Detroit Olympia Stadium, with fans hanging over the balconies and more of the blue-collar, rowdy attitude. The fans were more subdued in Minnesota at the Met Center. The crowd was back from the ice, and they were quiet for the most part. They were loyal fans and the building was modern and nice.

During our first trip to Montreal to play a league game, most of us went to the Giovanni Suit Factory. We could pick out material, and they would make us fabulous three-piece suits for one hundred dollars. We ordered two or three suits. Then when we played there again, we would pick them up and pay for them. It was one of the perks of playing in the league. Everyone loved to play in Montreal. It was always standing room only, and the crowd was loud and always into it. Montreal wanted to trade for me at one point when I was in Detroit. Ned Harkness liked me and would not trade me. Minnesota also offered a five-player deal for me, but Ned would not do it. He wanted to build for the future.

With the North Stars, I could see the personal conflicts with some of the players on the team. Bill Goldsworthy (Goldy) was a good friend and a great captain. He got along with everyone. He had the respect of the players and was a true leader. Dennis Hextall (Hexy) was opinionated and said what was on his mind. He was a good player, was chippy, and liked to mix it up. He was a good team-mate, and players hated to play against him. He centered Goldy, with J. P. Parise on left wing. Hexy did not like French hockey play-ers (frogs). He was verbal and could back it up in a fight. He wanted everyone to be more physical and fight. I remember when I got to Minnesota and the first time we had a beer together and talked. He said, "Great to have you, now we have four guys who will fight." He was referring to Goldy, Dennis O'Brien, himself, and, me as we were the only ones who would not back down from a fight.

Intimidation was a big factor in the NHL. When you would not fight or stand up for yourself, players like Hexy thought you were gutless and worthless, as did some coaches and management. On the North Stars, none of the frogs liked to fight and mix it up. That's why he did not like them. Just to anger J.P., during practices Hexy never passed him the puck while doing line rushes. He would always pass it to Goldy. The only way J.P. would get the puck was to get it from Goldy. Most of the time he would just skate up the boards by himself. After a while he would get angry and verbal, and they would argue. Then, on the next shift, Hexy would pass it to Godly again. After a while J.P. would not even skate down the ice with them. Around and around they would go; day after day all season long.

One time when we were playing in Boston, between periods in the locker room, J.P. was so mad at Hexy that he jumped over the top of me and sucker punched Hexy in the forehead. It started a brawl in our locker room, and we all jumped up and tried to stop it. Jack Gordon came in, started yelling at us, and calmed things down. It seemed the tension was always there during the season. We could play great at times and then fade, because of tensions, personalities and conflict. We had limited depth and talent base. We suffered, allowing other teams to take advantage of our lax situations and limited focus. We had some good journeyman players like Lou Nanne, Jude Drouin, Tom Reid, and Murray Oliver but very few impact players.

I was pressuring my lawyer, and encouraging him to get my contract together with the North Stars. I even talked to him about visiting with the Fighting Saints across town. I knew they were interested. Again, he said he was in touch with the management and they were working on a contract.

It was just after Thanksgiving, and we were in Pittsburgh. We played in Washington the night before and it was a travel day. We did not play until the next night and we arrived early. We went out to dinner and had a few beers. We sometimes did initiations for the rookies on the road and sometimes at home. We were going to do it to a rookie that night at the hotel. We gathered in one room, carrying on, teasing and having fun. Hexy came in drunk and started giving Jude Drouin trouble. He hated "frogs," and maybe it was Jude's turn to take some heat from Hexy. Jude got mad enough to take a run at Hexy. He grabbed him and pushed him out into the hallway. It seemed everyone was involved in this ruckus. Some punches were thrown, and players were grabbing and pushing each other to stop the fighting. We were a loud mob out in the hallway.

Goldy lost it and was so upset that he turned around and punched a fire extinguisher, giving himself deep cuts to his fingers and ligaments that required several stitches inside and out. By that time the management arrived trying to calm everyone down. After several minutes of pushing, shoving, having words with each other the players calmed down and finally went to their rooms.

Unfortunately, the press was registered and staying on the same floor as the players. This rarely happened, but this time it did. The reporters were standing down the hall and saw the whole thing. The headlines in the paper the next day stated "North Stars in bloody hotel brawl." Goldy was out for a month.

The drama and the personal battles among players continued throughout the season. It was hard to focus on playing with any consistency. We did not have the team camaraderie that we needed to win. We had personal problems with players who maybe should have been traded. The trouble was, players were not traded. Other players were traded for players of the same caliber. There was no significant difference. It seemed at times, the management was making trades to make trades, trying to make it look as if they were doing something. It did not help improve the team. Maybe they could not see or recognize what needed to be done.

I talked to my lawyer, Brian Smith again, and still the contract negotiations were not completed. He said they were closer and he wanted to get them finished before the first of the year. I had not seen Brian since the Boucha Bash, but we had talked on the phone. It would have been nice for him to come to Minnesota. He should have been able to sit down and visit with the General Managers of both teams, but I think Brian's wife Ann, got in the way and kept him on a tight leash. When I talked about this with other players, and about the way Brian did things or did not do things, they were concerned and thought he was out of touch and thought maybe I should get a new lawyer. Some of the players brought up things like insurance, investments, endorsements, retirement, contract guarantees, and bonuses that he should be working on for me, but he never brought up those subjects during our conversations. I took it all for granted. I thought he would be working and doing that for me. I overlooked a lot of things and trusted him too much. I assumed he was representing me well and he was not.

CHAPTER 51: MINNESOTA VS. BOSTON

We celebrated Christmas and the New Year with our family and friends. We had our holiday games too. I was still waiting for my new contract and I was looking forward to staying in Minnesota to finish what I hoped would be, a long and successful career.

On January 4, 1975, we were to play the Boston Bruins at the Met Center. It was a day just like any other game day. We came in for our morning skate and stopped to have some lunch before heading home for a nap before the game. We expected a big crowd and we wanted to start the New Year off with a big win. Beating Boston was a big treat for us. It did not happen that often. They had won the Stanley Cup in the early 1970s and still had the nucleus of the same team. Every team had some players who were borderline and were given an opportunity and brought up and sent down throughout the season.

On this night, I was playing on a scoring line with one of the top two lines. Ordinarily, the opposing team will throw out a checking line against you. That is what Don Cherry, Bruins Coach, did against us. I had Dave Forbes on my wing against me during the first period. He was one of those borderline players who were up and down throughout the season. He shadowed me throughout the game. Checkers like that, did their job by keeping us off the scoreboard. Forbes continued to brush me and give me an elbow here and there as he came by me, to distract me and to take me off my game.

MINNESOTA NORTH STARS.

Figure 76

It was more than usual, but I let it go. He seemed to take it a step further because I let it go. He was testing me more and more.

Later in the first period, I went into the corner in my end to get the puck. I saw him coming to lay a body check on me. I stopped quickly and jumped back, and he missed me for the most part and grazed my chin with his elbow. With that interaction, I turned around and grabbed him and threw a couple of punches and he went down. That is how you stop the intimidation and try to gain a little respect. He was down, so I didn't hit him again. But Terry O'Reilly came in and jumped on my back. As the third man in, he was removed from the game. Dave Forbes and I each received a five-minute major for fighting and two minutes each for roughing.

The game continued, and Forbes and I could not get back on the ice until the play had stopped. During our first few minutes in the box, we had a few words. I think he was embarrassed about the fight and wanted some revenge. After all, it was not good that he, as a borderline player, was beaten that decisively in a fight with the coach watching. He needed to prove more than that while playing with the main club. He was doing a good job until he stepped over the line, and he paid for it.

Bobby Orr cut Hexy during our time in the box and was given a five-minute major penalty for drawing blood. The game was getting rougher as the play continued. Some games were that way. I often wondered when Bobby Orr was in the box with Dave Forbes, if he might have encouraged Dave to do something when he got back on the ice. We'll never know.

With all of the stoppages in the game, it was close to fifteen minutes before Forbes and I were able to step back on the ice. There was a whistle and play had stopped. As I stepped onto the ice, I looked over at him to see if he wanted to fight again or if he had calmed down. He didn't make a move or say anything that would indicate a fight or that he was going to do anything. Usually, players will say something and square off to fight. Nothing was happening. So I looked over at the bench to see if I should stay on the ice or come off for a change. Someone said, "Look out!" As I was turning around to look, the butt of his stick hit me just above the right eye on the eyebrow. He had lunged forward and threw a sucker punch with his right hand and the butt of the stick was sticking out his right glove. The force of the blow was hard. I heard a pop and saw blood spurt out on the ice. I remember going down to cover up. I must have been in survival mode, because I immediately went to the ice and covered my head. A good thing I did, because Forbes then jumped on my back and punched me in the back of the head. He did that until one of our players grabbed him and stopped him and pulled him off me.

As I lay there, I was in between unconsciousness and consciousness. The trainer and team doctor were there to examine me and after a while, they called for a stretcher. They hauled me off through the Zamboni end of the ice, put me on a gurney and wheeled me into the first aid room. Those on the bench heard the pop of the stick hitting me. The cut was large across my eyebrow. They closed my cut, blood started coming out my eye, and someone asked, "Is his eyeball cut or damaged?" They called an ambulance and I was taken to the emergency room at Methodist Hospital.

In the emergency room they examined and prepped me by taking off my uniform and then closed up my cut with over thirty stitches. They admitted me into the hospital for observation. I was sick to my stomach from the medication, and they gave me something for that. It was a restless night and by morning my eye was swollen shut. They needed to let the swelling go down before examining me any further.

I received a call from Dave Forbes that morning telling me that he was sorry for what he did. After saying that, he said good-bye and hung up.

I seemed to be okay, although my eye was cut badly and was swollen shut. My brother Dave and family were there, along with Randi. The incident was national news that night. They reported that I was injured by a hockey stick, and people were calling to find out how I was. The team doctor was on staff at Methodist Hospital. They kept a close watch on me.

I was there for couple of days, and then they let me go home. Randi was an RN who worked at North Memorial Hospital. She stayed with me while I recovered. The phone rang constantly while I was at home with friends and family, and news reporters calling. Randi helped with the calls and that allowed me to rest.

After about a week, the swelling was starting to go down. They brought me back to the hospital for further examinations. When my eye was open a little bit my vision did not seem right. It looked as though the floor was uneven. After my x-rays and further examination, they concluded that I had an orbital fracture and the muscles around my eye may be damaged. They would not know for sure until the swelling reduced and they could examine me further.

Meanwhile the NHL gave Dave Forbes a ten game suspension until they could further investigate the incident. The North Star's office notified me that Clarence Campbell, the NHL commissioner, and his staff were coming to Minneapolis. They wanted to interview me as well as others who were close or were involved during the incident. In addition, the Hennepin County Attorney's Office called and wanted to interview me. They also wanted to take pictures of my eye. They were considering filing criminal charges against Dave Forbes for his actions on the ice. They wanted to charge him with aggravated assault.

CHAPTER 52: AFTERMATH OF THE INCIDENT

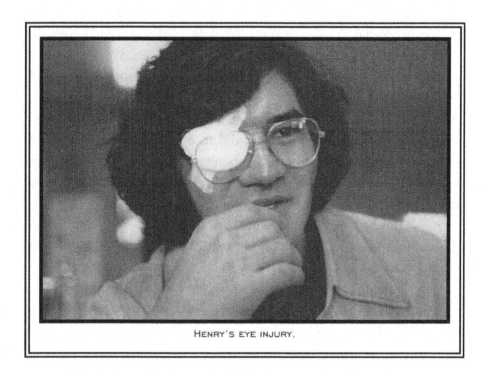

HENRY'S EYE INJURY.

Figure 77

The game was televised in Boston, locally in the Midwest and the game was sold out. The actual incident was not shown on TV replays, and no one had it on tape. Both stations went to commercial during the break. In other words, there was no tape of the actual incident—just personal recollections on what they saw and heard.

I had an outrageous interview with Clarence Campbell, Commissioner of the National Hockey League. He was in his 70's, and an attorney. I sat in front of Mr. Campbell and his staff, for no less than four hours. They questioned me about the incident. When I would answer a question, I had to do it slow enough so he could hand write out my answers on paper. I told them my side of the whole incident, in every detail that I could remember. He was in town for a week and interviewed a lot of people. His final decision for Dave Forbes was upheld: a ten-game suspension without pay. No one could believe it. That seemed too lenient.

Immediately, Gary Flakne, the Hennepin County, Minnesota attorney, filed aggravated assault charges against Dave Forbes. It was the first time in any professional sport that someone had been charged criminally for what they did in a game or on any kind of playing field. His reasoning: If someone did something similar on the street, e.g., hit someone with a club, the person would be charged with aggravated assault, and if found guilty, jailed and fined. Why would it not be the same way on the ice rink? Mr. Flakne was adamant and said if the league will not take care of this, then Hennepin County will take care of it.

Mr. Flakne maintained it took place in front of all these people, including kids. It had to be addressed. He went on to say, "It was televised in Boston, televised locally in the Midwest and there were over fifteen thousand fans at the game. If we let this go as part of the game, we will be sending a message to the kids that violence in sports will be tolerated. Kids would expect to get away with hitting someone without recourse or without getting penalized for their actions."

I was to be Gary Flakne's star witness. They took pictures of me and my eye, gathered all information about the incident, and had interviews with people who were there. He prepared depositions and prepared for the case against Forbes. It was big news, and this could be a landmark case.

The press was all over it. During the time that I was recovering, I flew to Warroad to visit my parents. While I was there, *Sports Illustrated* came, took pictures of me, and did a story. I still had my eye covered, and it was still black and blue and partially swollen. My injuries were never this serious before, nor did I have this much time off. I was restless. Hopefully, I would come back and pick up where I left off. But this time, this injury seemed different, more severe and more permanent. I thought about my contract. I thought about Brian Smith not completing the contract and negotiations. Now it may be too late. We would need to wait to see how my eye healed.

As the swelling reduced and the eye started to open, the damage was evident. I went back to Methodist Hospital to have my orbital fracture repaired. A week after my surgery, the problems continued. My eye was not working properly. The muscles around my eye were damaged. After some consideration, they thought the use of a troposcope to strengthen my eye muscles would help. I was scheduled at the Eye Center, University of Minnesota Medical Center for therapy. If I held my head straight, my upper eye muscles worked. I could see up and both eyes worked together, but when I tried to use my lower gaze, my damaged eye would not go down into that position. The muscles at the bottom of the right eye did not work and would not pull the eye down. I needed to see in all directions on the ice when playing hockey. The eye exercises were supposed to help strengthen those muscles. The proposed result would help strengthen and pull the eye down. I went there a few times a week for therapy.

Meanwhile, the team was faltering and they were on a losing streak. They were headed for the cellar in the division. They were only a point ahead of Kansas City in the cellar. The front office was getting desperate and wanted to stay ahead of Kansas City. They called me into a meeting. They were concerned enough to ask me to come back and play. If felt, they were not going to take no for an answer, as they were insisting. They needed my help. They said that I was a better player injured than most of the other players who were healthy. They said I could play on a power play and be used sparingly on the shifts but they wanted me back immediately. I thought this was crazy. I think they did too, but they were desperate. I could not see very well and had depth perception problems. I finally agreed to give it a try.

After being on the ice, it was obvious to me that I was not going to perform as before. My vision was not the same. It would take some getting used to. I had to make adjustments to see properly in different situations.

When playing in games, opposing players knew of my eye injury, and would give me room during play. When I was having trouble seeing the puck, they would not take advantage of the situation and put a hit on me. I appreciated that because there were times when I was vulnerable.

I was starting to get frustrated, emotional and depressed over my performance. I could not do the things that I did before and people looked at me differently because my eyes did not work together and I looked different. I was self-conscious about the way I looked. Randi did not care. I felt thankful to have her support. I was playing on the ice and I was doing okay, but I was not up to my expectations. I was drinking more than usual, and had some problems with the team as a result. I had an "I don't care attitude" and I was going through some emotional and personal challenges due to the head injury. I had not received any diagnosis of the extent of the head injury, counseling, or help adjusting to the changes. I was expected to play like nothing was wrong.

Finally, during one of those times when I broke curfew, I was sent home from Philadelphia for breaking team rules. I was experiencing depression, and some emotional problems but no one offered to help. The team was more interested in staying out of the cellar. No one seemed to care about me as a person and what the concussion and loss of vision did to me.

The team responded with better performance and we finished out of the cellar. It was another frustrating year for me as a player. Without a contract and with the injury, I was not sure how this was going to end up. I felt unsure of everything. I was insecure but Randi was there for me, when it seemed no one else cared. We were spending more and more time together. It felt good to have someone to share my uncertain life with.

When the season ended, players seemed to go their separate ways. There was no fanfare, no getting together with each other. It was over and it seemed final. I had gone through a lot in a few short months. I was still getting my eye therapy at the university and still under doctor's care. I felt I had an uncertain future in hockey. Randi was the only certain and positive thing in my life at the moment. We talked about marriage. I was leery; as I had not been close to anyone since Debby. I did not want to go through the hurt and loneliness of another relationship failure like that again. Randi seemed genuine, but she never introduced me to any of her friends or told me much about her life. She only told me what she wanted me to know. I thought that was odd, but I remember that I did not care or want to know. I never pressed it. She told me she had many relationships. Randi was a nurse. Previously, she did some modeling and she was pursued by men a lot during that time. It was in the back of my mind about her former relationships, but I never asked. For the moment, I was lonely and vulnerable. I thought we loved each other. I had experienced plenty of care free relationships too, and I would not let anyone get close. I always moved on. We were married on May 9, 1975, in Minneapolis with both families in attendance. We honeymooned at the Broadmoor Hotel in Colorado Springs. Her parents and family were some of the finest people I knew. I was thankful to be a part of her family.

HENRY AND RANDI'S WEDDING.
LEFT TO RIGHT: LLOYD AND JOANIE CHERNE, JOAN AND PHIL PETERSON,
RANDY AND HENRY.

Figure 78

I moved out of the apartment in Burnsville and Randi and I moved into a place in Bloomington, Minnesota. I still did not have a new contract and the future was a big question. I played out my contract with the North Stars and was a free agent. What a disaster with Brian Smith, no contract! I should have fired him right there but did not. He was scrambling around trying to get something together with the Saints, or the Stars. Now it was time to get down to business and get it done. Finally, Brian Smith came to town, and we negotiated with the North Stars and the Fighting Saints. After some back and forth negotiations, I decided to sign with the Fighting Saints in Saint Paul. The North Stars and Walter Bush did not budge and only offered a one year deal. My contract with the Saints was a guaranteed contract for four years, plus an option year. We waited for the lawyers to get things ready and to sign the contract. The criminal case against Forbes was pending and was on the docket with Hennepin County.

In late spring, the Dave Forbes trial was being held. It brought a lot of attention to Hennepin County, the Twin Cities, and the game of hockey. It was a drawn-out, two-week trial. I testified for the prosecution as the victim. There were a number of people called to testify. The trial was covered widely and had the interest of all involved with the game. Everyone was watching since it was the first time in the United States that an athlete was being charged criminally for actions while participating in a professional game of any kind.

The prosecution tried to prove that he intentionally tried to injure me. It was difficult and almost impossible to prove. Although we spent approximately fifteen minutes in the penalty box, and he was out to get me, they could not prove the intent. From the defense side, there was also a lot of "his glove made the cut," or "he hit his head on the ice," etc. With a blow that vicious, it had to be the stick. Several of the people behind the bench saw the whole thing. It was amazing how many different versions were told from people describing what they saw. With no cameras filming the incident, there was nothing but personal and spectator testimony about what actually happened that night.

It was a "hung jury" meaning, all of the jurors did not agree. The prosecution felt they got their point across and would not retry the case. It was over. Everything remained the same for the NHL and Forbes would receive only a ten-game suspension without pay. All criminal charges were then dropped.

CHAPTER 53: THE MINNESOTA FIGHTING SAINTS

Randi and I moved from Bloomington to West Saint Paul in midsummer, after the Dave Forbes trial ended. I also ended months of therapy at the University of Minnesota. There was no improvement. The Minnesota Fighting Saints arranged an eye appointment at the Mayo Clinic in Rochester, Minnesota with Dr. John Dyer. Dr. Dyer, a well-known eye specialist, thoroughly examined my eye, the muscles and the orbital fracture. He explained to me that there are six muscles around the eye that work together; they move the eyeball around, and both eyes work together. In my case, in my right eye, my lower muscles were damaged and were not working properly. As a result, those muscles would not pull my eye down. His suggestion was to move my upper muscles downward by reattaching them lower to help those lower muscles move the eye down. He said that I would not be able to look up as well, but it would give me some relief in looking down.

MINNESOTA FIGHTING SAINTS.

Figure 79

Later on, the procedure was completed and I recovered in the hospital in Rochester. I was released and went home to recuperate. I could tell a difference in my eyes mobility. After the examination and more testing, it was decided that the surgery was successful. It was better for hockey but I still had double vision, depth perception problems and poor peripheral vision. After more testing and after a couple of weeks, Dr. Dyer would try to relax and weaken my left eye muscles to force the eyes to work better together. With that procedure, they let me go home the same day. The doctor said, "Give it some time, and we will see how it all works." We tried to enjoy the rest of the summer and made a trip to Warroad to visit before the season started. My sister Darlene, her husband, Jim, and family from Idaho were visiting in Warroad. As always it was nice to see everyone. We had a great time and stayed for a few days before heading back to Saint Paul.

Years before, I promised my parents I would buy them a house. It had been on my mind for some time. While in Warroad, Randi and I looked for a small house for my parents. We found one next to the Warroad Nursing Home that we thought would suit them. We brought my parents and Jim and Darlene to look at it. Everyone seemed to like it and thought the location was good. We made arrangements to purchase it before we left. They would move once the abstract was up to date, and we had a title opinion and the deal completed. They were absolutely thrilled. It made me extremely proud to be able to do that for them. Once they moved into their new house, they rented out the old house and became landlords.

As training camp started with the Minnesota Fighting Saints, I was again excited to start the season. The camp was held at the Civic Center in downtown St. Paul. Instead of checking into a hotel for camp, the players were allowed to stay at home. It was different. There were a lot of Minnesota players on the roster. My eye was a constant concern but I went about my business and tried to do the best I could. That summer we found out that Randi was pregnant.

Both families were extremely happy for us and we were excited. She was due in late March 1976.

When looking at our Saints team on paper, I was excited. I knew most of the guys from Minnesota and I played against some in the NHL. The staff—Glen Sonmor, General Manager; Harry Neale, Coach; Glen Bostic, Trainer; and Don Niedercorn, Equipment Manager. We had a lot of talent and we seemed fairly deep. Our players included Pie Mackenzie, Boston Bruins, Dave Keon, Toronto Maples Leafs, Shakey Walton, Leafs, Wayne Connelly, North Stars, Rick Smith, Boston Bruins and Minnesotans; Jack Carlson, Mike Antonivich, Paul Holmgren, and Pat Westrum; also, my US National Team teammate Gary Gambucci, Olympic teammate Lefty Curran, and John Garrett and a few others who were good quality players. This team might be the best and most talented team I had played on.

The team was a cast of characters with colorful personalities. It was always interesting to be around them, because you never knew what was going to happen next. Glen Sonmor liked to have a team that was tough and would not back down from anything. He took the term *Minnesota Fighting Saints* literally. Harry Neale was an average coach but was able to put up with all those personalities. With that much individualism on the team, I am sure it was hard to coach and keep everyone happy. The season was going well and we were winning and having fun.

The truth about the instability of the team had been withheld from the public and the players for some time. Wayne Belisle, the team's owner and president had lost his investors just before the season and he tried to keep it private. The Saints needed eleven thousand paid fans per game to financially support them. We were averaging less than ten thousand per game. Toward the holidays the rumors were out about the team's finances. We had meetings, and Wayne Belisle assured us that everything was okay. With all of the rumors flying around, it was hard to play and stay focused. I liked playing in Saint Paul. It was more of a blue-collar town, like Detroit and a true sports town. The fans were great.

With the rumors, I checked on the status of my contract and I was stunned to find out that my contract was not guaranteed. My lawyer Brian Smith did not follow through on arranging the guarantee before I started playing. The money was supposed to be in escrow in the bank before I played a game. I think the management assured Brian it was there when in fact it was not. He took their word for it. Without the documentation in writing or guarantee from the bank, it would be no good. We all knew something was wrong with the financial status of the organization. I called Brian's office immediately. He did not answer, so I left a message. I wanted to find out about the money guarantee and about the status of the situation. I knew it was almost over and they would be folding. With no guarantee, I left the team first. I just walked out during a game.

Brian did not call me back right away. He knew about the trouble in St. Paul. He knew he screwed up big time. I was at home when I got the call from Brain. He was scrambling around and said Sid Abel, General Manager of the Kansas City Scouts of the NHL, offered me a contract and would match the one I had with the Saints. Would I be interested? Randi and I talked it over and we decided to accept the offer. They were stable and I would be back in the NHL. The next day I flew to Detroit and met Sid Abel and Brian at the Detroit airport. I signed the contract and flew back to Minnesota, packed my bags, and flew to Kansas City (KC) the next day for a press conference. I was not off the ice for more than a week, and I was under contract again but out the money in Saint Paul.

When I arrived in Kansas City, the staff picked me up at the airport. They scheduled me for interviews at three different TV stations and a couple of radio station before they brought me to my hotel. I was exhausted from traveling and the stress of the situation. I called Randi and we talked into the night, and then I went to sleep. When I got to the rink in the morning, I was introduced to the guys and I received equipment and a uniform. I was surprised to see Gary Bergman. I played with him in Detroit and he was in

Minnesota briefly, and now KC. The first thing he said was, "What the hell are you doing, following me around?" Gary was from my neck of the woods. He was from Kenora, Ontario, where most of my relatives live. Another player was Guy Charron, who I played with me in Detroit for a few years. It was good to see those guys and to meet the rest of the team. After skating with them, I could see the reason they were in last place. They were a bunch of cast offs with a thin talent base and no depth, and I was one of them.

CHAPTER 54: KANSAS CITY SCOUTS

I stayed in a hotel for about a week and then got an apartment in a complex where most of the other players were renting. The complex was in North Kansas City, about a half-hour drive to Kemper Arena. A moving company packed our belongings and transported them to Kansas City. Randi flew in and her parents drove our vehicle down for us. The weather was nice that time of year. It was warming up, and everyone seemed to have spring fever.

We played our regular schedule. The team struggled and lost most of the games. We didn't have the players to compete but managed to pull off some good wins here and there. During one game in Buffalo, Steve Durbano ("Durbo" a player most everyone hated to play against because he was so unpredictable and a typical goon in those days) was jumped by a Buffalo Sabre's rookie who started a fight with him. Steve had no chance of squaring off with him. The rookie jumped him from behind, landed on him on the ice and held him down while throwing a few punches. It was simply a rookie trying to make a name for himself, but it angered Durbo. I was on the ice standing by our goalie and waiting for a face-off while the teams changed lines. The Buffalo player was already in the penalty box and Durbo was at our bench getting a drink of water. Then all of a sudden Durbo took off across the rink with that water bottle in his hand and threw it at the Buffalo player in the penalty box. Well, all hell broke loose.

After Durbano had thrown the bottle, he raced down toward us. When I looked up, the whole Buffalo team jumped off the bench and was coming toward us; I thought I was going to die. I dropped my gloves and stick and skated out there to try to stop some of the guys, and all of a sudden everyone just stopped. They just stood there looking into the corner. When I turned around, there was Durbo, standing in the corner with two hands on his stick, swinging it like a baseball bat. They all knew how crazy he was and nobody from the Buffalo team wanted anything to do with that. Meanwhile, the referees got there. Fans were standing over the glass and throwing cups of pop and beer and anything else they could at Durbo. The referees escorted him off the ice and out the door and gave him a game misconduct. Durbano led the league in penalty minutes that year.

I did play against Dave Forbes that year in Kansas City. The newspaper built it up as a revenge match. I was told by the team, the league, and my lawyer not to do anything crazy or start something. The game was played without incident, and that was the last time I ever saw or heard from Forbes.

We were playing a game in New York against the Rangers late in the season when Randi was taken to the hospital to have the baby. Henry Jr. was born on March 28 and we celebrated when I got home the next day. He was such a cute little guy with a lot of black hair.

The National Hockey League wanting to expand their presence in the world and promote hockey, scheduled a couple of games in Japan that year. The Kansas City Scouts and the Washington Capitals were to play two exhibition games in Tokyo after the season. They were chosen because the league figured that the two new teams would not be making the playoffs. Henry Jr. a couple weeks old, was too young to make the trip. I did not want to go without Randi so we stayed in Kansas City.

KC Scout Caricature. Courtesy of J. White.

Figure 80

JOHN LANDBY, HENRY, AND AJ LANDBY AT MEET THE
KANSAS CITY SCOUTS DAY.

Figure 81

We heard the rumors the team may be transferring to Colorado. At the final team meeting, our coach said that Vickers Oil Company may be buying the team and moving it to Denver. Nothing was final, but they would keep us informed. The last thing our coach said as he walked out the door was," There is no more dough in KC, MO". We kept the apartment in Kansas City and stayed there throughout the summer except for trips to Santa Fe, Minneapolis, and Warroad.

With combined thirty-plus teams between the NHL and the rival WHA, the talent base available to stock the new teams in Kansas City and Washington was stretched pretty thin. In their first season, the Capitals would set an NHL record for futility, losing sixty-seven of eighty games and winning only one on the road. The Scouts fared only marginally better, and the 1974 expansion was widely seen as having been a mistake.In Kansas City, we suffered from inflated player costs, undercapitalized ownership, an economic downturn in the Midwest, poor performance on the ice, and poor attendance. We drew an average of just 8,218 fans during two years in the17,000-seat Kemper Arena (at a time when the league average was approximately 13,000). The team's thirty-seven owners, buried in debt, mounted a season-ticket drive to raise more revenue. However, when only two thousand tickets were sold, they concluded that the Scouts were not a viable venture and opted to sell.

CHAPTER 55: COLORADO ROCKIES

All players had been notified that the team had been sold to Vickers Oil in Denver. The new management would contact all players. When I heard the news that Johnny Wilson was hired to coach, I was thrilled. He was my first NHL coach in Detroit. I thought he was a great coach and he was what we needed for a competitive team.

During the summer, and after some animosity over the way things were handled by Brian Smith, we met Brian and talked things over. He apologized and smoothed everything over and we seemed to be back on track. We talked about a civil suit against Dave Forbes, the Boston Bruins, and the National Hockey League. He wanted to know what I thought about it. He said that he would like to look for a bigger law firm to partner with to help with the lawsuit. He convinced me that there was no alternative, as my eye was permanently damaged. After numerous attempts to contact Allan Eagleson of the Players Association, he did not return any of the calls. I was not playing productively because of the injury, longevity was questionable and we all thought my playing days were numbered. It was frustrating, because I could not arrange a discussion with the Players Association to review the status of my circumstances.

When I thought about a civil suit, it made sense, but could we win? How would this affect my career now? Randi was not so sure about Brian after the mess he caused me thus far. She wanted to change attorneys and use her parent's lawyer in Minneapolis. I had been with Brian for a long time. He helped me through the problems with Debby and I felt an obligation. Even though I was upset with him some of the time, I thought of him as a big brother and I felt comfortable with him. She reluctantly agreed. We did not file a suit until later.

In Denver, the management and everyone else assumed that I was about to sue Forbes, the Bruins and the league. It leaked elsewhere and when I arrived in Denver, the management already knew a civil suit may be pending. We had not filed anything yet but Ray Miron, GM was fairly cold to me. I sensed that something was wrong. I was under contract for another three years, and if I showed up and did my job, they had to pay me. It was uncomfortable for me to be around the management, so I avoided them as much as possible.

We started skating a couple of weeks before camp. The players chipped in, bought ice time and we scrimmaged. We were in a hotel for awhile and then we found an apartment. I could not get over the brightness of Colorado. The skies were bright and clear blue every day.

During training camp, I tried to stay positive. I felt with the addition of some new players and Johnny Wilson, we had a good chance of improving. I was excited about Denver and people were excited about the team. During our exhibition season, I was not dressing and Johnny Wilson came to me and said Ray Miron, GM, told him not to use me unless he absolutely had to. I practiced every day and did everything they asked. Johnny was nice enough to say something to me. Until then, I did not understand why I was being overlooked during camp. I had my suspicions. Johnny said, "He wanted to play me, but his hands were tied and he had to go along with management."

I understood the problem. I talked to Brian and told him about the situation and circumstances. He said the management was aware of the pending suit and decided to either punish me or make me want to quit. He figured the league was involved too. He thought maybe it was a tactical move by the league, without coming right out and forcing me out. It would be better for them if I quit and retired on my own. I had a contract for another three years. They had to honor it and pay me, but they probably did not want the publicity of forcing me out.

It was difficult during that time. I would practice every day and they would not dress me for games. I played in only nine games that year. When I did dress, it was because someone was hurt and they were short on players. I felt I should be playing on a regular shift, and Johnny Wilson did too.

During our time in Denver, Randi and I were having marriage problems. It seemed everyone on my side of things were more concerned about money and the lawsuit. Most of the decisions were made to protect the suit rather than my health and well being. I had to consider the inevitable, I may have to move on from my hockey life and find a different career. It is easier said than done. I was only 25 and would be 26 in June.

Finally, in early February the team made it clear that they wanted to settle my contract. I was put on waivers, and no team was interested in taking on my contract or me as a player. So after that, we went into negotiations on the settlement of the contract. Once we settled the contract, I was out. I was done. Hockey was over and life as I knew it would change. I had no idea what to do or where to live. I talked to Brian Smith about playing in the minors or in Europe. He said it was not a good idea with the lawsuit coming. It would look better if I did not play. I could see the lawsuit was more important to them than my livelihood. They went on to say, the suit would have more clout if I was forced out by the team and could not play. Every decision we made was from the lawsuit's perspective. I understood, they did not care about me; it was all about the money and prestige of winning a landmark legal case.

In those days, the Players Association or the league did not care about the athlete or person who had been injured or was suffering from a post head injury. You were on your own. If you were let go from a team, you had no medical coverage, only workman's comp, if you were injured. The Players' union had nothing to offer and never thought about career ending injuries or separation from the league at that time. Alan Eagleson, of the NHL Players' Association would not return our calls. My lawyer and I tried. He simply would not talk to us. Amazing!

Brian worked out a deal with another major law firm in Detroit to represent me in the lawsuit. The firm, Dykma, Goodnow, Spencer and Trigg had 125 lawyers and offices in the Renaissance Center in Detroit. The suit would be filed in Wayne County, Michigan. The papers were prepared by the law firm, and I signed them. Brian had twenty five percent split of the lawyer fees, plus expenses—a nice little deal for him. I thought Brian was a good friend and by then he seemed like family, but he did not do any favors for me. He made too many mistakes and he did not take care of me. In my case, he was not a good lawyer. I should have arranged for more professional mentors than just Brian. I was too dependent on him. I was so young and inexperienced.

The lawsuit was filed, and the firm started to do preliminary work and gather evidence and take depositions. No one knew how long it would take for this to go to trial. People thought this would be a landmark case, not only for the National Hockey League but for major league sports.

CHAPTER 56: SEATTLE AND SPOKANE

The contract with the Colorado Rockies was settled. I did not have any plans. It was just like walking out the door into another world. We did not know what to do or where to live. Randi wanted us to go back to Minnesota to live. I wanted to get away from hockey for a while. I had to find something else to do with my life and to carry on. After discussing our options, Randi and I decided to move to Seattle. I always liked Seattle and thought it would be a nice place to live or at least check it out for a while. I thought we could take our time and see what might happen. I thought about playing again, maybe in Europe. Every time I talked with Brian and the lawyers at the firm, they talked me out of it. I missed the game and the excitement of the competition. All players miss the limelight of playing at that level when they retire. It was hard, and I was not prepared for life after hockey. I did not have a particular direction and I was searching.

We rented a place in Edmonds, a northern suburb of Seattle. After we settled in, we looked around the city and got acquainted with the Northwest and the rain. It was springtime, and it rained every day for two weeks. I wondered what I got myself into. The weather in Denver was fabulous with all of the sunshine and clear skies. I looked at my options in the area and thought about employment. I went to a job agency and filled out an application. I realized then, that other than working at Marvin Windows in Warroad and working for the city as a kid, I had no experience or education to do anything. I did conduct hockey schools in Detroit. All I qualified for were labor jobs. So there I was with no formal education or job experience. My options were slim for the job market, unless I found an entry level position and worked my way up.

I had some money and thought about investing in a business, or maybe attend a trade school. I needed to do something that would keep me busy. I looked into business situations and various business options with a Realtor. I was a veteran, so I looked at the options that were available through the VA. I was trying to be smart with the next move. I remember thinking that I would be twenty-six in June. I was naive and green. I was in limbo and was searching, trying to fill the void. I was used to being very busy and having a lot to do.

We traveled to see my sister in Lewiston, Idaho, during the summer. I also took two trips back to Detroit because of the lawsuit. Randi spent some time in Minnesota visiting her parents. My brother Eddy got married that summer and we went to his wedding in Wisconsin. I was the best man. He married his long time girlfriend Linda Morello. They both lived in Milwaukee. They were married in Hurley,WI, her hometown. We had an absolute blast at the wedding. The family was there from Canada as well as my hometown of Warroad. We stayed and visited with friends and family for a while before heading back to Seattle.

The lawyers settled a workers' compensation claim for me, and they took their usual cut. I was looking at the newspapers and checking out different ads. I read an ad in the paper about a meat market for sale in Spokane. I remembered the meat markets in Kansas City and how interesting they looked. I also remembered the old meat market in Warroad and how fascinated I was with it. I thought it would be something that I might enjoy. I flew to Spokane for the day to meet a realtor and see the store and the city. The meat market looked good. The building had been updated and the business was profitable.

When I got back to Seattle, Randi and I talked it over and thought we should contacted a CPA to help me view the books and to find out how viable the business was and whether it was a good investment. After a week, he called me and had completed the review. We drove to Spokane and discussed the possibility of buying the meat market. After some discussion about financing, the Realtor said the owner would be interested in a contract for deed, with a down payment, and monthly payments. We crunched numbers with the CPA. We could cash flow the business. Randi liked Spokane. The climate was drier and it was a nice sized small city. We decided to make an offer and after a few back-and-forth negotiations, the deal was done. We set a closing date and figured out our move.

We were excited and we hoped this would prove worthwhile. We rented a place in the Spokane area and moved our things there in a U-Haul. Once we were settled, we closed the transaction, and I took over the business. The former owner stayed on and provided an orientation to the business and helped me for a few months.

Meanwhile, Randi was house hunting and found a nice house in the Spokane Valley. It was reasonably priced and we bought it. It took us a while to finally move in. Randi kept busy decorating the house, and her parents came to visit. Life was going well. I had relatives in Lewiston only two and a half hours away. I played a lot of golf, went fishing, water skiing and we were making new friends. Randi's sister decided to attend Washington State University in Pullman, so she would be close too. We had plenty of company during our time in Spokane. Business was holding it's own, and life was good.

For me personally, I was fighting depression and anger. I was emotionally bitter and felt I was in turmoil most of the time. It was hard to managed, but I got through it most of the time. I managed the store and things were going well. I was a good family man most of the time, but sometimes, I spent time away, drinking with my new friends.

I coached the Spokane Bantam team that winter. Sam Cozza a new friend helped as an assistant coach. Sam, his wife and his family became good friends of ours. We spent holidays together and had great barbeques and dinners. Sam and I were two peas in a pod, and spent a lot of time partying, probably too much. I thought my involvement in hockey would help me stay busy and focused. It was volunteer time and I felt it would help me give back to the community. I enjoyed being on the ice with the kids. It was good for me personally. It kept me busy and gave me some much-needed exercise on a daily basis. We played a good schedule and traveled around the area and to Canada for games and tournaments.

Ever since my injury on January 4, 1975, I had not been the same. It was a brutal injury including head trauma. I was suffering from a closed brain injury, and from my eye injury. I also was suffering from post-traumatic stress. Those are the terms used now. I was not thinking clearly sometimes. I hid my emotions well. There was something wrong, but I could not put my finger on it. I was emotionally bitter, depressed, and angry, and I tried to carry on with my life as usual and with some normalcy. The moods affected me emotionally, mentally, physically, and spiritually. I was looking for something that would help me. I prayed. I tried to go to church. I was looking for something that would change me, and settle me down and I would be at peace. I wanted to be a good family man. I could not control my drinking. I could not drink socially, once I started I could not stop.

People would look at my eye and ask me about it constantly. That upset me. I would try to be patient with people and tell the story over and over again. Having to explain the incident time and time again was mentally and emotionally draining.

RANDI, HEN JR AND HENRY.   HEN JR., HENRY AND RANDI.

Figure 82

Randi was pregnant again. Maybe she thought this would bring me around. She was desperately trying to keeps things together. I did not help. I was obnoxious and ornery and was walking around with a chip on my shoulder. It seemed that I did not care anymore. My friends introduced me to drugs, and I started using them as well. Things really started getting out of hand. Our wonderful daughter Bridgette was born on April 3, 1979. We brought her home amidst the turmoil of a possible divorce. Randi had talked with a lawyer about a divorce.

My meat business suffered, meat prices rose over 70% to make things even worse and more stressful. Small stores were closing everywhere. We were trying to compete with the super markets. I did not work and pull my own weight. I let the employees and the management do most of the work. We tried new advertising and

411

other business solutions. I felt I was spending good money after bad. I decided to close the store and put it on the market.

I was relieved once I made that decision. I was not in any shape to run a business. I was blaming everyone else for my problems. I was angry about losing my hockey career, the way I was treated by hockey management, the Players Association and by my own lawyers. Randi and I were getting a divorce and I felt my world was falling apart.

Emotionally, I was losing the battle with depression. I was drinking and drugging heavily. I thought that was the only way to survive and to relieve the pain. When I drank, I was in denial and I lost my inhibitions and did not have a care in the world. I dread the thought of how my son must have felt when he was waiting for me to come home after work. He would stand at the window and watch the cars go by, thinking it was me coming home. How disappointed he was when the car did not pull into the driveway. Those thoughts will haunt a man the rest of his life, and now I am truly sorry.

As the situation became worse, and my "do not care" attitude was evident, I stopped making payments on the contract and the owner started to foreclose. The store had not sold. Everything started to unravel. I had unpaid bills that needed attention, but I ignored them. Randi was at home and was getting the brunt of the calls. I let things fall apart, and I drank more and more to escape my life's situation. I did not need to let that happen. It was preventable. I was drowning in deep depression, anguish and self-pity.

Randi had no choice but to call her parents and request they come help her move back to Minnesota. They arranged for a moving company. I did not care at that point. I was engulfed in self-pity, denial, and obsessed in drug and alcohol abuse. Everyone knew that it was a matter of time before I would totally self-destruct, or had I already? Once they had the truck packed, they left. They flew back to Minnesota and left me with an almost empty house. I told her to take the furniture and everything. She left me with the furniture in the den. I was almost financially ruined at that point. I needed to get my act together and do something, but what?

I just sat there in the empty house for a few days, and I was in a deep depression. I knew I had to do something. I was in survival mode and sobered up, and when I came out of it, I packed my belongings and I moved to Lewiston, Idaho. I temporarily stayed with my sister Darlene and Jim. Before I left Spokane, I contacted an attorney friend and gave him power of attorney for anything that needed to be done. I left things in Spokane pretty much a mess. I let things fall where they may, and thought I would get them straightened out later. At that moment, I just wanted to leave. I stayed in Lewiston for about two weeks. It was good to get away from the situation and out Spokane at that point. I started thinking more clearly and made a decision to move back to Detroit and start over.

CHAPTER 57: DETROIT CITY

After I left Lewiston, I drove back to Minneapolis and saw the kids and talked to Randi. She needed time away with the peace and quiet after the ordeal I put her through in Spokane. I understood completely and I left Minneapolis and drove to Milwaukee. I stayed with my brother Eddy and Linda for a couple of weeks. I knew Randi and the kids were safe, the turmoil in Spokane was behind me. The problems of leaving Spokane would eventually catch up with me and I would need to deal with it, but for now, I felt free and needed a new and fresh start. The Summer Fest was going on in Milwaukee. Robert Marshall and Billy Freeburg from Warroad stopped and stayed for a few days. Tom Kohl came up from Chicago too. I also had a friend from Detroit fly over and we all enjoyed our time together. After my stay in Milwaukee, I drove to Detroit and stayed with a friend in Taylor, Michigan. I needed to re-invent myself and try to find something to do. While driving, I had time to think. Once a person is away from the problem, you have a different view of the situation. I realized that the problem was me; I had to try to fix me. I could not see that through the drugs and alcohol. The problem was mine and my responsibility. I had to deal with me, my feelings, my depression, my anger. I had to try figure it all out. It would take time.

After arriving in Detroit, I settled in and started looking at my options. I contacted several of my old friends and got re-acquainted. I called Brian Smith and set up a meeting with the other lawyers to see how the lawsuit was coming. We did not have a trial date set. The lawyers figured it would be the following year. I needed a job and went to see the management for Red Wings. I talked to Lincoln Cavalier, the president of the Olympia Corporation, who owned the Red Wings. He sent me to read for a spot as a color commentator with the local station that was carrying the Red Wing games. My old teammate Mickey Redmond got the job instead.

Then, I went back to see Ted Lindsay, the General Manager of the Wings. He hired me to work in the marketing department for the Red Wings. That was a good job and I attended all of the games and other functions. I also played with the Red Wing Old Timers in fundraising games and special events for charity. Things were okay, not great, but I was managing, and making changes. I was alive and maintaining a living and slowly coming to grips with my problems. It was not easy; it was a process, and a long and lonely one.

Meanwhile, it was good seeing all my old friends around the Detroit area. The Red Wings changed homes after some fifty years at Olympia Stadium. I played in the last game at Olympia Stadium with the Old Timers and continued to play with them the rest of the year.

I left my job with the Wings and I worked in the music business for a while, booking bands under Boucha Productions. I spent some time in studios with some up-and-coming bands. CDs were just coming out then. It proved to be a tough business. I couldn't take it to the next level. I did not have the capital to move forward, to invest, or make any commitments. I was more interested in making a living, and not taking any risks. I had been thinking about going home to Warroad for some time. I thought about other places too, but Warroad was always on my mind. I did not want to stay in Detroit much longer. Home always popped up in my mind, and I thought maybe I should follow my intuition instead of fighting it. My thoughts were to wait to see what happened with the lawsuit and go from there.

The lawsuit was coming along and there was talk of a settlement at some point. There were at least ten lawyers on the other side, and they all had a say. There were lawyers for Dave Forbes, the Boston Bruins, and a group from the NHL. By midsummer of 1980 we had a fall trial date set and were on the court docket. It was 5 years from the eye injury to get to this point. Talk of a settlement continued. My lawyers of course wanted to take it all the way. They wanted the glory and recognition and to set a president with the suit. It was glory for them, but then again they were thinking of only themselves, and not about me. If I would have let the lawyers do what they wanted, we would of ended up in the Supreme Court, and waiting another 10 years.

During the summer, Brian talked to me about testifying at the US Congressional sub-committee hearings on Violence in Sports in DC. There was a bill on the floor about taking action in fines and penalties, if the leagues could not govern themselves on violence on the field, rink or court. Brian thought this would get him some publicity and arranged for us to attend and speak at the meetings. Brian said that he was the one they asked and I was there to say a few words and agree with him. I prepared a statement, gave my testimony, and they asked me some questions. Representatives were present from all professional sports. Brian was not allowed to talk; they wanted to hear from me, not him. His plan backfired, and he spent his money for tickets, and hotel and was not allowed to say a word. So he lied to me about the situation, and lied to me for the last time.

I had enough of lawyers, enough of their greed and thoughtlessness of the individual/client. I told them to settle, if possible. About a week later the call came in that the National Hockey League, wanted to settle. They did not want to expose themselves with a huge public trial. Then the next week, attorney's for Dave Forbes settled (the insurance company), which left the Boston Bruins holding the bag. The Boston attorneys were visibly upset when they finally heard of the settlement of the other two parties, and went directly into conference. We knew we had them. They made an offer, and we countered. It was discussed and we settled the next day, although it took some time to get the paperwork in order. It was over and we got down to business. Randi and her family lawyer flew into town, and we settled with her. Our divorce was pending. It felt good to settle with her and to make arrangements for the kid's future.

After working on the final settlement costs, we settled other debts and the lawyers got their share of the money. I took a little cash up front, and chose to take the rest over a thirty-year period. I stayed in Detroit contemplating my next move.

CHAPTER 58: HOME TO WARROAD

It was the following spring by the time I decided to go back to Warroad. I was not sure if I was going home to stay or just to visit. My monthly settlement payments were coming in on a regular basis. When growing up we were never taught the value of money or how to budget. It would prove to be difficult. My parents lived off the land, and as long as they had a roof over their head, food, and a little money for gas and essentials, they were happy. They survived, like many people and families did during 1930's-50's.

Spokane was my bottom, my canyon and hopefully the worst was over. I still had my bouts with depression and a chip on my shoulder. I irritated a lot of people with my arrogance, poor attitude, and poor judgment. I was more of a binge drinker now. That meant I could go for days without drinking, but when I did, I went overboard and drank for a couple of days and then stopped for a while. We drinkers thought we were having fun and thought everyone drank, but when you sober up, and look around, you realize that hardly anyone drinks. I was able to stop temporarily, if had something important to do. I could hold off for a while, but then I would get restless and start drinking. I was better, but not totally okay. It seemed to me that I was looking for something and could not find it. I had this ball of energy and turmoil in my gut that I had trouble controlling.

When I arrived in Warroad, the family was happy to see me. It was great being home. I think the last time I was there was in

1976 when Randi and I visited in the summer. I stayed with my parents. The house was always full of activity. Friends and family would come and go all day long. It was good place to see everyone and to have a cup of coffee and visit.

During the weeks that followed, I spent time with friends Stu Wood and wife Sharon who owned Stu's Northland Tap in town. Stu had medical problems and he was struggling. They were thinking about selling the tavern. I told them previously that one day I would come back and buy the place. I agreed to buy the tavern on a contract for deed. Most people were thrilled that I was staying and buying the tavern. I was twenty-nine then and I could still skate. I was out of shape but I was still young and had a lot of spunk.

When I took over the bar, I had a grand opening. Things were going along pretty well. I had my binges once in a while, but all in all it was working. It was difficult tending bar and listening to people who had too much to drink or dealing with people who were rowdy and obnoxious, but that was the bar business. My friend Ron Umhauer (our Johnny Cash) and his band played in the bar on Sundays. We had some nice crowds during that time. I sat in with them and played guitar on occasion, and we had a lot of fun.

Hockey season came around, and I contributed financially to the youth teams. Cal Marvin asked me to play with the Warroad Lakers that year. I said that I would and I started skating. I committed out of respect, but my heart was not into it. I was out of shape, but as time went on I started to come back. I played in one exhibition game. I was suffering from tendonitis in my arm before the game but played anyway. I played one period, and then I took my equipment off. I had planned to go back and play the season, but I never did. I just did not have the heart or motivation anymore; I lost my desire for the game and could not bring myself to play.

I was bitter and I had an attitude about what I thought hockey did to me, instead of what hockey gave to me, and be thankful about it. My thoughts and feelings were in turmoil at times. I was still seeking help, and I did manage to visit with some professional people. Maybe I did not stay long enough, or thought they did not get what I was talking about. I did not hang out at the rink, and it disappointed a lot of people. My reputation and business suffered. In a manufacturing community as in most communities people drank, and the bar was doing okay.

However, during the winter, I lost interest in the bar business as it became more difficult to manage. Small community life seemed to close in on me and I felt a need to move on. I made arrangements with the former owners to return the bar.

During that time I had been seeing Elaine Olafson. She was and is a fine woman, strong willed, loyal, and conservative. We sometimes butted heads on issues. She worked at Marvin Windows and had an apartment in Warroad. We moved in together. Her parents were not happy. She was seven years younger than me. After I gave up the bar, I asked her if she wanted to go to Idaho for a change. She said "okay". We stored our things at my sister Shirley and Stan Flicks. We said our good-byes to the family and traveled to Phoenix to visit for a while. Then we drove to Idaho, camping and sightseeing along the way. We stayed with my nephew Dave and Pam Dorion, and then we rented a house. We traveled back to Warroad to bring the furniture to Idaho. We spent the summer in Lewiston.

CHAPTER 59: IDAHO

Lewiston is set in a valley on the confluence of the Snake and Clearwater Rivers. Clarkston was in Washington State just across the river. The name derived from the Lewis and Clark Expedition. Lewiston/Clarkston has a population of about 30 thousand and Clarkston was the smaller of the two. My sister Darlene moved there right out of high school and married Jim Dorion. My brother Georgie was killed there. I felt a connection and I spent time there with my brother Eddy in the summer of 1972. My mother took Jim, Eddy and I to visit Darlene and Jim when we were kids. We fished a lot when I was there before. The areas around Lewiston also had great hunting. I was excited to live there and get into the outdoor activities. I loved the mountains.

Darlene and Jim inherited a place on Slate Creek down on the Salmon River. They received the land from friends whom Darlene and Jim had cared for. They were about to put it on the market. They asked if I wanted to take a look at it, and maybe buy it. We were not sure we wanted to live down there; we didn't know anybody in that area. We decided to take a look and drove down with Jim and Darlene. When we arrived at Slate Creek, it was nice and sunny. It was really quiet and rural. It was a quarter acre of land. It had two trailer houses on it, an open shed, and a big garden plot. It had sixteen filbert nut trees, grapes, and pear and apple trees. It was also right on Slate Creek. I could walk out my front door and catch a trout. It was a quarter mile up from the main Salmon River. There was a ranger station at Slate Creek. Above us the road wandered up the creek into the Nez Perce National Forest. An older couple had a log house and shared the driveway. They were there in the summer and went to California in the winter. The nearest store was in White Bird, about ten miles away. There were other neighbors further up the creek, and a small community near the Ranger Station down below.

We went back to Lewiston and thought about it for a while. We only moved to Lewiston less than 6 months before. We liked Lewiston, and we were not sure if we would like it out in the country. Darlene and Jim said they would sell it to me on a contract for deed. They said they would sell his old 1966 Chevy pickup too. We were driving Elaine's car at the time. There were no jobs to speak of in the area. Most young people were moving out of the area to places like Lewiston and the bigger towns. For us, it was a lot to consider, but regardless it could prove to be a good investment. It was time to renew the lease on the house in Lewiston. We decided to go for it and bought the place. It was all new and exciting. We enjoyed exploring the contents of the property and the area. Darlene, Jim and the family took most of the good items off the property but there were still a lot of things there. We got to know our neighbors, and traveled around the surrounding area. It was amazing to us having come from northern Minnesota to see the nuts, pears, apples, and grapes in the yard in the spring.

We burned wood in the winter, and cut dry timber above us in the forest on Slate Creek. We hauled down about six cords for the winter. We hunted deer and had trout in the freezer. We also hunted elk with Jim and Darlene up on the north fork of the Clearwater River in northern Idaho. Our neighbors grew a huge garden every summer, and they canned, froze and haul it to California for the winter. They told us not to worry about a garden; their garden was big enough for us too. We helped them weed, and care for the garden, and took care of everything when they were away.

HENRY, HENRY JR., ELAINE, AND BRIDGETTE ON HORSEBACK IN IDAHO.

HUNTING CAMP IN IDAHO.

Figure 83

Slate Creek was an hour and a half south of Lewiston. In late fall, we hunted the North Fork of the Clearwater River near the Montana border. Jim took me fishing up there in summers before. Usually Jim, Darlene and his nephew Al Solom would go up ahead of us and set up camp. It was rough country. We hunted the elk trails on the side of the mountains, and on the creek side so we would not get lost. If you went over the top of the ridges, there was a good chance of getting lost. We packed a lunch and hunted all day, coming down in the evenings. We stayed in big tents on the river, and had wood stoves to keep warm. We hunted both sides of the river. Jim brought a small duck boat to paddle back and forth across the river. The area was massive. There were good elk trials up and down the ridges. The women stayed in camp during the day visited, tended the fire and did the cooking. It was nice having those hot meals when we returned to camp.

The country was beautiful. I loved to be up in the mountains. There were large tall pines and good trails, and you could find a nice sunny spot and take a nap. We usually hunted below the snow line. You could sit there and would hear the water running in the river down below or in a small creek nearby. With the wind blowing and swirling around, it was serene. When you sat there quiet, you could hear voices coming from somewhere. You were not really sure if they were real. Maybe they were coming off the road down below, or the spirits were talking to you and you couldn't quite make out what they were saying.

In summer we camped and fish for trout in different place around Idaho. There were many beautiful places. When you were walking and hiking around in the mountains, it was special. I was leery about the grizzly bears that were abundant up there. I was always a little jumpy, they were always a threat.

The winters were mild compared to northern Minnesota. It was mild most of the time and the days were around +20F. We did not do much during the winter; no one did. We would go into Lewiston from time to time to shop, get supplies or just visit. When traveling to Lewiston, we drove up White Bird Hill, and then across the Camas Prairie, and down into the Clearwater River Valley and down the river to Lewiston. It was always an adventure driving in the mountains.

We drove back to Warroad a couple of times a year. We drove the old 1966 pickup one way for about one hundred dollars. It had two 15 gallon saddle tanks, so we could go quite a long way on a full tank. Elaine worked part time and I did not work. We hunted, fished, and grew a big garden and canned our food. At first we did not have a TV so I had my nephew tape shows for us on VCR tape. We finally got a satellite connection and we passed the time watching TV. I hooked a cable to the neighbors, and they were thrilled to have TV too. Before that they read in the evenings and went to bed at dark and got up with the sun.

There was never anything going on, we were isolated. If we wanted any social life, we went to White Bird or Riggins and socialized, and sometimes we were invited to dinner at a neighbors. One year, a new owner of one of the bars in White Bird suggested that we start a Legion Club. People got enthused about it. There were retirees who got on board. We started our membership drive and unbelievably we had over a hundred and fifty members. We were looking for something to do as an event. Someone suggested that we start a powerboat (Jet-Boat Race) race that would run thirty-eight miles from White Bird to Riggins up and down the Salmon River. Everyone thought this was a great idea, and we went to work on that project. It was kind of a crazy idea, but everyone jumped on board, and we pulled it off. We had over fifteen thousand people down on the river watching this race. People brought their campers and camped out for the weekend. It brought a lot of business to the local businesses, and we made a little money. I was in charge of marketing and advertising the event. We made the *National Legion News,* which sent out representatives from the national office of the American

Legion. We had the Governor of Idaho and some staff there at the start of the event. We also staged other projects and fundraisers. It was a way to keep busy, and to help out the communities.

During the summers, I had summer visitation with the kids. I picked up Henry Jr. and Bridgette in Minnesota and brought them up to Warroad to spend time with the family. Other times they flew out to Spokane, and I would pick them up at the airport and bring them down to Slate Creek to spend a couple of weeks with us. We camped during the summers, traveled around the state. We made camp in the mountains, where we hiked, fished and explored.

Idaho was a nice place for me at the time. I needed to get away and have time to think and try to figure things out for myself. I knew I did not want to live there the rest of my life. After a while, things started to become clearer. Idaho was like my mountain top where you could look back, see your past and look forward to your future. I knew there was more to life than living like a hermit. We talked about moving home but had not made any firm plans. I had thoughts of building a cabin on the property and getting rid of the trailers. I thought, if I could get the cabin finished, and as an investment, it would bring a good price. We started saving for the cabin.

Elaine's mother and dad, Janet and Curtis Olafson, and aunt and uncle, Martha and Gordon Olafson showed up one day. We were surprised. They just showed up, unannounced. They went back to Minnesota the next day. They said they had a good trip but did not care for driving in the mountains. They were flat land farmers from Minnesota. I told them this is the only place a cow can fall out of the pasture. They all laughed at that fact, and after the drive through the mountains they understood.

That spring, I was restless and did not want to sit around watching TV. It was too early in the year to start on the cabin. Sometimes I would hike up to the top of the hills or on the fingers that ran down from the mountains toward the Salmon River. It was a thousand feet or more to the top. It would take me over an hour to climb to the top. There was a large ditch that ran for miles up the canyon and which carried water from the creek above Slate Creek down toward the Salmon River. It was somewhat level. The Chinese built it and used it for mining a sluice box back in the early part of the century. It was quite a feat to build something like that. All they had were shovels and pickaxes. It had not been used for years, but it was still there. There were snow patches here and there along my hike to the top. Once I reached the ditch, I followed it for a while, when all of a sudden in a snow bank, I saw a golden eagle lying there, dead. I picked it up, and it was frozen. I brought it down to the trailer. I knew we were not supposed to have an eagle in our possession. I knew it was significant to me as an American Indian. I thought about keeping it, but in the end I brought it over to the DNR at Slate Creek. They said it may have been sick, and that it had died during the winter. They were going to send it to the University of Idaho and have them examine it. I thought I did the right thing by giving it them.

Our building plans got under way later that spring when the weather warmed up. We lived in the small 12 X 50 two bedroom trailer. The other trailer was a 14 X 70 and basically used as a workshop. We sold that one and it was moved off the property. My brother Dave was a carpenter, and I invited him to come out to Slate Creek to help me build forms and pour the foundation. He stayed for a few weeks and we had a good time. He gave me a good start, and I had enough materials to frame it and get the roof on. Elaine's grandmother and husband came out late that summer to visit. They were retired and stayed for a month. We showed them the area and they helped worked on the place. Elaine was homesick, so it was good to have them with us for a while. Once the floor was on, we followed the plans and framed the 28 X 32 cabin. We put plywood on the outside, and cut out the windows. We continued to work on the cabin until the tongue and groove roof and plywood was on.

As I worked, I kept thinking about the eagle. Was it a sign of something to come? Although I did not want to learn about Indian culture and traditions when I was younger and growing up, it meant something to me now. I had no real knowledge of the Indian ways. I wished that I had learned about the culture when I had the chance and I was regretting it now. I was searching for a purpose; the more I thought about it, the more I was convinced that the sign was for me. I knew things did not change overnight. I would try being patient and waiting for the signs and for something to come. I would go with the flow and see where it led me.

That fall, we hunted early in September up near Dixie, and Elk City over near the Bitterroot Mountains. We hunted with a group of friends and had a nice camp set up. We stayed up there over a week. We fished the streams and took our baths in the hot springs at Red River. The weather was just about too warm to hunt; it was near 70 degrees up in the high country. It was not smart to shoot something down below and have to pack it uphill. It would have taken us days to get it out, and it would have spoiled. We shot a few blue grouse. We hunted in the early mornings and drove around some during the day. We called in a few bulls, but did not get close enough to shoot. We camped and visited. After a week or so, we packed up and went home to re-group. Our next hunting trip was with Jim and Darlene on the north fork. We usually hunted up there later on, in the first part of October. A two week break in hunting gave me a chance to work on the cabin and make more progress. We talked about going home for Thanksgiving and we would stay through Christmas.

We hunted the north fork with Jim, Darlene and Al Solom again. They only wanted to hunt the first week, so we stayed a few days longer. It was rainy, with wet snow and miserable that year. We were in the elk a few days and chased a few bull elk around, but we had bull tags only. No matter how miserable it was, it still was a treat to be hunting in that part of the country. It was beautiful and is there nothing like a good camp fire on the edge of a creek or river with the tall pines whistling in the wind and the smell of the camp fire.

Before we left for Minnesota, I had to finish getting the asphalt shingles on the roof. I worked hard and got that finished. The cabin was framed, the windows and doors were covered, and the roof was on. It was closed up for the winter. The neighbors and friends would check on the place for us while we were gone.

It was nice being home for the holidays. It was always a special time around my parents' house. One day, I got a call from my daughter Tara. She was fourteen at the time. I had not been able to spend much time with her over the years, only a few days here and there. Her mother selected the times that I could see her. She often selected times that were not convenient for me. I always thought she did that on purpose. Tara said, her mother agreed that she could come and live with me. It caught me by surprise. It was totally unexpected and I had a million thoughts going through my head. Tara said, she wanted to come live with me, but she did not want to move to Idaho. She asked me, if I would move home so she could attend school in Warroad. Without talking with Elaine, I said, "Yes, I would." We talked about moving home anyway. I asked her when she wanted to come and stay. She said, "Now or in a few days because it will take her a few days to get her things in order." I said, "OK, call me in a day or two." I would need to get things in order. When I hung up the phone, I sat down and told everyone. My family was excited and happy. I had some quick planning to do.

I decided the only choice was to get an apartment, and get it now. There was no time to get the furniture in Idaho. I would get some used furniture together now and try to make a home for Tara. I rented an apartment later that day, just a few blocks from my parents. Our dog Otis would have to stay with my parents. Mom and Dad liked the dog and didn't mind, and neither did the dog because they spoiled him. We got busy rounding up furniture and household goods. Everyone chipped in to help us put a home together in a hurry. I collected silverware, dishes, pots and pans, a couch, table and chairs, beds, and all the things you need to set up a home. We completed the move and Tara joined us a few days later. When the time was right, we would drive back to Idaho and get our belongings.

CHAPTER 60: OUR RETURN TO WARROAD

Our apartment in Warroad was now a home. Tara was in school, and we had a routine now that revolved around her. We had to do things that fit her schedule rather than our own. It would take some getting used to. We were getting to know our neighbors in the building. It was easier to see Henry Jr. and Bridgette now that they were closer. Things seemed to be working out. We followed my nieces and nephews as they played sports. I had five nieces and nephews who were real close in age to Tara. Whenever we went to any high school activity, there was always a Boucha relative on the team.

I started to skate again and played some games with the old-timers. I started coaching the Peewee B team. It brought me back into the good graces of some of the people in the Warroad. My nephew Mike Flick played on the Warroad High School hockey team that went to the state high school hockey tournament that year. We all went down and had a good time at the tournament in St. Paul.

I was working part-time with my brother Dave in his carpentry business. Elaine and I also cut and sold firewood. It was hard work, but we enjoyed being out in the woods. Dave had Boucha Construction and he was doing a few jobs in the area.

I had Tara to think about now and I settled down some. I was still driving my old 1966 Chevy truck. I never cared about what I drove or how it looked, as long as it got me around. The pickup was in fine shape. I kept the engine in top shape too, but the vehicle was old and looked it. It ran perfect. Tara was embarrassed to ride with me in that old truck. She kept bugging me to get a different car. I found out how serious she was when I brought her to school one day and she had me drop her off a couple of blocks away from the school, so no one would see her get out of the truck. I laughed all the way home.

In March, we still had our belongings in Idaho and we were making payments on the property and gaining equity. We planned to keep it and to go back in the summers to finish it and use it on occasion. At Easter break, we drove to Idaho with Tara. All three of us were sitting in the front seat. It was 12 hours to Billings, and that was only half way. I did not have a radio in the truck. I never listen to the radio anyway. I just drove, sometimes talking and joking. They read, visited, slept and looked at the scenery. Tara had not traveled much but she had made a trip to Spokane when Shirley and all the kids came to visit in 1979. She was nine years old then and she visited with us when I owned the meat store in Spokane.

The trip to Lewiston was about 1,325 miles, or twenty-three hours of driving time from Warroad. We usually stayed one night in Miles City or Billings, Montana. Once we got off the 2 lane roads north of Grand Forks, North Dakota, it was mostly freeway driving. We got on the I-29 freeway in northeast North Dakota and drove south to Fargo, then on I 94 all the way to Missoula. From there on the two-lane roads that took us over Lolo Pass and into Lewiston. We made the trip a lot and knew the roads well. In making plans for the move, I thought I would buy a two-axle trailer to haul my belongings back to Warroad, instead of renting a u-haul. That way I could sell the trailer once I got back. Tara was a little homesick that trip, she was not used to traveling, especially in the old truck. We stayed at Jim and Darlene's for a couple of days while I made my purchase, and then we headed down to Slate Creek to pack things up. I was not sure if I could get everything in the truck and the trailer, but it would be close.

WARROAD WALL OF FAME.

Figure 84

It was good to see our neighbors. We called Josephine and Jack Maynard and told them our plans and the situation. It was a small community and I am sure everyone knew we decided to move. They were happy for us and wished us the best. It took us a couple of days at Slate Creek to get organized. I managed to get most of the stuff into the pickup and trailer. It took us longer on the way home with the load. Tara was amazed, when I stopped in the middle of Montana, on a Montana Freeway next to a sign that had an 89 mile marker on it. I took it down in broad daylight and gave it to her. It was the year she was to graduate. We made it back to Warroad in one piece.

As time went on, Henry Jr. and Bridgette came to Warroad more often, and we went to the Minneapolis area to visit them and to see their school functions and games. It was wonderful to be able to spend more time with Hen and Bridgette too. It was a good move for me to be home in Warroad. Still, I loved the mountains, and we thought about moving back to Idaho after Tara graduated from high school. That never happened.

In the summers we fished and played mixed-league softball. Henry Jr. and Bridgette were there most of the summer and played summer recreation baseball and softball. Warroad was a good place for them in summer. Tara was pretty, had a lot of friends and a good social life. Tara had a good work ethic and she was not afraid to work. I was proud of her for that. It was easy for her to get a job and waitress at a local restaurant.

After working part time with Dave for a year and cutting wood, I went to work in the plant for Marvin Windows. I was there for a year before deciding to get my real estate license. I talked to Scott Pahlen, a local Realtor, about going to work with him. He thought it was a good idea and told me what I needed to do. I made the arrangements to attend real estate school in Minneapolis. I stayed with my friend Herb Trimborn while taking classes. The classes were hard for me. They crammed hours and hours of material into each day, and we had to study at night because of the amount of material they gave you. I kept thinking about working in the plant at Marvin Windows, and that motivated me. I was grateful for the work but did not want to make a career out of it. I went through the real estate classes and studied. I took the state exam on a Saturday and drove home that night. I waited a week before they sent me the results. The test was harder than I imagined, and I was not sure I passed. It was a two part test and four hours long. I was nervous when I opened the letter. It said "pass/pass." I was excited and immediately called Scott Pahlen. He came over and went through a company orientation with me. We went over the forms and materials that I needed for listing and selling homes and land. I still didn't know what I was doing. I put an ad in the Warroad Pioneer. I was a Realtor and I started working. I did advertising and handed out flyers. It all worked out, people started calling me and I started listing and selling property.

There were a few Realtors around then, but no one had a lot of business. So getting my market share was competitive but easier than expected. We did not have computers, lock boxes, or cell phones in those days, so it was primitive. We had a key rack in Roosevelt at Scott's house, where he had an office in a room downstairs. Carolyn, his wife, worked at Marvin Windows full-time and did his real estate typing and secretarial stuff at home in the evenings and on weekends. We only had a few listings. We talked about how we wanted to grow and expand. I started working Warroad, Roseau and the surrounding area. I remember my first sale. When it closed and I received my check, I thought, wow, this is easy. I could not believe how much money I made. I would have to work at Marvin's two weeks or more to get that much money. It really motivated me. I worked hard and I was successful. I worked with Scott Pahlen Realty for nineteen years.

In 1987, as my children and nieces and nephews were getting older. We as family were thinking ahead about college or being able to get our kids an education. We started our application for enrollment to the Indian and Northern Affairs Canada (INAC). They promised the Indians a free education. So we needed to get enrolled somewhere to take advantage of the situation. We applied to get our Canadian Indian Status. We had talked with Red Lake Band of Chippewa Indians, a Minnesota Tribe about getting enrolled as American Indians. Some of our relatives were enrolled there, but for some reason most Warroad Indians were taken off the rolls back in the 1940s. We wanted to know why they refused to enroll us again. They said we were Canadian Indians. When we first went to Canada, they said that we were American Indians because we were born or raised in the United States, a real Catch 22.

Frustrated with both sides of the border, we started our application in Canada. We had nothing to loose, and we started by documenting a family lineage on my mother's side, the Thunder family lineage. We knew we were from Buffalo Point but we did not know the lineage.

According to Indian and Northern Affairs we had to find and tie together the official documentation without a break in our lineage.

We needed birth certificates, baptism, census, marriage records, and whatever we could find to tie our families lineage together. My mother was alive when we started. My mother passed away in 1988. She had heart, diabetes and blood pressure problems. We lost a lot of the information when she passed that she could have provided.

We did the research on our mother's side first, and sent it into INAC. We celebrated and thought we had it completed and we were going to get our status. They sent a letter back informing us that we needed to do my father's side of the lineage sheet. It took a long time because we would wait 3 or 4 months for INAC to send us a letter stating that they received the documents. Then another two months to receive a letter stating what we needed to do next. They would always state they were short staffed and the documents would need to be verified, before being processed. Then another three months wait to hear from them again. After all of this time, we collected all the official documents and sent the full packet to Ottawa. Finally, after (13) thirteen years, we were enrolled in Canada in 2000 as full-blood Indians.

During that time Tara and all the nieces and nephews graduated from high school. They did not qualify for the INAC college education because we were not enrolled. They were denied their inherent right to receive their college education, when in fact they could have. INAC had the entire lineage on file, but never gave it to us. Some of the kids quit because of lack of funding. It is a ploy by the government to discourage Indian people not to apply for status. Come to find out later, the government had all the paperwork, lineage, and documentation. They could have simply given us our status within 6 months or less. It is still that way today.

CHAPTER 61: WARROAD TENURE

Late in 1987, the US Olympic Team came to play the Warroad Lakers in an exhibition game at the Warroad Memorial Arena. The US Olympic Teams played the Warroad Lakers in every Olympic year that I could remember. The 1988 Olympics were being held in Calgary, Alberta, that year.

There were some significant things that happened that year. Tara was a junior in high school. I purchased a car for her. We bought a house. I was contacted by the school and was asked to be on the Indian Education Advisory Board. Sadly, my mother passed away in July of 1988.

Jean Paul Boucha (JP) was born on February 4, 1988, in Roseau Hospital. We were still in our apartment when we brought him home. I was coaching then and had moved up to Bantams and I was enjoying it. I was still playing old-timer hockey and in some weekend tournaments. We also enjoyed watching the Lakers games.

Tara was prettier than ever. She was dating and playing volleyball and she was a basketball cheerleader. We would watch her cheer at the home games. Tara was more independent with her car now. She attended all the school dances—homecoming, was Frosty attendant, and prom—that year. She had good friends and a good social life.

We were going to Minneapolis to see Henry Jr. and Bridgette more often. Bridgette was a real cutie. They were up in Warroad for part of their Christmas vacation. We skated, played road hockey and had fun going to games and spending family time together. Hen was thinking of attending school in Warroad.

ALICE BOUCHA (MOM) AND HENRY.

PROM PHOTO: LEFT TO RIGHT: COUSINS TARA BOUCHA, (HENRY), DAVE BOUCHA JR.
(DAVE AND DONNA), SUE FLICK AND MIKE FLICK (STAN AND SHIRLEY BOUCHA FLICK),
NATALIE BOUCHA (DAVE AND DONNA) PAUSE AS THEIR DATES STEP ASIDE
FOR A FAMILY PICTURE.

Figure 85

I was attending the Indian Education Board meetings. In 1988, the US government passed a bill to require public schools to have an Indian Parent Committee, if a school district had ten or more Indian students. The board was to act as an advisory board to the school board to make sure that the needs of the Indian students were being met. We also addressed the Indian names and logo issue in response to the American Civil Liberties Union's challenges for schools using derogatory Indian names and logos. We designed a new Indian head logo for the school, and we developed a statement that supported the school using the name "Warroad Warriors." On board was the Indian community, the Indian Parent Committee, and the Indian Education Department.

My mother had not been feeling well that spring and early summer. She had heart problems and was frail. Unknowingly, she may have had Lyme disease along with all of her other ailments. She became very weak. Earlier mom worked with my sister Shirley at the nursing home as a cook. The nursing home was just across the street from her house.

In early July, the day before my mother died, I stopped in to see my parents at about 8 or 9 p.m. Mom was sitting in the living room and she was looking out the window. She said, "Who are those people over there? It looks like they are standing there waiting for something." I looked across the street to the nursing home lawn, where she said they were. I did not see anyone. Then she sat back and rested. She may have seen the spirits of our relatives who had come to take her home. They were waiting for her. I did not recognize it then, but later I understood. The next day she was taken to the hospital, where she passed away. My brother Dave said that, while he was in the room, Mom said, "What is Teresa doing riding her bike down by the beach?" Her spirit may have been traveling and she saw Jim's daughter Teresa riding her bike at the beach in Warroad. After coming in and out of consciousness, she finally said, "I am going home now," and she passed. It was a tremendous loss to us. She had been the pillar of the family. Now we would have to carry on without her. She had a good life. She made everyone around her a better person, and she was there for everyone through thick and thin. She is buried in the Riverside Cemetery in Warroad.

Later on that summer, we made an offer on a house. The offer was accepted, and we closed on the house in the fall of 1988. We moved in, and it felt great to have a home rather than an apartment. It felt good to have roots again. The house was just two blocks from the arena and only a block from the grocery store. It was in a quiet part of town.

I had come full circle. I was feeling better. I had come home. I had a chance to spend time with my mother before she passed. I thought about the eagle that I found in Idaho, and I connected that with the way things happened. It was a sign to come home. There is no other explanation of what it meant to me. There would be many new happenings to come. I was blessed to have it all; a home, a good job, a family, my kids around me. Really-what more is there?

CHAPTER 62: WARROAD-NEW LIFE AND HOME

Our new home had four bedrooms and a lot of square footage. That fall, Henry Jr. moved to Warroad. He wanted to live with us, go to school and play hockey in Warroad. He was twelve years old, in 7th grade and he would be playing with the PeeWee's.

Although we had a natural wood/gas combination stove, we burned wood that first winter. Hen had the job of bringing the wood from outside into our wood storage downstairs, a job he could do without. We eventually went to natural gas and took out the woodstove.

It was Tara's senior year. I was also asked if I could billet a young man from Williams who wanted to play hockey in Warroad. The Minnesota State High School League ruling stated that you had to attend the school in the district where you lived. Your parent or parents would need to move to that school district with you to attend school. The only way around it was to go through a legal adoption. I adopted Korre Pieper so he could attend the Warroad High School and play hockey. He was a great kid, and I enjoyed having him there. He was driving, and would go home to Williams on a regular basis. Williams was only eighteen miles away. After the adoption was legal and the league was aware of the adoption, he could stay at home in Williams and drive to school from there.

HENRY'S GUIDE BOAT, AND HOUSEBOAT ON LAKE OF THE WOODS.

Figure 86

Aside from our normal living and raising kids we hunted. In the fall we spent time hunting birds and spending time in the woods, we helped my dad cut and haul wood, he loved to burn wood. He cut wood into his 80's. It was always 80+ degrees in his house and he would spend time shoving insulation in ever crack he could find. He'd always say his house was drafty. Later in fall we deer hunted with my Dad, Stan and Mike Flick, Brother Jim and his sons John and Joe, Dave Amberg and some others who came and went over the years. It was good family fun and we enjoyed our time together. As winter came we would enjoy watching all the kids play their sports and spent a lot of time at the schools and arena watching them play. We always tried to attend as many games as we could. In summer we enjoyed the Pow Wow, fishing walleye, having cook outs and family time. I bought a boat and we enjoyed many hours on the lake fishing, exploring our old family sites at the Northwest Angle as well as other places on the lake. Later on I bought a houseboat and traveled the lake extensively finding pottery, looking for gold, visiting relatives, and locating our old family fish camps and places used by our ancestors during that time on the lake. It was a wonderful time for us. During that time period, I studied and received my Captains License from the United States Coast Guard. With all of our captains throughout our family history I thought it would be great to have one too. Our houseboat slept 8, with a nice galley, head and shower, generator, and we pulled a boat or two behind for fishing and recreation. Besides getting my captains license, I got a gold prospectors license from the Ontario Government. I prospected many parts of Lake of the Woods. We found small pockets of gold here and there. I was hard work, time consuming and expensive. It was a fun hobby.

The school asked me to be an assistant coach with the Warroad Warriors, and I accepted the position. I enjoyed working with the older kids and being a part of the game at that level. We would represent Section 8 at the 1989 State High School Hockey Tournament later that season, by beating our archrival, Roseau, in the section tournament. It was an upset, just like old times, and we enjoyed the moment. We proudly represented Section 8 at the Minnesota State Tournament.

HENRY'S FAMILY.
LEFT TO RIGHT: TARA, HENRY HOLDING JP, BRIDGETTE, HENRY JR., AND ELAINE.

Figure 87

Tara was nominated for Frosty Queen in high school, and my son Hen Jr. was nominated for Frosty King of the seventh grade. We were proud of both of them. The only one we were missing was Bridgette. She wanted to come, but Randi wanted her to stay in Minneapolis a couple of more years before she moved to Warroad. She was still young. It was a real joy, and I was counting my blessings having all the kids around that winter. It was great having the space; everyone had their own room, and a downstairs, where they could entertain. In the family, we celebrated everyone's birthday together. The meals we shared and family times we had were wonderful. We often had our whole family over for special dinners and special events during the year, and they all fit into our house. After dinner we would all get into a smear game for nickels and dimes and have a great time laughing and joking.

These are the precious moments, the processes, and the journey. All the money or material things in the world cannot bring you happiness. It is the love of family, friends and relationships.

CHAPTER 63: INDIAN EDUCATION

One of the highlights in my life was to be able to work with kids. Not only in hockey and other recreational programs but also with education, life's experiences and challenges. The opportunity came while I was serving on the Indian Parent Committee. A committee designated and designed by Federal law in 1988 to advise the school board on American Indian issues and to make sure the needs of our Indian children were being met.

The Indian Education Committee, but mostly Principal Ron Dietch wrote a grant to start an Indian Education Program at Warroad High School. The purpose was to provide tutoring and counseling to students who needed help. The grant was to provide one tutor/counselor for the school district's Indian students.

In addition, that person was to look for other funding and develop the program. At a meeting, we were asked if the board knew of anyone who would be interested. We thought candidates would need a teaching certificate or degree, but according to the Federal application, they did not need a teaching certificate. The committee would entertain applications from the Indian community. Nobody was really sure how all of this would work. I went about my business and attended the meetings. Later, the school district asked me if I would like to attend the Minnesota Indian Education Association annual meeting in Rochester, Minnesota. The district would pay for the conference and all of the expenses. It was to be a fact finding mission and if I went, I would come back and report to the board and committee. I agreed to go and represent the Parent Committee and school district.

HENRY BOUCHA AND THE BOYS: HEN AND JP.

IRENE BOUCHA BOBCZYNSKI, DARLENE BOUCHA DORION AND SHIRELY BOUCHA FLICK.

JP, BRIDGETTE, TARA AND HEN JR.

Figure 88

At the conference in Rochester, I went to the workshops and met several people who had programs in school districts throughout the state. There were a lot of programs statewide that provided tutor/counseling services to Indian kids, as well as traditional cultural and language programs. I thought this would be a great program for Warroad. It would give us a chance to provide those services to our kids, identify our Indian students, and develop a program to teach them our local history, culture, and traditions of our Ojibwa people.

We never had a program like that in the Warroad School District. In the past, there was a community program that taught crafts and provided a recreation space for the Indian people in the 1970s. That was closed after the funding ran out. This was new and exciting. I was enthusiastic and motivated by the possibilities of the program. It could be developed for our young people at the school and involve our Indian community.

At the next Indian Education Board meeting, I gave my report on the conference and how other schools developed their programs within the Indian community and the school district. I also told them that I would be interested in working with the school district to open and develop a program for Warroad.

Later that spring, Warroad had received a grant for the following year. The parent committee and the school district offered me the new position of Indian Education Director. I said, "Yes", and accepted the job.

I was selling real estate, and things were going well. I figured that I could do both. It was a new position, and no one knew how the program would work. We needed time to let it develop, grow and to see how things progressed. When I took the job, I made sure that it provided me time during the day to address a real estate matter, if needed.

I would work with the principals and counselors in each of the three buildings. I would try to address the identified problem areas and help find solutions. I answered to the superintendent, and the school district would provide the accounting and budgeting. I would be responsible for the Local Indian Education Committee, Indian Communities education needs, workshops, grants, fundraising, quarterly, semester, and annual reports. In addition, I was the community liaison, and I work with other community and county education, juvenile and developmental programs.

When school started, I was given a nice office in the middle school, and access to a secretary. The first problem I had was with some of the teachers. They were jealous, that I had my own office, used the staff lounge and that I did not have a degree. Some complained to the principals. Once they understood the program, most were okay with it. It was hard gaining the respect of some. Unfortunately, there are teachers even today who look down on the program and the staff.

I did not realize until I was there for a while, how difficult this job was going to be. Sometimes God has children's faces. It gave me the strength and courage to move forward to help these kids, and to work through the problems we faced. My goals were to educate the public about Indian culture and traditions, strengthen community relations, to help graduate more Indian kids, decrease the dropout rate by working on better attendance and reducing truancy. Also to help improve GPA's in all schools, work on parental involvement, and work with the juvenile justice and court system in Roseau County. One of the biggest challenges was to try to educate the churches about our spirituality. Most churches were taught that the Indians were "pagans." They didn't understand our spiritual practices. I would try to change that.

I did not understand the community until I started working at the school. When I interviewed students and visited with them one-on-one, I heard "everything." Students discussed parental views, and their comments and status about the different ethnic communities in Warroad. They also commented on other local communities. It was evident that the community had racism and discrimination problems. The students were learning those values at home. Not many people understood that we the parents were the first teachers. We were the ones that dictated our kid's views and morals. The kids listened and learned from the parents. It became their own views on racial issues, and sometimes their own values and morals. Parental involvement was critical when raising children, and needed to be addressed by educating some of the parents too. It was a problem that I wanted to work on through cultural education and sharing. This was a huge undertaking. We could make a difference.

I concentrated on the younger kids to make sure they were better prepared. I knew if we started in the elementary classes, we could prevent some of the problems we faced in the middle and high schools later on.

In addition to that, we wrote grants to hire staff. The principal decided to use the Indian Education Program as a new out, a new avenue to place problem kids. They started sending me not only Indian students, but students who were having discipline problems. Some kids didn't belong to the Indian Education Program, but we tried to help them all.

I received a call one day from Lou Vario, USA Hockey. He asked me if I would meet with a new group regarding a diversity program he was developing. I agreed to meet with him and the others in Minneapolis. In attendance were representatives from USA Hockey, the NHL, the US Olympic Committee, Ice Hockey in Harlem, Disney's Goals, Detroit Hockey Association, Saint Paul Mariucci Inner City, and myself. The organizations were selected to represent all ethnic groups in America. The goal was to introduce students to hockey, and provide ice-time, hockey instruction, and leadership training with an emphasis on education. We were to include all ethnic groups by encouraging community leaders to start hockey programs for their youth.

Figure 89

I started a program in Warroad called Warroad Indian Youth Hockey. We provided equipment, travel, fees and encouragement to parents and players. We provided equipment and services to other reserves (reservations) and programs in the area.

With the Indian Education Program, I worked on new and improved ideas all the time. I was always looking for ways to educate the community on our Indian Culture. It would help us understand our differences. I was out in the community all the time attending functions, speaking at meetings and churches. As a result, it forced me to learn my culture, and heritage myself. You do not know how many times I wished that I would have learned our culture and traditions when I had the chance. The eagle I found in Idaho was always in the back of my mind during these times of learning. I gained knowledge of the culture and traditions and move forward.

The first year, I held an all-school demonstration Pow Wow in our gym. I brought in Ojibwa dancers and drums from both sides of the border. We showed the kids how we danced and drummed. I brought a master of ceremonies, Vince Beyl, from the Bemidji Indian Education Program. He understood what I was trying to do. Over 1000 students and teachers and the community attended. Vince was a great teacher, speaker and educated everyone about the dances, the drum, the feathers, dancer's regalia, our customs, the pow wow's purpose, protocols, and our culture. It was a great afternoon and a huge success. At the end, we called for students to participate and there was no one left in the bleachers. They were all on the floor dancing. The next summer we started the Warroad Traditional Pow Wow, and it was a great community success. We were educating everyone about our culture and traditions. It was good to see firsthand.

I was counting my blessings. My daughter Tara was living with me, but now she was away at university. JP was in school, Hen was back and forth between Randi and I. Bridgette was in Warroad going to school. Jack and Deb Briggs son Koonse came to live with us and play hockey at Warroad. The Briggs were good friends and Koonse wanted a change and we thought this might help him out. I also took in Charles Redding who was having some trouble, got him back in school and tried to keep him on track. I was happily living in Warroad with Elaine, the kids, and family. I had a home, good jobs, coaching, and a wonderful opportunity teaching and providing cultural and traditional knowledge to both Indian and non-Indian students alike.

After a few years working with the school district, I was able to expand the program by bringing in more money. We were able to hire more staff. In 1995, I chose to resign. I stayed on as chair of the Warroad Indian Parent Committee and served there until 2006. The program was stable and sustainable.

Before I left the Indian Education program, I kept the Warroad Traditional Pow Wow. I founded, and developed Kah-Bay-Kah-Nong, a 501(c) 3, not-for-profit organization. Having the not-for-profit gave us the freedom to help the Indian community and those families that "fell through the cracks" with the other state and federal programs. Our mission was to promote and maintain the Anishinaabe (original people) culture and traditions as intended by the Great Spirit. It is also our cultural, moral, and social tradition to assist those in need.

We developed the Warroad Indian Youth Hockey, Ojibwa Crisis Center, Recreation and Sports Programs, Human Rights, Advocacy Program, and Mentorship Program, and History-Research and Documentation (Genealogy) Program. We assumed responsibility for the Warroad Traditional Pow Wow and continued to partner with several of the sponsors.

There was a lot happening during that time. Moses Tom from the Big Grassy Reserve in Canada contacted me. He asked if I would go to Kamsack, Saskatchewan to visit a medicine man/healer. Moses wanted to bring elders from the Big Grassy Reserve to see Lloyd Brass, a healer (traditional doctor and spiritual teacher). I told him that we would go along and help. Moses was married to my cousin Bessie Morrison. When I first met Moses, he was in good health. Later his health failed and he "doctored" with Lloyd Brass. Lloyd worked on my back as well as other ailments. Mosses, Bessie and family became close during that time, and we visited often.

One time at his house in Morson, Ontario, Moses was ill and passed out. The family thought he died because he was not breathing and there was no pulse. They were mourning and crying when the ambulance came for the body. The paramedics checked him over and verified that he had no pulse and that he was dead. They put Moses' body in the ambulance and went to the hospital some 50 miles away. As they were traveling down the road, Moses woke up and sat up. It scared the ambulance driver so much he almost ran off the road. At the hospital, they found nothing wrong with him. They kept him overnight for observation and discharged him the next day.

Through the years Lloyd Brass became my best friend. He was born March 5, 1944, and died September 25, 2008. He was also known as Kamanochiket ("he who dressed well"). In all the years I knew him, he never said an unkind word about anyone, anything, or any situation. He was raised by his grandparents, the Musqua family of Keeseekoose, Saskatchewan. He attended a residential school and a high school. He loved sports, especially golf. He was an excellent musician. He was devoted to his wife and family. His grandfather was a healer, and it was passed down to Lloyd. Lloyd was culturally astute and well respected. He healed many and was in demand until his passing. I miss my good friend, and I will miss the healing and the good times we had throughout our years of friendship. I always include Lloyd and his family in my prayers. He was the most powerful tradition doctor that I have encountered. His wife, Corrine, daughter, Karen, and other children and grandchildren live in Kamsack, Saskatchewan, on the Cote Reserve.

CHAPTER 64: UNITED STATES HOCKEY HALL OF FAME

What more can you ask for than to be recognized by your peers?

During the spring of 1995, I was nominated to the United States Hockey Hall of Fame. By midsummer, I heard that I had been selected. Amazingly, no one actually called me and talked to me about it. I heard it on the news and I saw it in the paper. People called me at home and congratulated me, and some people stopped me on the street and said congratulations.

HENRY'S INDUCTION INTO THE UNITED STATES HOCKEY HALL OF FAME (USHHOF).

Figure 90

1995 INDUCTION INTO USHHOF WITH FAMILY.

HENRY WITH THE STANLEY CUP.

UNITED STATES HOCKEY HALL OF FAME. HENRY IN HEAD DRESS, HERB BROOKS, JAIME SNOWDON, AND JP BOUCHA.

Figure 91

461

My induction, in Eveleth, Minnesota was well attended. Those in attendance included my former coach and presenter Dick Roberts and family, my Boucha family in its entirety, the Pahlen family, my friends Deb and Jack Briggs and family, and many residents from the Warroad and hockey community. Jack Briggs, President of Fon du Lac Tribal College, developed a scholarship in my name, and the American Indian Scholarship Fund gave me a picture stating my accomplishments. Herb Brooks, my good friend and teammate was the keynote speaker. Roger Jourdain, the former chairman of the Red Lake Band of Chippewa Indians who gave me my first Indian name. He presented me with a war bonnet and ribbon shirt.

It was remarkable to me, in just a few short years how my life changed, the path I was on and how that path led me to this point in my life. I was amazingly productive and blessed after finding that eagle on the mountain top.

IN CLOSING, ANYONE WHO DOES NOT BELIEVE IN MIRACLES, SPIRIT GUIDES, DIVINE INTERVENTION, AND GOD, THE GREAT SPIRIT IS NOT THINKING CLEARLY.

Secrets to a Long Life

Looking back at my life, I have come full circle. My highs and lows were sometimes super-high mountains and the deepest canyons. How I survived sometimes, I will never know but I suspect it was by the guidance of the Great Spirit/the grace of God.

Look around you; nothing is more real than miracles. Saying they are impossible simply puts you on the losing side each day.

I am thankful and I count my blessings every day.

Faith has kept me going. I always felt that there was something greater that I must do. I look to God/the Great Spirit, and try to stay close to family and friends.

Say and do what you mean. You are here for a reason; you can make a positive difference, no matter who you are or where you are.

Learn and travel all you can, and share the knowledge and love that was meant to be.

Keep family and friends close, and nurture the relationships. Be there when they need you, and they will be there when you need them.

Just be yourself.

A good teacher will teach you how to live, not how to make a living.

Never under estimate the power of prayer. Pray and have faith, and blessings will come. Stay wide awake and you will recognize the opportunities that arise for you throughout your life.

Stay clearheaded and clear minded and you will see the path. Listen to your inner thoughts and make the right choices. All of the answers are within you already. Learn to recognize them.

Remember, Pimatiziwin being the Sacred Gift of Life is not only the right but it is also a duty for we do not own our life. Believe that life was to be regarded as a sacred trust for the benefit of other life including our children and generations yet born. Life is a gift.

Highlights of My Career

1963: Minnesota State Bantam Tournament.

1964: Minnesota State Bantam Champions, Warroad's first state championship in any sport 1969: State of Minnesota Hockey Tournament; Three-time All-State selection

1970: United States National Hockey Team; Gold Medal, Group B World Championships

1971: World Hockey Championships; National Hockey League Amature Draft; sixteenth overall by Detroit Red Wings

1972: United States Olympic Hockey Team, Silver Medal; World Hockey Association number one draft choice; signed with the Detroit Red Wings; US Army Veteran

1973: Broke forty-one-year-old NHL record for fastest goal; Red Wing Rookie of the Year

1974: Traded to the Minnesota North Stars

1975: Eye injury incident; Signed with WHA Minnesota Fighting Saints

1976: Signed with Kansas City Scouts

1977: Retired from hockey at Colorado Rockies

1988: Appointed to the Warroad Indian Education Committee

1992: Selected as the first Indian Education Director, Warroad Public Schools

1993: Established USA Hockey Diversity Task Force

1995: First NHL/USA Hockey Diversity Program; established Kah-Bay-Kah-Nong, Inc.
United States Hockey Hall of Fame; Warroad High School Hall of Fame

References, Resources and Acknowledgements

Association of Minnesota Counties

Chapin, Earl V, *A Short History of the Roseau Valley*

Durham, J.W., *Minnesota's Last Frontier; Migration Story*

Federal Writers Center; Federal Writers Project of Minnesota

Godin/Morrisseau Family History

Hubbard, Stanley S. of Hubbard Broadcasting

La Vérendrye, Treaty #3, Warroad, Minnesota, Grand Portage, Minnesota, Grand Portage National Monument

Lund, Duane R., PhD, *Lake of the Woods, Yesterday and Today,*

Marvin Windows & Doors

Minnesota Historical Society

Native American History of Roseau County

NHL Archives

Northwest Angle #37 First Nation

Passamaquoddy Tribe at Pleasant Valley

Red Lake Band of Chippewa Indians

Roseau County Museum; Roseau, Minnesota

USA Hockey Archives

US Olympic Committee Archives

Vintage Minnesota Hockey—Lakers

Warner, William W., *History of the Ojibwa People*

Warroad, City of

Warroad Heritage Center

Warroad Historical Society

Warroad Indian Education Department

Warroad Indian Parent Committee

Warroad Museum

Warroad Pioneer

Warroad Public Schools

Wikipedia—1970 World Champions, 1971 World Champions, 1972 Winter Olympics

CPSIA information can be obtained at www.ICGtesting.com
Printed in the USA
LVOW04s0129310115

425077LV00008BA/161/P

9 780615 717449